Minnesota Women in Politics

Minnesota Women in Politics

Stories of the Journey

Billie Young & Nancy Ankeny

NORTH STAR PRESS OF ST. CLOUD, INC.

Published by
North Star Press of St. Cloud, Inc.
PO Box 451
St. Cloud, MN 56302

Printed in the United States of America by
Versa Press, Inc.
East Peoria, IL 61611

First Printing: November 2000

Cover design: Sara Klocke

Cover photo by: James L. Shaffer

All photos, unless otherwise noted, courtesy
Photo Department of the Minnesota House
of Representatives.

Photos of Ruby Hunt, Diane Ahrens, Barbara Carlson, Marge
Anderson, Karen Anderson, Choua Lee, Judith Dutcher, Joanell
Dyrstad, and Jean Harris were supplied by the individuals.

Dedicated to the Memory of Coya Knutson

Coya Knutson is the only woman to have been elected to the
Congress of the United States from Minnesota. From 1955
through 1959 she represented the Ninth Congressional
District (northwestern Minnesota) to the eighty-fourth and
eighty-fifth Congresses.

Among her accomplishments was sponsorship of the
first Federal Student Loan Program — legislation that is still in
force. Coya was defeated in her bid for a third term by 1,390
votes or one-half of one percent, after her opponents convinced her husband to write his "Coya, come home" letter —
an action the *Washington Post* of November 1996, called "the
most tawdry act of political sabotage in American politics."
Richard Reeves, the Kennedy family biographer, writing in
the January 1999, issue of *Forbes American Heritage Magazine*,
called Coya "the woman of the century." Coya's spirit of
courage and independence lives on in the careers of today's
women elected officials.

ল Table of Contents ৯০

Katy Olson
Born: October 24, 1928, Rock Valley, Iowa.
Elective offices held: Trimont School Board, 1962-1974; Minnesota State School Board, 1976-86; Minnesota House of Representatives, 1986-1994.

Gladys Sinclair Brooks
Born: June 8, 1913, Minneapolis, Minnesota.
Elective offices held: Minneapolis City Council, 1967-73; Metropolitan Council, 1975-83.

Joan Anderson Growe
Born: September 28, 1935, Minneapolis, Minnesota.
Elective offices held: Minnesota House of Representatives, 1972-1974; Minnesota Secretary of State, 1974-1998.

Phyllis L. Kahn
Born: March 23, 1937, Brooklyn, New York.
Elective office held: Minnesota House of Representatives, 1972-.

Mary Forsythe
Born: May 23, 1920, Whitehall, Wisconsin.
Elective office held: Minnesota House of Representatives, 1972-1990.

Phyllis Mae Onsgard
Born: September 6, 1928, Hillsboro, North Dakota.
Elective office held: Moorhead City Council, 1974-1977.

Lona Ann Minne Schreiber
Born: February 4, 1943, Hibbing, Minnesota.

Joanne Cushman
Born: July 8, 1932, St. Paul, Minnesota.
Elective offices held: Roseville Area School Board, 1982-1985; Roseville City Council, 1985-1993.

Marjorie (Marge) Anderson
Born: April 21, 1932, Mille Lacs Reservation, Minnesota
Elective offices held: District Representative of the Mille Lacs Band of the Ojibwe, 1976-1987; Secretary-Treasurer of the Band, 1987-1991; Chief Executive Officer of the Band, 1991-2000.

Marlene M. Johnson
Born: January 11, 1946. Braham, Minnesota.
Elective office held: Lieutenant Governor, 1982-1986.

Joanell Margaret Dyrstad
Born: October 15, 1942, St. James, Minnesota.
Elective offices held: Mayor of Red Wing, 1985-1990; Lieutenant Governor, 1990-1995.

Joanne E. Benson
Born January 4, 1942, LeSueur, Minnesota
Elective offices held: Minnesota Senate, 1990-1994; Lieutenant Governor, 1995-1999.

Karen Jean Anderson
Born: March 14, 1940, Chicago, Illinois.
Elective offices held: Minnetonka City Council, 1986-1994; Mayor of Minnetonka, 1994 -.

Marion "Mindy" Gail Greiling
Born: February 28, 1948, Rochester, Minnesota.
Elective offices held: Roseville Area Board of Education, 1987; Minnesota House of Representatives, 1992-

Alice Hausman
Born July 31, 1942, Bremen, Kansas.
Elective office held: Minnesota House of Representatives, 1989-.

Martha Rappaport Robertson
Born: September 14, 1952, Boston, Massachusetts.
Elective office held: Minnesota State Senate, 1992-.

Ellen Ruth Anderson
Born: November 25, 1959, Gary, Indiana.

☞ Acknowledgements☜

Writers of nonfiction are peculiarly dependent on the generosity of others. For this project, special thanks are due to:

The political women who took the time to speak candidly about their lives and experiences and let us write about them with the belief that each generation builds on the achievements of those who have gone before.

Ruby Hunt who responded immediately to calls for information with precisely the material needed.

The St. Paul Public Library and the Commission on the Economic Status of Women whose researchers were always ready to hunt for one more elusive fact.

Marcia Aubineau, Honors English teacher at Stillwater High School who wields a red pen like a scalpel, carves up paragraphs that change direction, questions undocumented assumptions and eliminates irrelevant phrases. (Anyone who questions the rigor of Minnesota's public schools must meet Marcia.)

Our families and friends who have been with us on this journey.

To all of them, our gratitude and appreciation.
Biloine (Billie) Young and Nancy Ankeny
July 2000

ca Foreword so

Minnesota Women in Politics: Stories of the Journey had its genesis in 1997 when, in partial fulfillment of the requirements for a degree of Doctor of Psychology, Nancy Ankeny conducted tape-recorded interviews with thirty-nine Minnesota women in politics.

She hoped to learn more about the characteristics of these women who had taken on the roles of elected officials and had exposed themselves to the buffeting of a political campaign. She also wanted to identify shared themes from their early lives. Are their stories similar, she wondered, and what themes do they share? Who are these women who have been pioneers in the political world, have stepped forward to formulate policy and express themselves in the political arena as elected officials?

Under the guidance of the Department of Psychology of the University of St. Thomas, thirty-nine carefully selected women were invited to be interviewed about their childhood and young adult experiences and to share stories of their lives. Seventeen of the women identified themselves as Republicans and twenty-two as Democrats. Having been elected to city, county, and state offices, these women came from all parts of the state and from rural, suburban and urban areas. They ranged in age from twenty-eight to eighty-four years old and represented four racial groups.

Of the thirty-nine women interviewed, twenty were the first child or an only child and ten were second born.

When the interviews with the women were analyzed, seven themes emerged: affiliation, the importance of connection and association with other people; self-efficacy, the individual's sense of personal power and control over her own life and circumstances; commitment to community, the personal responsibility to make changes that would enhance the entire group; optimism, a sense that change is possible and that life can be made better; persistence, the conviction that hard work and perseverance are necessary to produce change; curiosity, the quest for information and experiences; and integrity, a sense that honesty and trustworthiness are absolutely necessary.

The dominant theme that emerged from all of the interviews was the sense of affiliation, which formed the foundation upon which all the other themes were built. Every participant, as a child and young adult, saw herself in a context of other people, being cared for, loved, guided and mentored. Each woman talked about family members, teachers, friends, community members, or neighbors who believed in her, expressed that belief and support by providing a safe space for her to grow and mature before moving out into the world. "One of the messages that I got clearly from both of my parents was 'you can be anything you want to be.'"

When describing the meaningful relationships of their early years, sixty-two percent indicated that both parents played an equally significant role, fifteen percent described their father as most significant, five percent indicated that their mother was the most significant adult in their early lives, and five percent reported that that role had been played by their grandmothers. Almost half (forty-six percent) of the respondents remembered grandparents providing significant support and nurturing. "My grandmother was the one person I could always go back to. She was very important to me . . . an overwhelming sense of love." Another said, "My grandfather was the only man that I have ever loved completely, totally, without any kind of reservation. He was so good to me." Eighteen percent of the respondents had grown up with an alcoholic parent. (This is in line with national statistics that report that almost one in five adult Americans [eighteen percent] lived with an alcoholic parent while growing up.) All of the participants who grew up with an alcoholic parent reported that they had significant adult role models and mentors, other than the alcoholic parent, who provided mentoring and support to them.

Teachers played a major role through encouragement and mentoring for eighty-seven percent, and religious institutions were influential in the lives of seventy-seven percent. One said, "School was always a place where I was successful even when things were turbulent at home." And "I had a teacher who would go over my work with me . . . I needed someone to believe in me and she believed in me."

A second theme that was expressed by all of the participants was a sense of self-efficacy, that, as a child or young adult, they had a sense of their own personal power. In their early years, they learned how to listen to their internal voices, to notice how they felt or what they believed and to trust themselves. The characteristic of self-efficacy includes such traits as competence in school, confidence in self, being strong-willed and stubborn as well as independent, self-reliant and courageous and not being fearful of challenge or conflict. One participant recalled, "I grew up as a minority who had to justify her existence from day one. I learned from a very early age to defend myself verbally." Another reflected, "You're responsible for yourself, your actions, what you do. It takes a lifetime to build a reputation and a minute to destroy it. Do the best you can." Every participant said that as a child or young adult she had an early sense of her own personal power and believed that she could speak up and have an affect on events around her.

Another characteristic reflected in many of the stories was a passionate belief in social justice and fairness. As young people, they felt a sense of commitment to others and believed they had a responsibility to speak out and to give something back to their community.

Helping others and participating in community service was valued by almost three-quarters of the women during their childhood. "It was expected of me to give back to the community. You shouldn't just be a taker — you ought to be a giver too." And "I greatly value public service . . . giving back . . . making the world a better place. I think in a way you live on through that." More than half said that, as children, they were compassionate, considerate, and kind to others and described themselves as being action oriented.

All thirty-nine of the women in the study, on looking back at their childhood experiences, saw themselves as having been optimistic and hopeful as well as capable problem solvers and decision makers. They believed that change was possible. Even those who experienced difficult family circumstances as children continued to be hopeful about life and the future. As one put it, "I have a sense of possibilities . . . vision . . . I always believed that good things were going to happen . . . that I would be a part of it."

Studies done on the American electorate suggest that the American people want leaders who are optimists, who tell them that their problems will be solved. Optimistic people anticipate the best possible outcome and thus have faith that the future holds hope for positive change. Research suggests that optimistic women may be more likely to become actively involved in politics. Political women tended to express significantly greater optimism than women who were not political.

Thirty-eight of the women also identified themselves as persistent, hardworking or tenacious. They indicated that the achievements of their youth and adult lives did not occur magically but happened because of their persistence and hard work. Almost three quarters of the women reported that, even as children, they were organized, methodical and systematic in their work. More than half remembered themselves as having been determined, feisty and persevering. One respondent said, "I'm a hard worker—sometimes to the point of compulsivity. I don't ever remember my parents asking me if I had my homework done. They knew that I was just going to do that. It was a family message."

Curiosity, inquisitiveness or adventurousness emerged as another theme for eighty-two percent of the participants, reflecting their early quest for information and experiences. The women valued education and many reported that they liked to read as young people. "Learning was an integral part of the culture in my family and it was something that was discussed around the kitchen table," one respondent said. Forty-nine percent of the women described themselves as being good listeners, attributing their listening skills to being curious about what others were saying and doing.

Discussions of politics and world events whetted many of the women's interest and curiosity about the world. In their youth, as part of their families or communities, seventy-seven percent of the women indicated that they discussed or heard the adults discussing politics or current events. Their consciousness-raising experiences ranged from World War II and the Kennedy assassinations, to the Women's Movement and involvement in the PTA and League of Women Voters.

In addition, sixty-four percent of the women made the point that a sense of integrity and trustworthiness became a core part of who they were as children and young adults. Early in life, they learned that being honest and truthful engendered trust from their families, friends, and associates and that this trust enabled them to move into positions of responsibility. One remembered, "In the dime store somebody gave me the wrong change—a nickel too much—and I gave it back. It was an inbred thing with me to be honest. It came from my parents and grandparents. They trusted me that I would be honest."

Of the thirty-nine women interviewed by Nancy Ankeny for her doctoral project, twenty-nine gave permission for the authors to use their edited transcripts in this book about Minnesota women in politics. Most of the twenty-nine women were re-interviewed and two additional subjects were added. The result is a record of the childhood and experiences of thirty-one women who, when they reached adulthood, defied the conventions of the past to become political leaders in their state.

⚬ Introduction ⚬

*"The single most impressive fact about the attempt of American women
to obtain the right to vote is how long it took."* – Alice Rossi

January 10, 1992, did not start out to be an historic day in the
Minnesota State House. Rep. Alice Hausman arrived at her office on the
fourth floor of the State Office Building a little before 9:00 A.M., and in
going over her calendar for the day, noted that the women representatives were scheduled to have a group picture taken at the end of the
afternoon session. Mollie Hoben, editor of the *Minnesota Women's Press*,
was planning a feature on women in politics, and the photograph was
to be a centerpiece of the story.

Almost as a reflex, Hausman glanced at the mirror in her office, then
shrugged and picked up some papers on her desk. She would have
almost four hours to work before she would leave her office to walk
through the tunnel to the Capitol where the photograph would be
taken.

Rep. Dee Long, newly elected Speaker of the Minnesota House of
Representatives, had remembered the date with the photographer
before she dressed that morning and had chosen to wear a double
breasted, tailored suit with an open-necked blouse and a single-strand
necklace. Long was the first woman to have been elected Speaker of the
Minnesota House of Representatives, and the picture was to record
what was for Dee a significant and moving event. She was only the
fourth woman in the United States to have been elected speaker of a
state legislature. Her election to the leadership post had taken place a
few days before, and her workload had almost immediately doubled.
Dee had arrived at her office on the fourth floor of the State Office

1

Building that morning before seven, hoping to get almost a full day's work done before she would leave for the afternoon session and the taking of the picture.

Others who were to be in the photograph drifted into their offices. By ten most were at work—on the phones, conferring with colleagues, shifting the piles of papers on their desks. Each one had noted the time scheduled for the picture and most made a mental note not to be late. Though they were accustomed to posing for photographs, this one would be different. This time all of the women of both parties who were serving in the Minnesota House of Representatives would be standing together. They formed one of the largest classes of women in the leg-

The women of the 1992 session of the Minnesota House of Representatives. Back row (left to right): Ann Rest, Phyllis Kahn, Kris Hasskamp, Dee Long, Katy Olson, Mary Murphy, Kathleen Blatz, Jean Wagenious. Third Row: Karen Clark, Edwina Garcia, Alice Johnson. Second Row: Becky Kelso, Teresa Lynch, Connie Morrison, Joyce Henry, Kathleen Vellenga, Harriet McPherson. Front Row: Becky Lourey, Linda Runbeck, Linda Wejcman, Mary Jo McGuire, Alice Hausman, Gloria Segal, Sidney Pauley, Peggy Leppik, Sally Olsen, Hilda Betterman. Not pictured: Eileen Tompkins. (Photo courtesy Minnesota House of Representatives.)

islative history of Minnesota. In the center would be Speaker Dee Long. Although it was Long who was the powerful Speaker of the House, they all felt some reflected glory, a special pride, and kinship because, despite the recent swelling of their numbers, Long was still a rarity in politics. Dee Long, like them, was a woman.

Women first became eligible for election to the Minnesota Legislature in 1920, when they won the right to vote. Two years following the passage of the enabling legislation, four women made it through the electoral process and took their seats in the House of Representatives. Three were from Minneapolis, and one came from Otter Tail County in the northwestern section of the state. The three Minneapolis women were Mabeth Hurd Paige, a civic leader with a legal education; Sue Dickey Hough, a business woman in real estate and the great grand-daughter of John Quincy Adams; and Myrtle Cain, a labor leader and activist in the National Women's Party. The woman elected from Otter Tail County was Hannah Kempfer.

Prior to her election to the Minnesota House, Mabeth Paige had been president of the Women's Christian Association and had helped found the Minneapolis chapter of the Urban League, serving on its board for twenty-five years. She had been a leader in the campaign for women suffrage. When Mabeth decided to run for public office, her candidacy was turned down by the Republican Party so she ran as an Independent. She served for twenty-two years in the Minnesota Legislature.

Sue Dickey Hough had been urged by friends to file for one of the District 34 seats in the House. At first she was reluctant, but when she was elected she found that she "loved every minute" of her service as a legislator. She served only one term though she made four attempts to be reelected. A staunch Republican, she believed that her business experience in real estate made her especially qualified to hold public office.

Myrtle Cain was active in the first strike in 1918 of the Telephone Operators Union and later served as a board member of the National Women's Party. After the passage of the Nineteenth Amendment, she was elected to represent District 28 in Minneapolis, a working people's neighborhood. In 1923 she was one of seven members of the House to sponsor a bill "Granting Equal Rights, Privileges and Immunities to Both Sexes." The bill was highly controversial, and, perhaps sensing that the times were not right for such a measure, the three other female members of the legislature were against it. Hannah Kempfer is credited with having killed the measure by moving that it be indefinitely postponed.

Cain was fifty years ahead of her time. She never gave up on her beliefs in equality for women and in 1973 was present at the Minnesota capitol when the legislature voted to ratify the Equal Rights Amendment to the United States Constitution. Cain was defeated in 1924 by thirty-nine votes, but she remained active in the labor movement throughout her life.

The legislator from Otter Tail County was Hannah Kempfer, an Independent. Hannah was a tall, thin, forty-two-year-old farm woman when she was elected to represent District 50 in the state legislature. She would serve for nine terms and hold membership on all but one of the permanent committees. Hannah's early life read like an adventure novel. She had been born out of wedlock to a stewardess sailing on a ship in the North Sea. Placed in an orphanage in Norway, she was adopted by a Norwegian couple who brought her at the age of six to the United States. Their lives as struggling immigrants were hard, and Hannah worked as a hired girl, teacher, and farm wife. She must have been an extraordinary woman, for, besides representing her district for eighteen years in the Minnesota Legislature, Hannah sold eggs, trapped animals and tanned their hides, made fur coats, canned and sold produce, raised pigs and turkeys, and even worked in a nearby county store — taking goods in lieu of cash wages. Though she and her husband never had biological children of their own, they brought many children into their home to live with them.

Hannah had a deep love for animals and was responsible for setting limits and seasons for fishing and hunting. She was dedicated to the cause of conservation, and, when her committee approved a fifty-cent annual licensing fee for fishing, she was severely criticized by her constituents, almost losing her next election. Though conservation was her major interest, she was also active in health and welfare issues and the rights of children born out of wedlock. In 1923, along with her three women colleagues in the house, she worked to extend the same rights to children of unmarried mothers as were enjoyed by children deemed "legitimate."

The *Minneapolis Tribune* for January 3, 1923, in its article on the swearing in of new legislators, commented on the extraordinary sight of four feathered hats on the floor of the House of Representatives of the

State of Minnesota. While the presence of the hats made for an amusing line in the reporter's story about the convening of the 1923 session of the state legislature, most Minnesotans saw the presence of the four women as an aberration. If anything, lawmaking was being trivialized by the women's presence, as the reporter implied in his remark about the hats.

Scarcely two years had passed since women won the right to vote, and the struggle for suffrage had been a long and bitter one. Since the science of polling and the sampling of public opinion had yet to be developed, there is no way to know for certain how Minnesota citizens felt about the emerging idea of women holding elected public office. However, it is highly probable that Minnesotans, along with most of the rest of the world, believed that women had little business being active in politics. (Mabeth Paige's law professor husband did not want his wife, a law student, to take the bar examination because he thought it would be unwomanly for her to appear in court.)

Women, according to the conventional belief, represented the private world of family and sex, a concept dating as far back as Aristotle, who believed that men belonged in the public arena and derived their nature from their mental, spiritual and political capacities, while woman's nature developed from her sexual characteristics. The distinction was absolute. Aristotle referred to women as "failed males" the result of something going wrong in the womb. He wrote with sublime conviction about women's limits and capacities, about the appropriateness of women for household duties and the obvious inappropriateness of their participation in the primary activity of life, which he defined as politics. Men, Aristotle declared, belonged to the public arena and women belonged in the private one.

Writers in the centuries that followed did little to change Aristotle's assessment. Machiavelli warned men that a state can fall because of a woman. Advising the prince against allowing women to become involved in public debate, Machiavelli held that women were not only outside the bounds of political life, but were a threat to the order and security of the state.

Philosophers from Bacon to Rousseau, from Kant to Engels—not to leave out the medieval Christians—tied female virtue to sexuality. Human nature was believed to consist of two parts, mind and body. The mind was identified with men. Men's minds were believed to be able to do abstract critical thinking and moral reasoning, to conceive of concepts such as rights and justice. The "body" half of human nature was the realm of women. Women's minds were held to be irrational, subject to extreme fluctuations of mood, and tied to the rhythms of their bodies. Abstract thought was believed, for the most part, to be beyond their capacity.

Seventeenth-century New Englanders believed that extensive learning for women was inappropriate if not dangerous. John Winthrop wrote in 1645 of the "sad infirmity, the loss of her understanding and reason" that afflicted the wife of the governor of Hartford, "by occasion of her giving herself wholly to readings and writing and had written many books. If she had attended her household affairs and such things as belong to women," he continued, "and not gone out of her way and calling to meddle in such things as are proper for men, whose minds are stronger, she had kept her wits and might have improved them usefully and honorably in the place God had set her." In the nineteenth century gynecologists warned that use of the female intellect, from reading novels to taking college courses, could cause the uterus to, quite literally, wither away, foreclosing any opportunity for motherhood.

At the time of the Seneca Falls Convention of 1848, women lived lives of profound subordination to men in marriage and society. Because colleges did not admit women, they could not enter the learned professions and thus were at an enormous disadvantage educationally and economically. Women were denied access to positions of power in the churches they supported and were prohibited from any role in politics. A married woman had no legal existence apart from her husband. She could not sue, contract, or even execute a will on her own. The woman herself, her estate, and her wages became her husband's property when she took his name. No woman voted, though all were subject to the laws. Unmarried or widowed women who held property were taxed without their representation. According to Blackstone's Code, which informed laws in Britain and the United States, women were legally in the same category as children and "idiots."

For over two thousand years the belief that women should personify virtues of chastity, shame, and modesty left few other conclusions than that the keepers of those virtues could best serve their God-given function sequestered in the sanctity and privacy of the home. This ideology of domesticity, assigning women a limited and sex-specific role to play, primarily outside the public sphere, prevailed from Victorian times into the twentieth century.

Consequently, those few early women who aspired to participate in politics received little encouragement from society. Regrettably, and to most contemporary women, illogically, many women—even those in the recent past—did not live up to their intellectual potential because they feared the consequences of success. Success and achievement were defined as masculine. In order to achieve success in a traditionally male profession, women were compelled to deny or repress basic aspects of their nature. Achievement and femininity were believed to be mutually exclusive.

Despite the pioneering achievements of the Minnesota four who won state elective office in 1922, attitudes about women in public life were slow to change. As late as 1977, surveys revealed that almost eighty percent of women believed men wanted women to make their political contribution in ways other than running for office. Almost half of the women surveyed in the mid-1970s agreed with the men, namely that women should contribute to public life in ways other than putting their names forward as candidates.

A study written in 1974 by Jeanne Kirkpatrick, ambassador to the United Nations, described women who ran for elective office as exhibiting "deviant behavior" since their actions deviated so far from the social norm. Her study also observed that women who sought political office, far from being peculiar, were similar to male candidates in that they had a conservative personal style and reflected traditional values. Elected women were found to be as likely (or more likely) than other women to be married and no more likely to be divorced, widowed, or single. Women officeholders tended to have the same number of children as women in the general population.

By 1992, however, gender played an important role in voting patterns with the emergence of identity politics. Women tended to vote for female candidates, with feminist consciousness emerging as a significant factor shaping women's voting behavior. As women entered the labor force in greater numbers their political attitudes and voting patterns began to change.

When Coya Knutson (the only woman ever elected to Congress from Minnesota) ran in her first bid for office for the Minnesota House of Representatives in 1950, no woman had served since 1943. In that same election, Sally Luther, campaigning in Minneapolis, won her seat. Until their election, the state legislature had been all male for seven years. In the decade of the 1930s, six women served. No new female office holders were added in the 1940s. Three women won election in the 1950s and six in the 1960s. Up until 1977, only thirty-two (2.25%) of the 1,445 individuals who had served in the Minnesota Legislature were women. Twenty-nine of the thirty-two were in the House, and three were in the Senate. (Laura E. Naplin served in the Senate from 1927 through 1933. Nancy Brataas was elected in 1975, and Emily Anne Staples came in 1976.) Women's tenuous hold on elected office was illustrated by the experience of Knutson who, after serving in Congress from 1955 to 1959, was defeated when her alcoholic husband made public a letter he had purportedly written to her titled, "Coya, come home."

The idea that women's participation in elected bodies should be a token at best is revealed by Sidney Pauley's experience when she was door-knocking in 1973 during her campaign for a seat on the Eden Prairie City Council. A man came to the door and, when she explained that she was running for city council, he exclaimed, "But we already have a woman on the city council!"

The deep-seated cultural bias against women in the legislature can be illustrated by the case of the capitol rest rooms. Adjoining both the House and Senate chambers in the Minnesota State Capitol building are two rooms called "retiring rooms." The retiring rooms are for the exclusive use of members of the House and Senate (the public cannot enter) and are held in such sacred regard that even members of the House are not allowed into the Senate retiring room. Members of the legislature can leave the floor and go into their respective retiring rooms without having to pass through public areas of the capitol.

Until 1989, the retiring rooms had restrooms for men only. Male members of the House of Representatives could go to the private retiring room and use the rest room, while women representatives had to exit the chamber into the public area and run the gauntlet of lobbyists in order to use a former men's room with the urinals still in place behind a temporary wall. The construction of a women's bathroom was considered a political coup. "When they built us a restroom, at least they knew we were there," commented one woman legislator.

In 1977 only six percent of the members of the Minnesota State Legislature were women. By 1997 that number had increased to thirty percent. In the year 2000, thirty-five women (26.1 percent) were serving in the Minnesota House of Representatives, and twenty-two (32.8 percent) were in the Minnesota Senate. That placed Minnesota just ahead of the national mean. In 1999, 22.3 percent of state legislators were women; Washington State had the highest number with women holding 40.8 percent of the seats and Alabama the lowest with just 7.9 percent. Women have made the most gains in the western states holding 36.5 percent of the legislative seats in Nevada, 35.6 percent in Arizona, thirty-three percent in Colorado and 32.7 percent in Kansas. (Research indicates that the socioeconomic development of states is the most important predictor of women's representation in state politics.) In 1997, sixty-six of the 447 Minnesota County Commissioners (fifteen percent) were women. Minnesota women held 780 of the 2,593 school board seats (thirty percent) and 790 of the 3,477 city council seats (twenty-three percent).

At the beginning of the twenty-first century an increasing number of women are formulating public policy and expressing themselves as elected officials. Though the social climate has changed from hostility to grudging acceptance of a female presence in governmental affairs, women previously denied any role in public life are taking up the challenge and are making their voices heard in legislative bodies. Who are these women who are changing history? What stories do they have to tell about their childhood, their young adult lives, and their development into political women?

There is no specific background that predisposes an individual to political office. Shared themes do not imply causality. Yet it would be equally wrong to say the events of these women's lives are without significance to their development as political leaders. The roles they play as adults are built on the foundation of past experiences and relationships. Childhood incidents influenced their careers as adults. Certain early events may have propelled them in later life into politics.

Aside from the fact that, as a matter of equity, careers in politics should be as open to women as to men, does it make a difference to society, in the long run, if a significant proportion of elected officials are women? Is electing women to political office merely a striving for political correctness or do women bring a unique perspective? Are the bodies politic different because women have become players of the political game?

According to the Center for the American Woman and Politics, women in political office are ideologically more liberal than men and tend to be more interested in women's issues such as equal rights for women, abortion, and child care than are men. Women in political office report different emphases in the performance of their official duties than do men.

The participation of women in public affairs is changing both the content and the style of governmental decision making. Many female elected officials believe that women bring a different style to government. They frequently describe women as wanting to work collaboratively, as a team, to build consensus. Women are not as concerned about party politics and who gets the credit as they are about finding a compromise, the middle ground, a resolution to the problem.

Psychologists have noted that women generally develop and mature through a process of connection with others. A woman's autonomy and sense of self as an authoritative being come about within the context of relationships, through a process of connectedness with others. Much of what we think of as female morality is organized around the ideas of responsibility and caring for people — the expectation of limitless female giving and self-denial. (This may explain why most of the envelope stuffing for political campaigns has historically been done by women.)

The search for connection can lead women into situations that create serious emotional problems when the only forms of connection available to them are subservient affiliations. These subservient affiliations demand that women sublimate their feelings, needs, and thoughts for the sake of a relationship. Many adolescent girls learn to think in a way that is different from the way that they feel, creating a chasm between their self-knowledge and what they say. Often girls will not voice conflict, disagreement or anger for fear of losing a relationship. Girls and women have more difficulty than boys and men in asserting their authority or considering themselves as authorities.

Research on female elected officials has found them to be generally more intelligent, more assertive, more venturesome, more imaginative and unconventional and more liberal than women in general. Political women rate high on measures of sociability, optimism, and willingness to take risks. Women who run for political office are seen as being confident, having high self-esteem and strong egos.

An examination of the early lives of political women reveals that a common experience includes a break with the status quo. Many have changed religions, stopped or reduced church attendance, made major geographic moves, attended coeducational schools. By choosing to revolt against the authority structure of their society, many political women feel that they are working toward a world where the opportunities available to both men and women will be greater.

Though all of the women in this book held elected political offices and have characteristics in common, the stories of their early lives are vastly different. They came from rural areas, small towns, and large cities. Some were reared in poverty, others in affluence. Some were children during the Great Depression, others were influenced by the Vietnam conflict and the Civil Rights turmoil of the 1960s. What follows are accounts of the journeys of a group of women who chose to enter the political arena as elected officials and whose actions, in the public arena of politics, have powerfully influenced the lives of every citizen of Minnesota.

"Although the world is full of suffering, it is full also of the overcoming of it." — Helen Keller

Though Katy Olson and Gladys Brooks both took political office in the decade of the 1960s, the two women could hardly have had more different backgrounds. Katy was a child of rural poverty, whose early years were more typical of the nineteenth century than the twentieth, and who had to defy her father to be allowed to attend secondary school. Gladys had sophisticated parents, advanced education, and foreign travel. Nevertheless, both women faced similar difficulties as they moved into the public realm. Though they were unaware of it at the time, both stood on the cusp of change in America.

The year before Katy Olson was elected to the Trimont School Board, President John Kennedy had created the President's Commission on the Status of Women, chaired by Eleanor Roosevelt. The year following Katy's election, the Equal Pay Act, proposed twenty years earlier, was finally passed, establishing equal pay for men and women performing the same job duties. The act was a feeble token, failing to cover domestics, agricultural workers, executives, administrators, or professionals, but its passage introduced the concept of equal pay into the political discussion.

In 1965, only two years before Gladys Brooks entered politics, the Supreme Court overturned one of the last state laws prohibiting the prescription or use of contraceptives by married couples. By the following year, fifty state commissions on the Status of Women had been established and convened in Washington, D.C., to report their findings. Not content with the slow rate of progress in ending employment discrimination, in 1966 twenty-eight women, among them Betty Friedan, author of *The Feminine Mystique*, founded the National Organization of Women (NOW) to function as a civil rights organization for women the way the NAACP worked for African-Americans. The ideas in *The Feminine Mystique* and the legislation urged by NOW permanently altered the psyche of America.

If white American males, who were in power when the sixties began, had been paying attention, they would have noted the fury that ran through African-American literature. Writers such as Langston Hughes in the 1930s, Richard Wright in the 1940s, and James Baldwin in the 1950s had seen problems developing as a result of America's treatment of its black citizens. But it took a pacifist and a woman, Rosa Parks, to ignite the spark of civil disobedience in the civil right's movement. Her feet hurt, and she was not willing to give up her seat on the bus even when ordered to do so by the white bus driver. "I had been working all day [at a dry cleaning establishment] handling clothes that white people wear," Rosa explained. Rosa symbolized the passive resistance, espoused by Martin Luther King, Jr., that began to be practiced wherever there was discrimination.

Additional dissonance was added to the political cacophony of the sixties by the involvement of the United States in Southeast Asia. Minnesota's Sen. Eugene McCarthy was an early foe of the war in Vietnam. When no other Democrat dared to challenge Lyndon Johnson in the 1968 presidential campaign, McCarthy decided to run. He became an instant favorite with college students, who campaigned unceasingly on his behalf, though his candidacy split the Minnesota DFL party into warring Humphrey—McCarthy factions. The whole enterprise was to end tragically with the deaths of Martin Luther King, Jr., and Robert Kennedy, the invasion of McCarthy's headquarters by Chicago police and the taking over of the civil rights movement by strident young radicals who wanted to do away with the establishment altogether.

A similar take-over occurred in the women's rights movement. Those who wanted to participate in the system were drowned out and marginalized by the extreme elements, one group of which even crowned a sheep Miss America. It was in this frenzied and contentious political atmosphere that two novice Minnesota politicians began their public service careers.

The world of ideas beyond the concerns of the farm and her immediate family first opened up for Katy Olson through the medium of the PTA organization. Katy embraced it eagerly. Gladys, whose view had always been outward into the world, perceived in the late 1960s a new platform for women on the City Council of Minneapolis and stepped on to it. Though the decade saw only six women elected to the Minnesota House of Representatives and none serving in the Minnesota Senate, feminist inroads were being made on the local level. Katy was elected to the Trimont School Board in 1962, and Gladys Brooks took her seat on the Minneapolis City Council in 1967.

Katy Olson was the second to the youngest in a family of ten children. Her father had gone bankrupt farming in Iowa, so in 1936, with the help of a friend, he moved his family to a Minnesota farm. At the time of the move, Katy was a thin, eight-year-old tomboy, dressed in overalls, her hair cut short. She hated housework and worked like a man at the heavy chores on the farm. She milked the cows, rode the horses, hauled sugar beets, and ran all the heavy equipment. Katy was cultivating fields with a team of horses when she was five years old. It was two days before Christmas when, in the depths of the Depression, the destitute Olson family moved to Minnesota. Katy remembers two things about the move: the ground was white and it was moving. "The ground on the whole place was moving with rats. Inside this old house and outside, the ground just moved. It was terrible."

When Katy's family was still living in Iowa, her father had been on the council of the local Dutch Reformed Church and became embroiled in a conflict over the pastor. Olson had supported the minister, but the other members of the council were opposed and, though he fought to the end, Olson lost and quit the church. Olson never joined another church, but Katy's mother took her and her brothers and sisters to church in Minnesota. Despite his displeasure with organized religion, Katy's father daily read passages from the Bible to his family at mealtime. "He felt being a Christian gave him the strength he needed. My parents read the Bible and prayed."

Katy described her father as being a large man, six feet, four inches tall, a strict disciplinarian who was highly critical of his children. "We never did anything good enough. Sometimes you kind of wished he would say, 'Hey, you did a good job,' but he never did. At least he made you try the best you could." It was a teacher in her small country school who changed the life of this overall-clad farm girl. Though Katy had never been fond of school, the teacher, Miss Miller, worked with her to improve her reading and give her more confidence in herself. Miss Miller also emphasized the importance of education. That was crucial for Katy as education was not valued in the Olson home. Only one of Katy's eight brothers and sisters ever attended high school.

Katy's parents had immigrated from Holland, and her father desperately needed his children's help on the farm. Katy's help was especially valuable to him as she could do the work of a full-grown man. "My dad didn't want me to go to high school. He wanted me to stay home and work," she remembers. However, encouraged by Miss Miller, the determined eighth grader resolved to attend school even though it meant challenging her father. On the morning high school was to begin, when Katy's father came in the back door of their house, she crept out the front door and got on the school bus. Earlier, her mother had warned Katy what would happen if she disobeyed her father and went to high school. "You know you'll get a beating," she had said. Katy had replied philosophically, "That's probably the price you have to pay for some things." When Olson returned home from her first day of high school, her father beat her with a strap.

"Now are you going to stay home?" he asked?

"No," Katy replied.

Realizing that his daughter could not be beaten into submission, Katy's father negotiated an agreement. Katy could attend high school if she would milk the cows every morning before leaving for school and stay home to help with the farm work in the fall and spring of the year. As a result of that agreement, Katy, every year, missed the first six weeks of school in the fall and the last six weeks in the spring. "Dad was a male chauvinist," Katy explained. "He said women don't need an education to be wives and mothers."

Two issues came up during Katy's high school experience that concerned her. The first involved women's athletics. In Iowa high school girls were allowed to play basketball. To her puzzlement and regret, Katy learned that Minnesota had no basketball program for women. The second problem concerned courses she was not allowed to take. When Katy asked to take shop instead of home economics she learned that the school did not allow the girls to take shop. Manual training was only for boys. This made no sense to her, and she refused to be put off. Katy argued her case with the school principal and the superintendent, gradually working her way up the bureaucracy to the Board of Education, asking each authority for permission to take the course in shop. Everyone turned her down.

When Katy realized that she could not get the policy changed, she did not give up. Instead of asking permission, she simply went to the shop class on her own. "I spent many hours at shop when I was supposed to be in home economics. I would stay until the teacher came and got me. I was sent to the principal's and superintendent's office a few times, but that didn't bother me a whole lot. They weren't mean. We would sit and argue. I said that a lot of girls were interested in shop and would do that better than sewing. 'Why do I have to take sewing? I am never going to sew,' I asked. I didn't care about cooking and stuff like that. I asked why I couldn't learn to do things I liked to do. But of course, it was the policy — always a policy."

The school authorities did not realize what they were up against. A young girl who would accept a beating from her father in order to attend high school would not be deterred by a mere policy against girls taking shop. Katy's sense of personal power, her need to take control of her life and be responsible for herself were traits that, later in life, would carry her to Minnesota's statehouse.

One of Katy's regrets in her life is that she did not do better in high school. If only she could have attended regularly and had been allowed more time to study, she says. Her favorite subjects were mathematics, geography, and science. Though Katy's mother was unable to defy her husband over the issue of her daughter's education, she showed her silent support by buying Katy some decent clothes to wear to school. Nevertheless, when Katy graduated, neither of her parents attended the ceremony. The only members of her family to come were an older sister and her sister's husband. Since her parents gave no graduation party for their daughter, Katy attended those of her friends and tried not to let the neglect bother her. "That's the way they were," she remembers.

Earlier, thanks to intervention by the school authorities, Katy's older brother, Ari, the fourth from the oldest child, also graduated from high school and went on to college. "The superintendent of schools came out to the house and talked with Dad about Ari's capabilities in mathematics. He talked Dad into letting Ari accept a scholarship to go to Luther College in Decorah, Iowa." Ari graduated from Luther, went on to get his Ph.D. degree, and became the head of the mathematics department at Augustana College.

Katy dreamed of attending college like her brother Ari, but she had no money and no support of any kind from her parents. With her family unable to help her, Katy found a job, worked and saved her money. In 1947, she finally left home to enter Luther College when the second semester began in January. Katy's father was again opposed to his daughter's decision. He told her in anger, "Once you go to college, don't come back home." She replied that she wouldn't return unless he wrote her a letter and invited her back. When the Easter break came, Katy's mother wrote and urged her daughter to come home for the holiday. Though Katy was lonesome and homesick, she refused to return until her father wrote and told her she was welcome. The standoff ended when Katy's father finally put a sentence on the bottom of one of her mother's letters to her inviting her home for Easter. Katy could afford to attend only one semester of college. "It was a great experience. I wished and wished I could have gone further." Unable to pay her tuition, Katy left Luther after one semester and, by the next year, she was married.

Katy Olson's political career began with the Trimont PTA. Though she was busy rearing five children and farming, she took her PTA membership seriously. "I went to the meetings and learned what PTA policy and standards were." On one rare occasion when she missed a meeting, her fellow PTA members took advantage of her absence and elected her president. Katy credits attending PTA meetings on the state level with getting her involved in issues and eventually politics. "I made it a point to work hard to learn about school boards and education. Maybe that's why women are better board members and better legislators. We know we have to work harder at it and I think we do."

It was while she was lobbying a PTA issue at the state legislature in 1971 that she first got the idea of running for an elective office. She had found, to her surprise, that many of the representatives knew less about school issues that she did. "I felt, well, if they could be a representative, so could I." An out-of-town speaker at the state PTA convention also inspired her. He was impressed with Katy and told her she could do anything she wanted to if she wanted to do it badly enough. "He said to just get involved. Get involved in your local government, get on the school board and things like that. So that's what I did." Katy's service with the PTA had also convinced her that "if you really want to make some changes in your home school, the way to do it is get on the school board." The first time she ran she lost. A few years later she ran again, and that time she won.

Katy was elected to the Minnesota State PTA Board in 1962 and a member of the Trimont Board of Education in 1976. Once on the board she was surprised to find that her fellow male board members took their jobs for granted and, in her opinion, did not put their whole hearts into it. "When I first started on the school board we would get our packets of information in the mail and most of the guys wouldn't open the packets until they got to the board meeting. Heck, I had already gone through the material and talked to people about it. After a while they also did that."

In 1986, fifteen years after she had been inspired to seek public office by the PTA convention speaker, Katy, at the age of fifty-eight, ran for and was elected to the Minnesota House of Representatives, the first woman to have been elected from her district. Her interest, based on her ten years as a school board member, was in education, and she soon found herself on the education committee. As she had done on the school board, she made sure she knew the issues. She was also placed on the agriculture committee, a rather "low-priority assignment." It was immediately apparent to Katy that she was the "token woman" on the committee. The other members talked around her and generally ignored her presence. Only when she began speaking of ridge-tilling farm practices, the horse-power of tractors, and fertilizer applications, did the men tumble to the fact they had a life-time farmer in their midst. As she said, "They had a hard time stumping me."

Katy relished being a legislator. She felt that if she told the truth, explained the facts to peo-

State Representative Katy Olson

ple, most of the time she could convince them. She soon learned that when voters were against an issue, she would receive stacks of mail, but would seldom hear from her constituents when they agreed with her stand. "I would say, 'why didn't you write, why didn't you call?' 'Well, we knew how you felt,' they would reply. 'We knew you would do the right thing.'"

Throughout her political career, Katy was guided by her inner feelings on issues. For example, her strong beliefs in freedom for women led her to her pro-choice position on abortion. "I hated abortions as much as anybody, but I didn't want the government telling us what was right for our family. It was like the burning-the-flag issue. I didn't like people burning flags, but maybe some of those demonstrations we had during the Vietnam War saved a lot of lives by helping bring the war to an end. My cousin in Holland said that when Hitler took over, if you just looked at the Nazi flag wrong, you were shot. I have strong feelings about freedom."

Katy served in the Minnesota House of Representatives until 1994 when she decided not to run again. "The worst decision I ever made," she now says. During her final term she was assistant majority leader of the House, and Irv Anderson was House Speaker. While she got along with Anderson personally, she was opposed to many of the things he did. "It was a good old boy's club type of thing. I had a real problem with that. If you wanted to get a bill heard you had to do certain things. If you didn't do them, you couldn't. I said, ' I'm not going to beg anybody. If a bill can't stand on its own merit I'm not going to support it.' I told him I didn't think he had the right to decide. But that's how they would try to whip you in line. I did not react well to threats."

Some of Katy's votes for speaker did not sit well with the party leadership. "I always voted for the right speakers but they didn't win," she remarked. "I did not vote for Irv when he ran for Speaker, and he never let me forget it." Katy also did not vote for Dee Long when she ran for the same office. Before the vote Katy had spoken with Dee, saying she wished she could vote for her, that she wanted to see a woman elected, but she felt she had to support the other candidate who came from a rural area near Katy's district. "Rural people have to stick together," she explained. "Dee never held my vote against me and always treated me fairly."

When Katy began talking about not running again, most of her fellow legislators tried to talk her into staying in the legislature. "Except for Irv Anderson," she said. "I don't know if he was glad I was leaving or not, but he didn't do anything to encourage me to run again." When she looks back on her legislative career, she says there were occasions when she felt she lacked the background to do as good a job as she wanted. "There were a lot of times when I felt dissatisfied with the job I was doing as a legislator because I felt I didn't have the intelligence or some of the capabilities I needed to really do a good job. Like Ann Wynia, for example. She could get up and speak on things and do a beautiful job of it. She was very capable. I felt better about being a school board member than I did about being a state representative. I worked hard at it."

Olson is philosophical about her experience: "You've got to do the best with what you've got. I was really rewarded because it was such an honor to be a representative for eight years. It was the biggest honor anybody could have. It was a very demanding job—365 days a year, seven days a week. Now I regret quitting. I really do. I thought I was getting to the age where I haven't got a lot of time left, and I had better quit and relax and golf and fish and do some of those things. But I wish I hadn't left. I need challenges in my life."

Another notable election of a woman to Minnesota office in the sixties was that of Gladys Brooks, Minneapolis City Council member and the first woman to run as a major-party candidate for mayor of the city. Gladys also describes herself as having been a tomboy as a child. There were no girls living on her block in Minneapolis. As a result she played games with the boys and was a starter on their baseball team. She did not realize that there was anything unusual about a little girl playing with the boys until she was riding the streetcar with her grandmother and overheard two women in the seats ahead of them talking about the children in the neighborhood. One of them said, "That Gladys Sinclair. She's such a tomboy. She plays with the boys all the time." The remark did not bother Gladys at the time, but it is significant that seventy years later she still remembers it. Always in good health, Gladys walked the eight blocks from her home to Margaret Fuller Elementary School, making the trip four times a day as she came home for lunch. Her interest in athletics continued through high school at Washburn where she would be chosen captain of every basketball or volleyball team on which she played.

The other characteristic Gladys remembers about herself as a young girl was her comfort with adults. "I wasn't afraid of older people," she remembers. Her ability to be at ease and even familiar with adults sometimes got her into difficulty with her parents. Gladys' father was politically active, and in 1924 he managed Robert LaFollette's campaign for president. LaFollette was a senator from Wisconsin and a member of a prominent Wisconsin family. LaFollette came to the Sinclair home for dinner and took the time to chat with ten-year-old Gladys. When he left at the end of the evening, Gladys ran out to the car and called out, "Good luck, Bob." Her mother was embarrassed and told her daughter, "You don't say that when you are talking to a senator."

From her mother Gladys learned a love of reading. "She loved to read Stevenson and Bobby Burns," Gladys remembers, "but more than anything my mother was interested in peace." Gladys' mother was an early member of the Women's International League of Peace and Freedom and was instrumental in getting signs reading NO MORE WAR placed in the downtown streetcars. "When World War II came, she felt so bad. She wanted a peaceful world more than anything else," Gladys remembers.

Because her parents traveled and were away from their home much of the time, Gladys grew close to her grandmother and credits her with having had a great deal of influence on her. Gladys' grandparents had been homesteaders on a western ranch located fifty miles from the nearest railroad. Her grandmother told Gladys how, in 1896, she and Gladys' grandfather had ridden their horses fifty miles so he could vote for McKinley for president. It was from her grandmother that Gladys learned to value and respect all people, regardless of their economic or social station in life.

When Gladys was in the tenth grade, her parents moved to a suburb of New York City. It was a difficult change for the fifteen-year old. Part of her problem was that no one knew where Minneapolis was, "People didn't think there was anything beyond Chicago," she remembers. Once when a young man asked her where she was from, she thought to herself that he would not know where Minneapolis was so she answered, "Near Chicago."

"Oh," he replied. "Out where the pigs and wheat are."

Despite being a newcomer from an unknown city, Gladys became a member of the Pelham High School French Club, the International Club, and her church youth group.

She attended Wells, a women's school in upstate New York, that had been recommended by her mother's friends. When Gladys had been there a year, she decided that she wanted to major in political science, but when she looked through the catalogue she found Wells had only one political science course, one in economics and only two in history. "This isn't for me," she decided. "I have to go to a place where I can learn more." She transferred to the University of Minnesota. Her grandfather had attended the University of Minnesota and her father, as well as an aunt and an uncle, were graduates. Gladys enrolled in political science only to find herself one of only two women in the department. Her classmate was Eric Severeid, and due to the alphabetical seating arrangement Severeid and Sinclair quickly became good friends. ("Poor Eric. In those days we called him 'Arne,'" she remembers.)

Despite her friendship with fellow students in the Political Science Department, Gladys found the going difficult because of the professors. They would not call on the women students, and their comments were pointedly directed at the men in the class. One professor in particular, who taught "American Political Parties," roused her ire as he would never call on her or give her an opportunity to participate in discussions. "Regardless of what we did, and there were a lot of things going on over there," she recalls, "they would always select the men."

While at the University of Minnesota, Gladys became involved with the Progressive Party and was a member of the group of students who protested United States involvement in the Spanish War. "We never thought about going in to the president's office, like they did in the 1960s," she says. "But we did stand on the steps north of the auditorium and point our fingers at Coffman over there. Richard Scannon, who was the son of the dean of the Medical School, was part of that group, as was Lee Loevinger, who's now a judge in Washington. We were kind of obstreperous while we were at the university."

The year Gladys graduated from college, she got a big break. She was selected to participate in a United States-Japanese student conference in Japan. Of the forty students selected from the United States, five were women, and when she got to Japan, she found that, of the forty

Japanese students who had been selected, only four were women. The trip brought home to her the under-representation of women in public affairs and launched her on a campaign that was to continue for the rest of her political life.

Because her father's business took him to Europe frequently, Gladys had opportunities to travel, both with her family and alone, throughout the continent before the Second World War. She had spent some time in the summer of 1935 at the University of Geneva, and, in 1939, she told her father she wanted to go back and see what was happening in Switzerland. Gladys' father was not enthusiastic about the idea because it was obvious that war was about to break out. He said, "Okay, but stay close to the border and in case anything happens, get back to France and then come back."

Gladys went to Europe by herself in August of 1939, and while she was in France, learning that Eric Severeid was also there, she arranged to meet with him. Severeid, by now married to Lois Finger, daughter of the University of Minnesota track coach, discussed his career with Gladys. He told her that a man had come over to Paris from London to ask him if he would be interested in doing any radio broadcasting. Severeid was wondering how he should respond, and he asked Gladys, "Did you ever hear of a guy named Ed Murrow?"

It was during this trip to Europe that Gladys met George Bernard Shaw. Her father was representing MGM and Paramount pictures, which wanted Shaw to release some of his plays. Gladys' family was in England from May until early September 1939, and during that time Shaw took an interest in Gladys' mother. As a result of his interest, she invited Shaw to lunch. The author accepted, but stipulated that no other guests were to be invited. The Sinclairs had a wonderful visit with Shaw, who told stories of his life in Ireland before he came to England. At the end of the lunch, Gladys' father asked permission to take a picture of his two daughters with the illustrious writer and Shaw agreed. Just before the picture was snapped, he told the girls to look at him instead of the camera. They did, and Gladys still has a copy of the picture of her sister and herself looking fondly at George Bernard Shaw. The German invasion of Poland took place in August of that year, so the Sinclairs sailed hastily for the United States.

Gladys became involved in the civil rights movement in the early 1950s when a black woman journalist applied for membership in the

Minneapolis chapter of the American Association of University Women (AAUW). Though the young woman was fully qualified, many members, as well as the local president, were opposed to her membership. Gladys was a member of AAUW as well as the Minneapolis Women's Club, neither one of which had minority members, and she argued for the black woman's admission. When the black woman was finally admitted, many AAUW members resigned and went over to the Women's Club in protest.

A year or two later, a friend, Rhoda Lund, called Gladys and said that a black teacher from Edina wanted to join the Women's Club. "What do you think?" she asked. Gladys thought about it overnight and called Rhoda back. "I think it is great that she wants to belong," she said, "but let's find four other black people as well. Let's get five black members." Rhoda agreed and, with Rhoda's and Gladys' help, five black women were brought into the Minneapolis Women's Club, some of whom are still members.

In addition to being influenced by her grandmother, Gladys credits her father for her interest in politics. "Politics was always a topic of conversation with us," she says. Gladys' father took his two daughters on trips throughout the United States, believing that it was important for them to know about their own country, and he taught Gladys to enjoy different kinds of people. "I like people," she says, "The more people the better as far as I'm concerned. I go around and talk to them and enjoy what they're doing. I like to find out what people are doing."

Gladys Brooks was fifty-four years old in 1967 when she ran for a seat on the Minneapolis City Council. Though her children were grown, she still encountered the criticism that she should be home caring for her children instead of running for political office. Her friends would say to her, "How can you do it? My husband wouldn't let me!"

The ward to which Gladys was elected to represent, Ward 11 at the south end of Minneapolis, was a large one, extending from Lyndale to Cedar Avenue and from Forty-fifth to Sixty-sixth streets. Only one woman, Elsa Johnson, had previously served on the Minneapolis City Council, and Elsa had become ill and did not serve her full term. Gladys was elected the following year and was the first woman to serve not only her first full term but two additional ones. Because Gladys represented the eleventh ward, she was put on the Ways and Means Committee, which controlled the city's expenditures. According to Gladys, the representatives from the eleventh, seventh, and thirteenth wards were always on the Ways and Means Committee because they represented Minneapolis's wealthiest citizens. "When, after three years on the council, the men discovered I knew something about economics, they made me the chair," Gladys said. When businessmen came to testify before the committee, they were invariably surprised to discovered Gladys, a woman, sitting in the chairperson's seat.

After serving three terms on the city council, Gladys resigned in 1973 to run for mayor of Minneapolis—the first woman from a major political party to make the attempt. She had two reasons, she says, to run—one was to depose the then current mayor, Charles Stenvig, and the other was to serve as an example to other women that they could run for major political offices. Gladys was defeated by Al Hofsted, but she was not too disappointed. "Al was a good friend of mine," she says. "He had been on the council with me for one term, so we had a good time. We had fun getting rid of Stenvig." In 1975 Gladys was named to the Metropolitan Council, serving until 1983.

Soon after she resigned from the Minneapolis City Council, Gladys

Minneapolis City Council Member
Gladys Brooks

was asked to be the first woman to serve on the board of the Farmers Mechanics Bank. While she was serving on the bank board, a request came in from the YMCA Fund Drive Committee for $75,000. Two weeks later the YWCA Fund Drive Committee asked the bank for $50,000. Both requests were sent to a bank committee for study. The report that came back to the board, recommended that the YMCA be given $50,000 and that nothing be given to the YWCA. Gladys objected. "This is not fair," she said. "Why do you give to one and not to the other?" John Davis, a fellow board member, joined her protest. The two requests were sent back to the committee, which returned with a revised recommendation. This time the YMCA was again given its $50,000 and the YWCA $15,000. Gladys was still not satisfied, but felt it was better than nothing.

Toward the end of her nine-year service on the bank board, Gladys invited all of the secretaries of the Board of Management to lunch at a downtown restaurant. A few days later she met the bank president, who said, "Gladys, I hear you took the secretaries to lunch. What a great idea. We never thought of that." For over forty years Gladys Brooks has taken the staffs of organizations with which she works to lunch once a year "to thank them and tell them what a good job they are doing."

When Title IX was enacted in the 1970s, requiring equity for women in school athletic programs, Gladys was asked by the president of the University of Minnesota to be a member of an advisory committee on women's athletics. She became the first chair of the committee and has continued working with the organization ever since. Realizing that raising money is a special problem for women, who typically receive less than half the political contributions given to men, Gladys became one of the founders of the Women's Campaign Fund. In her opinion, too many women, when asked to give to a political campaign, still reply, "Oh, my husband does that." "What women don't realize is that they have to give to other women," she says. Despite what seems like women's slow progress in winning political offices, Gladys looks with satisfaction at the Minneapolis mayoral races. "Who would have thought a few years ago that a white woman and a black woman would have been running for mayor," she says, and adds, "It was just twenty years after I ran for mayor that Sharon Sayles Belton was elected."

$\alpha2\omega$

"We're half the people; we should be half the Congress." — Jeannette Rankin

The 1970s was the decade when the horizon brightened on the political scene for Minnesota women entering elective office. Prior to the 1970s, the highest percentage of women members of the legislature had occurred back in 1928 when 2.5 percent of the legislators had been women. After that year, the percentage hovered between half of one percent and one percent. There were no women at all in the legislature from 1943 through 1948, and in 1970 only one lone woman, Helen McMillan, was serving. Then, in 1972, six women, four from the DFL Party and two Independent Republicans, were elected to the House, raising the percentage of women to a thumping three percent.

What events propelled the sudden increase? The causes were many, and some were not immediately apparent. It was a cigarette advertisement that captured the mood of the decade. "You've Come a Long Way Baby" proclaimed Virginia Slims' billboards and magazine ads, tying cigarette smoking to women's liberation. The slogan embodied for many the triumph of the women's movement during that decade.

The emerging feminism shattered many established traditions of female subordination in American life and opened up formerly closed occupations to women. The women's liberation movement revolutionized women's and men's sense of their gender roles and transformed literary theory, art, and social analysis. New disciplines of women's studies appeared on college campuses. A host of injustices in American life were challenged. Like the civil rights movement, the social effects of feminism were widespread and powerful and, because they were so far-reaching, they sparked controversy and opposition.

One of the most significant demands of the women's movement was equal pay for equal work. More and more women were entering the labor force and found themselves earning fifty-seven percent of male wages. Women were further shortchanged by turn-of-the-century labor laws that prevented women from working overtime. Many women found themselves working at the lowest-paid, most menial jobs. Though some institutional changes took place — the Ivy League universities went co-ed, the Lutheran Church in America and the American Lutheran Church (although not the Missouri Synod) agreed to ordain women, and Las Vegas hired female blackjack dealers — many significant areas stayed the same. At the end of the decade, women's wages were still an average of fifty-seven percent of men's.

In March 1973, the Equal Rights Amendment overwhelmingly passed Congress and was quickly ratified by thirty states, including Minnesota. Then its momentum was stalled. Phyllis Schlafly, an activist in the right wing of the Republican Party, claimed passage of the ERA would lead to a loss of alimony in divorce cases, the drafting of women into the military and the creation of unisex bathrooms. Schlafly's supporters, organized into such groups as WWWW (Women Who Want to Be Women) and HOW (Happiness of Womanhood) flooded state capitols with telegrams, phone calls, and homemade breads and pies. The real power of Schlafly's organization lay in its ability to tap into the grassroots fear of many Americans that social change was proceeding at too fast a pace. In 1979 the ratification period expired. Though Congress passed a three-year extension, not a single additional state approved the amendment.

A seemingly unrelated but nonetheless important event propelling women into public life was the passage of Title IX, the federal legislation that prohibits sex discrimination in any educational institution that receives federal aid. "No person in the United States shall, on the basis of sex, be excluded from participation in, be denied the benefits of, or be subjected to discrimination under any education program or activity receiving federal financial assistance." Though the act applied to all programs within schools, not just physical education and athletics, its greatest impact was on sports programs for women. Athletics became a major influence in the lives of many girls who later entered public life. The quality of women's sports experience and its impact on their careers is defined by whether it occurred before or after the watershed passage of Title IX.

The year (1972) that six women began serving in the Minnesota Legislature was also the year *MS Magazine* began publication, Barbara Jordan became the first Black woman elected to Congress from a Southern state, and police arrested five men for breaking into the Democratic National Committee headquarters at the Watergate Hotel in Washington, D.C.

Joan Growe, future legislator and second woman to hold the office of Minnesota Secretary of State, grew up in the small town of Buffalo, Minnesota, the daughter of the owner of the local hardware store who also served as the town mayor. As a young girl, Joan built forts with the neighborhood boys and played in the woods and creeks around her home, pretending to be an early pioneer settler. She attended the local Catholic school where the nuns, in dark habits that reached the floor, taught the children their catechisms and the proper observance of all of the religious holidays of the Roman Catholic calendar. The school was small with two classes to a room. Joan was a good student who enjoyed her school as well as life at home where her mother, a stay-at-home mom, looked after her and her younger brother.

The disciplinarian in the family was Joan's father, a gentle man, who, disliking controversy, debates, or anything unpleasant, ruled through his wife. If Joan wanted to stay out later than the curfew her father had established, she would ask her mother who, in turn, would inquire of Joan's father. Back would come the answer. "No, you have to come home when your father said." Joan has no idea what her father might have done if she had disobeyed his rules, and she says she never tried to find out.

Joan's family was small-town and middle-class. Her father worked six days a week at the hardware store and on the seventh, while his wife and children attended Sunday mass, he did his paper work. "Everyone was very careful about money and we didn't squander it," Joan remembers. "My parents didn't go on trips or travel. We had one car which was common then." Joan felt that she and her brother always had what they needed. She never felt deprived, but there were not many extras.

At the end of her ninth year in parochial school, Joan transferred to the public high school of Buffalo where she found the student culture to be vastly different. Instead of walking quietly through the halls, speaking in lowered voices and showing great respect for teachers, she found herself surrounded by fellow students who were loud and demanding.

They shouted and screamed, were rude to teachers, pushed and shoved in the halls, swore and were disruptive in class. Despite the dramatic difference between the schools, Joan adjusted and thrived. She became a part of the town clique of girls, as distinguished from those who were bused in from the country, and participated in the school newspaper and dramatics. She was popular but not part of the crowd that went to the dance halls and drank, both because she knew her father would not have allowed her and because those activities did not interest her. The most disruptive activity Joan participated in as a young person was, with her friends, stealing and eating watermelons from a farmer's patch and moving outhouses onto the highway at Halloween.

Looking back on her childhood, Joan believes the first time she ever challenged authority was in college at St. Cloud State University where dormitory closing hours were still in force for women. She and her friends thought it was very daring to slip out of the building after hours using the fire escape. With fake IDs, they would order beer in the local establishments. "We thought we were quite grown up," she recalls.

Joan's parents had encouraged her to attend college. While a senior in high school, Joan dated a fellow student and was reluctant to move away from him. It was Joan's mother who insisted that her daughter go away to school, telling her, "You've got to get a college education so if something happens to your husband someday you will be able to take care of yourself." Reluctantly Joan acquiesced, and, after she was in college at St. Cloud for a few months, she says that she "totally forgot the boyfriend."

Though Joan's father was the mayor of Buffalo, Joan did not think of him as "being in politics." The father of one of her high school friends was a state senator. In Joan's mind, he was in politics, but she did not consider that her dad was. "There's a difference between being a small town mayor and a state senator," she says. Joan does not recall ever seeing a piece of campaign literature for her father or working for his election. The only indication of her father's political activities came when people would call their home to complain about a neighbor's cat in their yard or when her mother would grumble that they could seldom have a meal without the phone ringing.

Occasionally friends of her parents would look at Joan and her younger brother and remark, "I suppose you'll be going into politics like your dad." When they said it to Joan, they would laugh and treat it as a joke, but when they said it to her brother, it was a serious comment.

"I remember not liking the feeling that there was something they were saying that was fine for my brother and laughing about it for me," she recalls.

Most of the time the comments about a political career went over Joan's head. She had no idea what she wanted to do, and the idea of politics was as far from her mind as being an astronaut. Though her parents had encouraged her to get an education, even such professions as medicine or law were beyond her expectations. "No one set that kind of a goal or vision out for me," she says, "and I didn't have it for myself."

At the age of twenty, Joan married a man who was a senior at St. Thomas College in St. Paul. Following their marriage, he entered the University of Minnesota Law School, and Joan went to work teaching the second grade in the Bloomington Public Schools to support them. She also had children, one each year. The children were spaced so close together that the second and third were born in the same calendar year. When her husband graduated from law school, they moved to Tracy, Minnesota, Joan's husband's home town, where he opened up a one-man law practice.

It was in Tracy that Joan's marriage fell apart. To her dismay, she discovered that her husband was an alcoholic and physically abusive. Until her marriage at the age of twenty, Joan had led what she calls "an incredibly sheltered life. I didn't know that people drank too much. I didn't know that men hit women." Joan had worked to put her husband through law school and had three babies in three years only to discover that her husband was an abusive alcoholic. "I was living something I had never heard of in my life," she says. "I was just devastated. I had expected to be married for the rest of my life and live happily ever after. I really believed that."

Forty years ago alcoholism, particularly in a native son who was a graduate of a law school, was not something anyone talked about. Few people were aware of treatment possibilities. There were no safe houses for women and children. Women in Joan's situation were expected to just stick it out. As Joan struggled with her situation, a conspiracy of silence settled around her. Though everyone in Tracy knew what was going on, the small town mores prevented anyone from doing or saying anything, or from coming to Joan's aid. When she began to fear for her children's safety, she decided it was time to leave.

Taking sixty dollars that she had managed to save from her household money, Joan packed up her three children, all under the age of four, and fled to St. Paul. Because her teaching certificate had expired, she was not able to get a job in the better paying public school system, so she took a position in a Catholic school for severely retarded children. She had no car, so she rode the bus that went around to pick up the children for the school, and, when the school day ended, Joan rode the little bus home. Her salary was $300 a month, out of which she paid $125 for rent and $100 for a baby sitter to care for her children while she worked, leaving $75 to feed and clothe her family for the month. At the same time she was teaching at the Catholic school, Joan was also taking night classes at the University of Minnesota to get her teaching certificate renewed.

The stress of her situation resulted in a gum infection. Though she had no money and no insurance, she went to see a dentist. The compassionate doctor treated Joan, though he knew she had no money and could not reimburse him immediately. Joan later paid the dentist's bill at the rate of $2.00 a month, walking the ten blocks to his office to save the cost of a stamp.

Though it had been a struggle and a hardship, taking the night classes at the university finally paid off. That spring Joan was hired by the St. Anthony School District to teach mentally disabled children. However, though her job would finally pay a living wage, it would not start until September. The Catholic school, like the public schools, was on summer break, and Joan had to figure out how to live through June, July, and August. She tried to find a position that would earn enough to pay child care for the summer and discovered that there were none. In desperation, she went to the welfare office and applied for AFDC (Aid For Dependent Children). After a few days she was visited by a case worker, a young woman about eighteen years old, who tried to give Joan helpful hints on how to save money. "I completely ignored her," said Joan, "because there was no money to save."

Welfare recipients in the early 1960s were given bulk commodities to take home and use. Joan remembers that "you had to go stand in line on Central Avenue in Minneapolis at the AFDC office, and they would give you bulk grains—rice, cornmeal, and things, which are very 'in' now but they weren't thirty-five years ago. We had to be there a certain day of the week, and there was one person giving it out at the door.

Everyone driving down the street had to know what was going on. There I stood on Central Avenue with everyone passing by, my kids hanging on to my skirt, to pick up our bulk products. I would take them home, and some I used and some I gave away to a neighbor. The experience was humiliating. The line was made up of all women." When school started in the fall, Joan was earning enough to take care of her children. She had been on AFDC for three months.

In looking back on the experience, Joan says that "my spirits had to hold up. You are into survival, and you take one day at a time. If I had thought too far into the future I wouldn't have been able to cope. My goal was always to earn enough money so I could hire the baby sitter to take care of the kids." Joan's parents came to her aid during this period bringing clothes and toys for the children. Her father would take one of his grandsons to the grocery store "to buy some cookies" and would come back with enough groceries for a week.

By 1965 Joan had remarried, had had a fourth child, and was living in Burnsville, Minnesota. One day she saw an advertisement in the paper announcing the organization of a new branch of the League of Women Voters. Anyone interested was invited to attend. "I thought it was the most exciting thing I had ever heard of," Joan recalls. She went to the organizing meeting, and before it was over she had been named to the board of the new group and assigned the task of voter service. "The idea of talking about something other than housework and cooking and children was stimulating to me. One of the things the League did was conduct a study of the local community, and I thought that sounded fascinating. Burnsville was a growing community, and I didn't know much about it."

One memory Joan has of that early League was the copy machine. It consisted of a flat tray filled with a jelly-like substance. Joan would put the machine on her kitchen floor to use it, hoping she could get a copy of something made before the cat or one of the children stepped in the jelly and mooshed it all up. "We thought that was high tech," she remembers.

Joan and her family lived outside of Minnesota for a year, and when they returned it was to the community of Minnetonka. Before the moving boxes were even unpacked, Joan had called the local League to tell them she was back. Within a short time the president of the Minnetonka-Eden Prairie League, Janet Johns, knocked on her door to ask Joan to co-chair the League finance drive. From finance, Joan moved to the issue of housing.

Minnetonka was a growing community in Minnesota, and there was no moderate or low-income housing for people. It was the League's position that there were people with low and moderate incomes living in the community for whom appropriate housing should be provided. Joan organized League-sponsored forums where citizens could learn about and discuss housing issues and, in time, get the city council to act. Janet Johns, the former League of Women Voters president, had been elected to the Minnetonka City Council where she was the lone vote in favor of moderate-income housing.

By the early 1970s, what had been a closed political system in Minnesota began to open up. Reapportionment created a new legislative seat in Joan's district. At the same time, there was pressure to give women more responsible positions. The old system of naming men the chairmen of the committees and expecting women to do much of the detail work was breaking down. By 1972 the DFL had a rule that half of the delegates to conventions from every level had to be women.

When it came time for the IR endorsing convention, Joan's good friend, Gwen Luhta, an active IR member and then president of the League of Women Voters, resigned her League position to seek her party's endorsement for a senate seat. The women in the League were excited as they thought Gwen would be perfect in the legislature. League members attended the convention only to watch in frustrated silence as the Republicans endorsed one of the men who had been active in the party for thirty-five years. "That is typically what happened in those days in districts the party controlled," Joan says. "They put forth male candidates. This district was about sixty-seven percent IR, so you knew a Republican was going to win." League members were "incredibly disappointed."

When it came time for the DFL endorsing convention for the district, the DFL Party did not have a candidate for the new House seat. With the district barely thirty-three percent DFL, none of the party regulars wanted to run since they were sure they could not win. Friends came to Joan and said, "You ought to do it." Joan thought to herself, "Why should I do this? I am just going to lose." Nevertheless the idea intrigued her. She had been to the state legislature lobbying for the League of Women Voters and had sat in the gallery watching the legislators voting in ways that she thought were wrong. "I can do this as well as they can," she thought.

The calls kept coming. "There is no Democratic candidate," her friends pointed out. "This guy (the IR candidate) is going to win. But at least, if we have a good DFL candidate, we can educate him on the issues." Joan finally told a friend, Connie Hudnut, that she would run for the endorsement at the DFL district convention if someone would get her a baby sitter for that night and a speech. Connie accepted the challenge and produced both the sitter and the speech. The speech that Connie supplied was written on recipe cards. It was the exact same speech that Gwen Luhta had given in her unsuccessful bid for the Republican convention endorsement. Joan just changed IR to DFL and gave it. "It was a typical good League of Women Voters' speech," Joan remembers, "and it got me endorsed." Actually, the convention had no choice, Joan was the only person running. "The Democrats were plead-ing for somebody to run. They were looking for a live body. That's how the DFL operated in those days. They were happy to endorse women for seats they weren't going to win," Joan said.

When she got home that night, Joan actually felt sick to her stomach thinking about what she had done. "I don't know anything about run-ning a campaign," she said to herself. If she had known it was possible to withdraw she would have. A few days later she invited some party activists to her home to tell her how to run a campaign. About fourteen people sat in Joan's living room giving her advice, but as they filed out only one person, a woman, Nancy Wangen, gave her a check.

Just as Joan was about to truly panic, her friend Gretchen Fogo returned home from a vacation. When she learned what Joan had done, Gretchen and Nancy Wangen set out to organize a campaign. Since Gretchen, Nancy, and Joan were all former teachers, they ran the cam-paign like a classroom exercise. Gretchen wrote elaborate lesson plans and charted out a precisely planned campaign. Joan remembers that "it was a production you could never reproduce because we had all these capable women who were not working and had time and were so excit-ed. No one paid any attention to us because I was not supposed to win. The chair of the state DFL Party lived in my legislative district, and I never met him until after the election. We did not get any help."

Joan and her campaign workers decided that their main hope lay in door-knocking. The year 1972 marked George McGovern's bid for the presidency, and the women knew that all the odds were against them. The first day Joan went out to walk the sidewalks door-knocking, she wore high-heeled shoes. By the next day she had switched to oxfords. Joan door-knocked from noon until after dark, every day, from the day she was endorsed in July until the second Tuesday in November. Workers took turns bringing casseroles to her house and baby sitting her children. Other women volunteered to drive her around.

Ted Kennedy came to town, and the legislative candidates were invited to a reception to meet him. Joan loved and respected the Kennedys, but the reception was at 5:00 P.M. and she felt she should not give up the door-knocking time, even to shake hands with the senator. On the night before the election, Joan was out in Eden Prairie in a snow-storm talking to a man who was skinning a deer in his garage, trying to convince him to vote for her.

The women organized coffee parties, two or three a day, in people's homes. The district was half in Minnetonka and half in Eden Prairie and people had a lot of questions. Many of the queries concerned school finance, and Joan was prepared. One of her friends, Diane Henze, had acted as her tutor. "I knew the complicated formula for school financing better than anyone in the state of Minnesota," she said. "It was important because people didn't expect a woman to know about finances. I could make that my big push at the coffee parties, and I knew more about it than did my opponent, Richard Stranik, a businessman and one of the party faithful."

Toward the end of the campaign, Gretchen and Nancy divided up the community into blocks of thirty to forty homes and assigned each block to a woman worker. Volunteers hand-delivered campaign literature to the designated residences. The campaign committee met every week, with child-care provided. The process was totally democratic; the women discussed and voted on everything, on colors for campaign literature, on whether to have bumper stickers, on the size of campaign posters. Working with Joan was the "in" thing to do. It became a matter of pride that women were running the campaign.

As election day drew near, Joan, Gretchen, and Nancy looked at their excited workers and wondered what they could do to lower their expectations. They were still convinced that Joan could not win. Tactfully, they tried to tell their workers not to get too excited, and not to feel too let down when Joan lost.

Joan, of course, did not lose. She defeated her IR candidate with fifty-five percent of the vote. When her election returns were in, Joan and Gretchen decided to go down to DFL headquarters in Minneapolis. However, neither of them had ever been there before, and they did not know where it was. When they found it and went in, they encountered Rep. Martin Sabo pacing the floor and muttering in disbelief, "Joan Growe won? Joan Growe won?"

During her first week at the legislature, Joan, along with the other newly elected lawmakers, was briefed on her duties. The assumption behind the briefing was that the work connected to the various committees and subcommittees to which the legislators were assigned was complicated and difficult to coordinate. As she listened to the briefing, Joan laughed to herself. Keeping her committee assignments straight was nothing compared to managing the school, sports, activities schedules, and transportation needs of four children.

The year before Joan was elected, there had been only one woman, Helen McMillan, in the entire legislature. Elected along with Joan were four more women, three Democrats and one Republican. For her maiden speech in the legislature, Joan decided to speak in support of the Equal Rights Amendment. Television had just been introduced into the House, and Joan was terrified at the thought of making her speech before her colleagues and whomever might be watching on television. Adding to her discomfort was the fact that the House floor was noisy. Few members actually paid attention to the speakers and most carried on conversations or did paper-work during speeches.

When Joan stood up to make that first speech, she was shaking, and the other members were still carrying on their own conversations. As soon as she began, however, the House suddenly fell silent. A woman's voice in the chamber was still a novelty and the legislators were startled into giving her their attention. Joan persisted, looking into the TV camera, and giving her Equal Rights Amendment speech to a hushed and attentive audience.

Two years after winning her legislative seat, Joan decided to run for the office of Secretary of State. At the time, the seat was held by Arlen Erdahl, a Republican whom Joan described as "a very decent, a very good man." Erdahl had announced his candidacy for Congress so the Secretary of State seat was, presumably, to be open. However, when Erdahl went for his party's endorsement for the Congressional seat he lost, so he came back and ran for Secretary of State again.

The IR refusal to endorse Erdahl for the Congressional seat made running for Secretary of State far more difficult than Joan had at first anticipated. Besides having to win the DFL endorsement contest, Joan would have to run in the DFL primary, and then, in the general election, would have to run against her friend, the incumbent Arlen Erdahl.

Joan's opponent in the endorsing contest was Al Loehr, the mayor of St. Cloud. A woman had never been endorsed for Secretary of State for as long as anyone could remember and people were skeptical of the idea. Joan traveled all over the state so people could look her over. "I thought I looked pretty normal," she said. "I didn't wear chains or short leather skirts." Joan believes she defeated Al Loehr because she out-worked him. "I called every delegate three times, and I traveled all over."

After winning the endorsement, Joan had to face the primary contest. Her opponent was a man named Noonan, from whom no one ever heard or saw during the entire campaign. Other than filing for the position, Noonan did nothing. Nevertheless, he almost won. On primary night, Joan was at her headquarters until 3:00 A.M. waiting for the paper ballots from northern Minnesota to come in. "The election was very close," she remembers, "Noonan's success must have been because he was a man. I never saw him, and he never did any campaigning."

For the general election against Erhdal, Joan went to every county in the state of Minnesota. She would go to the court house, introduce herself to the county auditor, who would take her around and introduce her to others in county government. Joan had a driver, and they would try to hit ten to twelve towns in a day.

Joan lost fifteen pounds during the campaign. She became so thin that, even in the summer, she did not dare wear short sleeve dresses because she looked anorexic. When she arrived in a town, besides the court house, she would visit the newspaper, the radio station, and would walk up and down Main Street, introducing herself and hanging posters in store windows. At night she wrote thank-you notes to the shop owners thanking them for sharing their window space.

Joan remembers that "it was the kind of campaign where we would stay in people's homes at night because we couldn't afford a motel. The driver would get the basement room, and I slept in people's bedrooms with their kids and their dogs. They would feed us in the morning and we wouldn't eat again until we went to some event. It was a hand-to-mouth, grass-roots campaign, and people were incredibly kind and generous. We were well organized—scheduled within minutes. If we had ever kept to the speed limit, we could never have kept to our schedule. We had about twelve minutes between towns."

The political pundits expected all of the Democrats running for statewide offices to win except for Joan. Wendell Anderson, Warren Spannus, and Jim Lord, all of whom were running, were thought to have easy contests. Only Joan was believed to be in trouble. The race was indeed a close one. When the ballots were counted, Joan Growe had just squeaked by. Again, she had outworked her opponent. Joan was elected Secretary of State in 1974 and served until she retired in 1998.

The highlight of Joan's twenty-four-year career as Minnesota's longest-serving Secretary of State came when she was asked to be a United Nation's observer during the first election in South Africa in which every citizen, regardless of race, was eligible to vote. Joan was asked to participate and represent Minnesota because of the state's stellar national reputation for voter turn-out and participation. Expecting to be impressed by what she saw, Joan was overwhelmed by the sight of hundreds of people standing in the pre-dawn in a long line leading

Secretary of State Joan Growe

to the voting station. About that experience she said, "People walked three or four miles just to join the line and then stood five or six hours in the mid-day sun to vote, even if disabled or infirm. Many of the elderly were helped by their children or grandchildren. One man was brought to the station in a wheelbarrow. Many were frightened to be voting for the first time. Some trembled. Others cried. One woman, when asked who she wanted to vote for, kept saying, 'the old man, the old man.' For clarity she added, 'the one who was in prison.' What drew hundreds of people to the voting station at dawn? Not fear, but hope. Not reward, but faith."

What made Joan Growe run and work so hard to win? Looking back on her life, Joan credits the trauma of her first marriage and her struggles to support herself and her three children with instilling the fierce determination and tenacity that she brought to politics. These experiences changed the inner core of her being. "Always in the back of my mind was the thought that nothing could be harder than what I had already done," she said. "Nothing could be more exhausting. If that had not happened I would have been just a nice housewife all of my life."

Two others elected to the legislature at the same time as Joan Growe were Phyllis Kahn and Mary Forsythe. Phyllis Kahn's first great interest, which began when she was about ten years old, was major league baseball. Her home was near Ebbett's Field in Brooklyn, New York, and she remembers 1947 as the year the Brooklyn Dodgers brought Jackie Robinson onto the team. From then until she graduated from high school, Kahn was immersed in baseball, paying to attend games, sneaking into games, cutting school to go to games on ladies' day. She was not alone in her enthusiasm. "It was very much of a neighborhood thing," she remembers. "All the kids were fanatic Dodger fans." Later, at a feminist gathering when Phyllis was asked to name a role model for herself, she said "Jackie Robinson."

One year, when she was in elementary school, the playoffs pitted the Brooklyn Dodgers against the Philadelphia Phillies. The first game was to be at Ebbett's field, and Phyllis wanted desperately to attend. The problem for the Kahn family was that the game happened to fall on the Jewish holiday of Rosh Hoshana. Nevertheless Phyllis was determined to go to the game and argued the point with her father.

Phyllis's plan was to go to the ball park with a friend the day before the game and camp out all night at the box office so as to be in line for the early fifty-cent bleacher tickets. Fortunately for Phyllis, her father understood how important it was for his daughter to attend this game. His problem was what he would say to his own mother when he appeared in the synagogue on Rosh Hoshana without his daughter. After much discussion, Phyllis reached a compromise with her father. She would be allowed to attend the game, but she could not camp out overnight and, besides going with a friend, she would have to take her little brother along with her.

The three children arose very early on the morning of the game and found places in the ticket line. Before going to the synagogue, Kahn's father stopped by the stadium to make sure the crowd was not too unruly and that the children would be safe. Phyllis, her brother, and friend got into the stadium without incident where the Dodgers, unfortunately, were defeated by the Phillies. For years Kahn believed that the reason her beloved Dodgers had lost the game was because she and her brother had gone to the game on Rosh Hoshana instead of to the synagogue. It was years before it occurred to her that she and her brother had not been the only Jewish kids in the stands.

Like many of the other women who later entered political life, Phyllis, as a child, was free to roam without restrictions through her neighborhood of the city. The children climbed fences, walked the railroad tracks, played on the subway line—jumping over the third rail—and got into fights with neighborhood gangs. "I lived in a tough neighborhood. If you crossed the boundary line and your foot went from the Jewish section to the Irish section, gangs of kids would get you and beat you up and make you apologize for killing Christ." The first time this happened, Phyllis went to her mother (her father was away in World War II until she was eight) to ask her what this meant. Her mother replied, "Oh, we didn't do it, but you can tell them you are sorry anyway." Phyllis took her mother's advice and learned how to say she was sorry about Christ's having been killed without having to admit to anything. But she only did that, she adds, when she was seriously outnumbered.

Phyllis' grandfather was an immigrant who had helped organize the garment workers on New York's Lower East Side. Her parents, and Phyllis as well, continued the liberal tradition. "My father, to his dying day, never crossed a picket line." Phyllis, who was seven years old at the time, remembers the 1944 presidential election between Franklin Roosevelt and Thomas E. Dewey and her mother talking about the election with a neighbor on the street. Roosevelt was a great hero to Phyllis' parents and relatives. The neighbor was wearing a Dewey button, and Kahn could not understand how her mother could be having such a friendly conversation with this woman who was obviously an enemy. "Why wasn't she ripping the button off her blouse?" she wondered.

(Phyllis tells the story now as evidence of how she has mellowed.) Phyllis also remembers having seen President Franklin D. Roosevelt riding down the street in a convertible although the memorable aspect of that encounter for her was that Roosevelt had his dog, Fala, with him.

Though Phyllis was an excellent student, she continually got into trouble during her elementary school years, either for talking out of turn or for reading ahead in her reader. When the readers were handed out Phyllis would consume the entire book (which was supposed to last the entire semester) on the first day. She also smuggled her own books into the class and would read them instead of paying attention to the teacher. Her punishment for these offences was being ordered to sit under the teacher's desk. It was not until she was in the fifth grade, when the emphasis shifted from behavior and became focused on creativity and ability, that she began to like school.

Phyllis' community was made up of immigrants who were upwardly mobile, liberal and homogeneous. During the 1948 presidential election, her junior high civics class held a straw vote. Of the thirty-two students in the class, thirty voted for Henry Wallace and two for Norman Thomas. The students were quite obviously voting for the candidates their parents supported. Phyllis was one of the two who voted for Norman Thomas. She explained her vote by saying that she wanted to vote for a candidate for whom no one else would vote. The school vote reflected the liberal, intellectual and progressive nature of the community. Phyllis remembers that no one discouraged girls from trying to be smart. "Nobody ever said you shouldn't act as if you're smart because you're a girl. I don't know how I would have reacted if that had happened. In this community, girls were smart and boys were smart and everybody was bound for good colleges."

The Brooklyn Botanical Gardens, not a formal school, provided the first significant early learning experience for Phyllis Kahn. At the Botanical Garden, across the street from her home, Kahn was given her own plot of soil with seeds to plant in it and suggestions of experiments she could conduct. In the winter, the children were taught how to start seeds and do simple research. This experience and the summers her family spent at Woods Hole in the environs of the Oceanographic Institute fostered the young Phyllis' early and lasting interest in science.

Because she was in a hurry to get through school and into college, Phyllis talked her parents into letting her attend a special accelerated program in junior high that would allow her to graduate a year early. The school was in Bedford-Stuyvesant, a deteriorating neighborhood where her parents were fearful for her safety. Nevertheless she was able to convince them to let her attend and so was able to graduate ahead of her classmates. Her parents' only requirement of her was academic excellence. If she brought home a ninety-eight on an examination paper, her parents did not comment on how well she had done but, rather, asked what had happened to those other two points.

There was never any question but that Phyllis and her brother would attend college, and their parents were prepared to pay all of their expenses. "My parents were actually very well off except they did not like to spend money," she remembers. In a competitive examination, Phyllis was awarded a New York State scholarship that paid about one quarter of her expenses. The world expanded for Phyllis when, at age sixteen, she went away to college. "I didn't meet a white Protestant until I went to high school, and I didn't meet a Republican until I went to college," she claims. Phyllis majored in biology. At one point in her academic career, she wanted to take a course in calculus, but when she talked with her advisor about it, he advised her not to take it. The advisor had the idea that "girls didn't do well in calculus" and if she got a low grade in calculus she would not be able to get into medical school. Phyllis replied that she was quite sure she would do well in calculus, and, besides, she was not planning to attend medical school anyway.

Phyllis took the calculus course and, as she had predicted, did well in it. Her success with the calculus course was a factor in her decision to leave biology and go into physics as she put it, "to get away from these people who were telling me I couldn't take these things." Phyllis continued her education through graduate school, receiving a Ph.D. in biophysics from Yale University in 1962, and went on to take a research position in genetics and microbiology at Princeton University. She worked full time for three years while caring for two babies. "I only missed seven days on a graph I was doing once because I had a baby . . . it was a flat line, straight . . ." she remembers.

Phyllis came to Minnesota in 1964 when her husband, Donald, was offered a position at the University of Minnesota. After they were settled, Phyllis began looking for a job at the university for herself. "I wanted something like a research position. I did not want to put myself in line for a full faculty position because of our children. Besides, I had never seen a women in a full faculty position—only women researchers. There were not any role models."

When Phyllis began job hunting at the university, she ran into a stone wall. "No one was willing to look at my credentials," she remembers. She also discovered that her standards for work appeared to be higher than were those of the other scientists. She had been accustomed to working with full professors at Yale, MIT, and Princeton who were at the top of their fields—members of the National Academy of Science. "It never occurred to me that not everybody worked that hard. I had thought that all academics did that. Here [in Minnesota] they were not that much on the cutting edge of research. I had never thought that maybe life was a little slower in Minnesota."

Eventually Phyllis found a professor in the department of genetics who was willing to put her on a grant for which he was applying. She was so grateful for anything that not until later did it strike her as strange that, while she was the one applying for the grant and would be doing all of the work on it, she could not apply for the grant under her own name. The male faculty member had to be listed on the cover as the principal investigator. When she inquired as to the reason, she was told that the dean would not allow "non-regular" faculty members to have grants in their own names. Phyllis thought, "Well, Okay, that's the way it is." She did not object until three years had passed.

During those three years Phyllis became involved in the women's movement and the campaign for abortion rights. NOW (National Organization of Women) had been formed and her friends got her involved in it. "My consciousness was raised," she remembers, "and soon I got involved in the campaign to remove gender references from the classified advertisements of the newspapers." Phyllis and her friends were sitting around one evening discussing the problem of the newspaper ads when Phyllis, becoming impatient, said, "Let's just call John Cowles, the publisher, and ask him to make a change." She got a phone book, looked up Cowles' home phone number and dialed it. When Cowles answered his phone, Phyllis explained who she was, told him that the editors of the *New York Times* had taken all references to gender out of its classified ads, and suggested that if Cowles wanted the *Minneapolis Star and Tribune* to be considered superior newspapers, he should do the same. Cowles thanked her for her call and a few weeks later all references to gender were removed from the classified ads in the *Star and Tribune*. (The EEOC was to rule in 1968 that unless employers could show that a bona fide occupational qualification existed, sex-segregated help wanted newspaper ads were illegal.)

Phyllis' women friends were taken aback by her abrupt phone call to the publisher. They were used to engaging in a long period of discussion to achieve group consensus before taking any action. Some complained that she "acted like a man." Hearing this, the husband of one of Phyllis' women friends laughed and said, "Phyllis doesn't think like a man. I know exactly how she thinks. She thinks just like a physicist. That's how she's been trained — to figure out the cause of a problem and then do something to solve it."

After three years as a "non-regular" faculty person, Phyllis decided the time had come to do something about her status. "It was time for a real position," she said. "There were some openings at the university but when I applied, suddenly they just weren't available." Then, in 1968, Phyllis was invited to take a high-powered class in electron microscopy of micro-organisms at Oak Ridge, Tennessee. There was not enough money in her grant to pay for her participation in the class so she asked her department to pay for it. The department chairman refused her request. "You are not a 'regular' faculty member," he told her, "and we have these opportunities available only for regular faculty members."

When the people who had invited Phyllis to Oak Ridge heard that her own department would not support her, they gave her a scholarship to pay her way. "We are inviting the top people in the United States to take this class," they told her. "Since you are one of them, we'll pay for you." That experience reinforced Phyllis' decision that she had to do something about her career. "Okay," she said to herself, "It's time I became a regular faculty member."

"So then I started applying. I was told I could apply for positions when they came up. The field I was working in was the most cutting edge field — the field that became recombinant DNA — genetics between micro-organisms — and no one was doing as good work in that field as I was. I was invited to the conference that is considered to be the first conference on recombinant DNA and molecular DNA in the fall of 1972 in Honolulu, Hawaii. Thirty United States scientists and thirty Japanese scientists were invited, and I was one of the thirty United States scientists who was invited."

Still, the University of Minnesota had no place for her. So Phyllis filed a discrimination suit. In the meantime, a friend asked for her help in lobbying for abortion rights at the legislature. "I put my test tubes down, and we went to the legislature. It was the first time I had ever been in any state capitol, and I kind of got hooked on it," she remembers. The women were lobbying for three issues: repeal of abortion laws, the addition of gender to parts of the Human Rights Act, and some child care facilities legislation. The first two issues went nowhere, but Arne Carlson, a freshman legislator at the time, authored the child care legislation, and it passed.

At the university, Phyllis applied for a two-year grant from the American Cancer Society to support her research. Again, she was told she could not put her own name on the grant, but had to use that of a regular faculty member. Though she was furious about it, she complied. During the review process, her grant application ended up on the discard heap at the Cancer Society because, as she explained, "the first thing they look at is 'who is submitting this grant application and what do we know about them.' My name was on the thirty-second page of the application." Purely by chance a professor from New York University was leafing through the discarded applications when he saw and was intrigued by her proposal. "What is this weird situation?" he asked. "You are clearly the person who is doing the work. Why aren't you the principal investigator?" He called the dean at the University of Minnesota and heard the explanation that only "regular" faculty members could sign as principal investigators. "Well, Okay," he said. "That is Minnesota. Kahn is qualified but that must be their bureaucratic way of handling it."

Phyllis was awarded the two-year grant but she had to rewrite the application. When it was finished, she had the papers signed by the dean, signed by the chairman of the department, and then walked the document over to Morrill Hall for the final stamp of approval and mailing. She had returned to her laboratory and was working at the electron microscope when she got a call from the dean to come see him immediately. When she appeared in his office, the dean told her he had pulled her grant application and changed it so that it would be funded for only one year instead of two. Phyllis was astounded. That was like throwing money away. The dean explained that he did not want to guarantee two years because Phyllis had filed a discrimination complaint with the university, and he could not guarantee her employment for two years. She might be fired because of her actions.

State Representative Phyllis Kahn

Phyllis replied that this was the most outrageous thing she had ever heard. "I was smart enough to insist that I get the dean's story in writing—that I could only apply for one year because I had filed the complaint. The date of the dean's letter was five days after Title VII had been signed prohibiting discrimination and retaliation in employment." Not until years later, when she became a plaintiff intervenor in the Shawala Rajender case, was her complaint finally resolved with a financial settlement.

The immediate result of the dean's action was that Phyllis made up her mind about going into politics. "That was when I just decided, I've had it," she said. "I'm running for office." Redistricting had taken place, and Phyllis decided to run for a House seat. A man in the College of Biological Science had run for office four years before, so Phyllis went to him to learn the accommodations the university had made for him to serve in the legislature while also working at the university. Then she ran. "Nobody paid very much attention to me because I was running against Matt Stark, the head of the Civil Liberties Union, and a much better known person. Then I won the primary. The next day the dean pulled me into his office. 'How was I going to do my work if I were elected?' he wanted to know. 'How was I going to handle both?' Fortunately, I had a copy of all the decisions that had been made for the other faculty member when he was running. He hadn't been elected. So they just backed off and didn't do anything. I'm sure if I had not had a copy of those decisions they would have made me take a full leave of absence or resign."

Phyllis continued at the university for two more years, through 1974, and then resigned. "The legislature was a much more useful place to accomplish things," she said.

One of Phyllis Kahn's most memorable pieces of legislation was the 1975 Clean Indoor Air Act. The legislation had been suggested to Phyllis by Ed Brandt, the Republican legislator from her district, who had not run again. The bill did not call for a ban on smoking, just the separation of smokers from non-smokers. Compelling people came to testify for the bill including Charles Mayo of the Mayo family and an impressive group of doctors. When Phyllis went to the Rules Committee with her bill, the Speaker of the House was Martin Sabo, a chain smoker. The newspaper reported the meeting between Phyllis and Sabo with the headline, "She Huffs and He Puffs" and wrote that when Phyllis came into Sabo's office with the bill, he blew smoke rings at her.

The public responded with outrage. Sabo's secretary called to ask Phyllis to drop the clean air issue because of the nasty letters Sabo was receiving. The upshot was that Sabo ended up signing onto the bill as co-author. (Phyllis remarked that "Sabo always knew which way things were going, and he had seen all this support.") "It was very helpful to have a chain smoker supporting the bill. The people who were opposed were the bar and restaurant people."

In drafting the bill, Phyllis had decided that she would deal only with public places and would exempt bars and restaurants from the bill. However, an early draft of the bill included the separation of smokers from non-smokers in restaurants. When the restaurant association lobbyist came to her office to complain about that provision, she told him, "Okay, I'll take the restaurants out." The bill passed the House and went to the Senate. In the Senate committee, Skip Humphrey looked at the bill and said, "What's this about taking restaurants out of it? Restaurants are the only places I care about." Humphrey promptly put the restaurants back into the bill, and it passed the Senate.

When restaurants were put back in the bill, the restaurant lobbyist came back to Phyllis and complained. "You promised me you weren't going to have restaurants in there," he said. "You have to go to the conference committee and take them out." Phyllis explained that she had removed restaurants from the House version of the bill but she had not said anything about the Senate version. It was the lobbyist's job, not hers, to lobby the Senate. The House accepted the Senate version and the Clean Indoor Air Act became law.

Other legislation proved to be more difficult to get passed. One was a bill allowing women to keep their own name when they were married. To keep her own name a woman had to go to court. Some judges would refuse to approve women's keeping of their maiden names. (Opponents to the measure claimed children would be upset if their mothers had hyphenated names or names different from their fathers, that the whole name situation would be too complicated for children to understand.) Women were forced to go judge shopping. Also, when a woman got a marriage license her voting record was automatically changed, whether she wanted it to be or not. If she did not reregister again under her married name, she could not vote. Eventually the law was amended to say a woman could select the name by which she wanted to be known. Phyllis found it hard to believe this was not something women could just do and that a law was required to accomplish it. According to English common law, a person can use any name she wants to unless it is done for the purpose of fraud.

When she began working on bicycle legislation, Phyllis found that many legislators considered "bike" to be a four-letter word. Working through Willard Munger's committee, she was able to pass legislation dealing with bicycle safety, registration, and the development of a network of trails.

One of the things politics did for her, Phyllis says, is change her sleep habits. "I went from being a night person to being a morning person. I had two kids without ever being happy about getting up in the morning. In the legislature the first thing I had for several years in a row was an eight o'clock Appropriations Committee meeting. I actually didn't stop being a night person; I just sort of stopped sleeping."

The oldest of three children of a physician in the small town of Whitehall, Wisconsin, Representative Mary Forsythe grew up in a town that itself played the part of an extended family. Like the children in the imaginary community of Lake Woebegon, the youngsters in Whitehall were all above average. Mary recalls that her senior class of around thirty-five students had the second highest IQs in the State of Wisconsin.

Mary's parents were loving but strict, and her father enforced a curfew. Mary remembers going to a movie and failing to return home by the appointed hour. Her father went to the theater, found her, insisted that she leave immediately, and brought her home. "I was probably a freshman in high school and was very embarrassed. But I didn't say a word; I wouldn't have dared."

Despite his strictness, Mary was proud of her father and believed that he used his influence to benefit the community. Mary's father was particularly upset by children's use of fireworks at Fourth of July celebrations and was active in passing the ban against them in Wisconsin. "Kids with their fingers blown off would come to the house on the Fourth of July. One year a guy came who had had his leg blown off," Mary remembered. "They can sell fireworks in Wisconsin, but they aren't allowed to use them," she explained, shaking her head. "So they sell them to Minnesotans who can't use them either but who do."

Mary was impressed by the way her father, on his own initiative, did things that needed to be done for their community: "He and a friend laid out a community golf course." Mary's father got a group of people together to plant trees on a hillside outside of town just because he thought it would look nice. He was a Boy Scout leader. And he attended all of the high school games—just sat and watched—so that if anyone was hurt, he'd be there." Mary's brother became an Eagle Scout, and her mother, who was a music teacher, became a Girl Scout leader so that the girls in the community would also have a scouting opportunity. Mary became a Golden Eaglet, the Girl Scout equivalent of the boy's Eagle rank. Mary still has her Golden Eaglet pin and wore it one day when the Girl Scouts came to the Capitol. One of the leaders recognized it. "Isn't that a Girl Scout pin?" she asked, pleased that Mary had worn it for the occasion.

Life in a small town taught Mary the important lesson that, in a small town, all the citizens have to contribute if they are to maintain a viable community. Residents had to be active in many organizations. For instance, Mary, who considered herself to be the world's least skilled athlete, played basketball because if she hadn't, there would not have been enough players to form a girl's basketball team. She and her friends belonged to and participated in almost all the organizations in her high school. The importance of contributing to every aspect of her community became a basic lesson of her childhood. She also was expected to run to the Lutheran Church in her small Wisconsin community every time the church bell rang, which was often. "I was very active in the Lutheran League and whatever else they had: Sunday School and Confirmation. I sang in choirs and participated in all of the activities."

Describing herself as a child who was "fat but happy," Mary was required to get up early in the morning so her family could have breakfast together. Her physician father did all the surgery for miles around their Wisconsin community and had to be at the hospital by 7:00 A.M. Since her father might not be home for lunch or dinner, he insisted that the family eat the first meal of the day together. They also had family devotions before he left for the hospital. Looking back, Mary feels she was fortunate. "I had a good family. I went through the Depression and never even knew it. I didn't even know that my family and friends were poor. None of us even thought about such a thing. My father lost a lot of money, but we didn't pay any attention. We were eating well."

Growing up in the small safe world of her Wisconsin community may have shielded Mary from some of the realities of the larger world, but it also gave her a strong connection with people, the desire to contribute, and a sense of optimism about the future. She believed that change for the better was possible, and that, if called upon, she would be able to make a difference.

Mary was fifty-one years old, a mother of five children—most of them grown—when she asked herself the question many women confront at some point in their lives: "What am I going to do with the rest of my life?" She began by reviewing her skills and what she felt she knew how to do. She had a music degree from St. Olaf College and had sung in the St. Olaf College Choir under F. Melius Christiansen. ("If God is perfection, you're as close to God as you are ever going to get with the St. Olaf Choir," she declared.) She had taught music in the public schools and Sunday School for many years. "I was a Girl Scout leader forever, even before I had children of my own."

When her husband, Robert, was Assistant Secretary of HEW under President Dwight Eisenhower, Mary became part of the Washington, D.C., political scene. She soon became involved with the PTA and a member of the county PTA board in Virginia where sixteen new schools were under construction. "As parents we had to do a great deal for those sixteen schools because there wasn't the money to do extras along the way. I was put in charge of hanging pictures on the walls. I made the horrible mistake, one day, of suggesting they put the picture of Abraham Lincoln on the wall. They didn't do that in Virginia."

While living in Washington, D.C., Mary was a member of the Cabinet Wives Club. Every month one of the wives would give a presentation on what was going on in the department in which her husband was involved. When it was Mary's turn she spent weeks studying for her presentation, not realizing that the other women just read a report someone from the department had written for them. Mary didn't do that and was proud of herself because, when the topic was opened for questions, she had the information and could answer them. Mary became known as a person who did her homework. "You don't just jump in with an opinion," she said. "You have to know what you are talking about."

As Mary pondered the decision of what she should do in the future, politics came more and more into her mind. She had become involved at the precinct level after a friend who she knew in Washington became a precinct officer in New York City. "I thought, if he can do it, so can I. I decided to go for it. It wasn't hard to get it as nobody wanted to be precinct chair. I learned a lot there. We didn't have computers, thank goodness. I had nice little shoeboxes full of cards."

Eventually Mary decided to make a run for a major elective office. She ran for a seat in the Minnesota House of Representatives, and in 1972 was elected to the first of eight terms. She was a little concerned when she ran because she did not think a woman had ever been elected to anything in Edina before. "I block worked and, do you know, people were really mad at me because then all the other politicians had to do it too. Some of them didn't like it at all." A senator friend of Mary told her she would love being a legislator from Edina because "they vote for you and then leave you alone." Mary says it did not work out that way for her: "I would encourage people to write to me, and I got a lot of mail," she remembers.

In 1972 the legislature was not receptive to women. "Nobody even told us where the women's restrooms were, nothing, zero. There was no mentoring. I think they resented the fact that there were a few women there. It took a while for the men to get used to women being there. The year before I went there was just one woman, Helen McMillan, in the legislature. The year I was elected there were five of us—an increase of 500 percent." Mary and her fellow freshman, Phyllis Kahn, were named to the Appropriations Committee—the first women to hold those positions. Individuals testifying before the committee were not used to the women's presence and kept addressing the committee members as "Gentlemen." The protests of the two women members of the committee were ignored. Finally Mary and Phyllis decided that the next time they were addressed as "gentlemen," they would get up and walk out. "We did it and slowly they learned," Mary remembers. "Maybe it was a habit, and they didn't mean anything by it. But we kind of thought they did." Mary eventually became chair of the Appropriations Committee.

One of the most controversial issues in which Mary became involved was the seatbelt law, which she authored. People sent her hate mail over it. To get the bill passed, she had to water it down to the point where an offender would get a ticket but would not be charged and could only get a ticket if the driver was being stopped for something else. "Some of the members were mad as hornets at me. It was a very difficult issue. People all over the state hated it, including my husband. I got a letter one day telling me that my husband was not wearing a seatbelt. 'That's why I'm doing this!' I replied."

Mary was active in the National Conference of State Legislatures. When she went to a meeting of women legislators, she was concerned to discover that there was no information available about incarcerated women. "At this time women in prison were not being given any education. It was a real problem. They came out of prison much worse than when they went in. There was no opportunity for them whatsoever in prisons. And here were all these women legislators, and not one word was said about women who were incarcerated. So I got up and said that if women legislators did not speak up about it, who else was going to?"

Mary was shocked to find that women prisoners in Minnesota were being confined in a building that was a firetrap. She also learned that, while male prisoners were being given opportunities for education and rehabilitation, none of these services were being provided for females. The issue had been studied and studied by the legislature over the years, but no action had been taken to correct the situation. Mary visited the institutions to see the conditions for herself. When a bill for a new women's prison was introduced, the recommendation was made once again to study the issue. At this Mary exploded and, for the first time in her life, pounded on her desk. "We have studied this for ten years," she said, "and I'm tired of studying it. We've come to the same conclusion every year. Now let's do something." Money for a new women's prison was appropriated that session, and the education building was named after Mary Forsythe.

Not everyone was happy with Mary's votes. One measure, which dealt with the setting of alimony, infuriated a woman from Duluth who called Mary to complain. It seems that the woman's husband and four other men had raped a girl. Through blood tests doctors found that the woman's husband was the man who had impregnated the girl. The man was now having to pay the girl child support, and his wife's earnings were being garnished as well. Mary's thought, upon hearing the story was, "That sure is a terrible price to pay for one night of revelry." Like most other women legislators, she

State Representative Mary Forsythe

also received calls telling her she should stay home and care for her children. (At the time she received these calls, all but one of Mary's children were in college and two were married.)

Looking back on eighteen years at the capitol, Mary says she made "some real big booboos in the legislature, voted for things that, when I think back on it, I don't know why I would do such a thing. Nobody can tell me that everybody isn't in the same boat. You really don't know what you are voting on all of the time. There is so much. If anybody thinks the members of the legislature know all about everything they are voting on, they are wrong. I went into the legislature thinking I wasn't going to vote on something I didn't know anything about. That lasted only a week or so." She is respectful of the role of lobbyists in the legislature. "Don't think for a second that they aren't helpful. They are. There is all this talk about how horrible lobbyists are. Nobody talks about how great they are. They don't last long if they don't tell you the truth."

Mary found that "it takes guts to run for office. You have to be able to take it because you're going to find that a lot of people aren't going to agree with you. And you just have to accept it. You have to know where you stand. You have to listen to people. Maybe they were right, but if I thought I was right I would say so. Some people just go off the deep end. You will never be able to change them, so all you can do is be quiet, let them say their piece, and hope that maybe then they will feel better afterwards."

Mary is convinced she is "not the leader type, not a strong personality. In the legislature I had respect, and they would listen if I said something. That's because I didn't say anything very often. I used to get so disgusted with people who went on and on and never said anything more than they could have said in five minutes." Mary believes the atmosphere in the legislature has changed. "When I first got there some of my best friends were Democrats." (Mary is Republican.) "It wasn't as free in the end, you had to stick with your own party." Nevertheless she found her service to be "the most educational experience I could imagine. When I left, I just felt that it was time to go. I was getting to the age where I felt it was sensible to leave. But I did miss the people very much. When I saw pictures of the Capitol I would cry."

०३ ३ ८०

"The world taught women nothing skillful and then said her work was valueless. It permitted her no opinions and said she did not know how to think. It forbade her to speak in public, and said the sex had no orators."
— Carrie Chapman Catt

The future Moorhead City Councilwoman Phyllis Onsgard, first elected to office in 1973, grew up in the thirties and forties on a farm eight miles west of Hillsboro, North Dakota. The only girl in the family, with one brother eleven years older, she thought of herself as an afterthought. She became a reader early in her life, and her father would often find her sitting under a favorite tree on the farm reading a book. Because there were no other children to play with, Phyllis dressed her cats up and pushed them around in a baby carriage. She enjoyed animals. Like many solitary children, Phyllis engaged in imaginative play, staging tea parties for herself on the porch of her house during which she carried on conversations with imaginary guests.

One afternoon her mother, hearing Phyllis chattering away on the porch, supposed she was conducting one of her solitary tea parties. When she looked out a window, she was surprised to see a large black man sitting at the tea table chatting amiably away with the little girl. He was a farm worker, come to help with the threshing, who had accepted her invitation to tea.

Phyllis' family was close knit. She remembers winter evenings when the chores were done and her father would help her mother roll *lefsa* and make potato dumplings. For entertainment, her mother would bake a pie and invite neighbors to come over and play cards in the big farm kitchen.

Phyllis attended a rural school with grades one through eight in the same room. Some years there would be only two students to a grade

with the result that Phyllis received a great deal of individual attention—enabling her to skip the fourth grade and graduate from high
school at age sixteen. She had started private piano lessons at age eight
and continued with music through college, winning state honors at
recitals. Aware that pianists' minds will occasionally go blank when
they sit down to play a solo in a recital, friends would ask her mother,
"Why doesn't Phyllis ever forget?" "I don't know," her mother would
reply "but she never does."

When she was in the eighth grade, Phyllis entered the speaking contest for the North Dakota Citizenship Day award. Her memory did not fail
her, and she placed first in her school, and then first in Traill County, giving her the opportunity to compete in the finals in Bismarck. There she
won the state competition with her speech on how to be a good citizen.

Phyllis' ideals led her to rather innocently run afoul of her Lutheran
pastor's sense of morality when, as part of her preparation for confirmation, she was asked to write an essay about a person whom she
admired. Phyllis chose her grandfather, a kindly German immigrant
who distributed the fruits and vegetables from his garden among his
neighbors. As part of his daily routine, her grandfather always had a
glass of beer, and when he ate Sunday dinner at her home, Phyllis'
mother always made sure the glass of beer was on hand for him.

When Phyllis put the detail about the beer drinking in her essay, the
pastor did not approve. She should not admire a person who drank
alcoholic beverages, he told her. Caught between her grandfather and
her pastor, both of whom she revered, Phyllis chose her grandfather.
The pastor called her parents, who backed up their daughter's decision,
and eventually the incident was overlooked. Phyllis was confirmed on
schedule in the Norwegian Lutheran Church. (Phyllis suspects the fact
that her grandfather was a member of the rival German Lutheran
Church in the same community may have had something to do with the
dispute.)

Phyllis traces her interest in politics back to the days when, as a
child, she went with her father to township meetings. Her paternal
grandfather had been a member of the North Dakota State Legislature,
and her father was active on school and township boards. Supper table
conversation often concerned politics and agricultural affairs. After
school, Phyllis would be given a choice of going to the ladies aid meetings at the church with her mother or attending the township board

meetings with her father. Phyllis chose to go with her father. "I liked to see the men sitting around visiting about the different things, asking,' Should we build this road? Do we have enough money?' That's where I really got interested in government."

The first cause that Phyllis publicly advocated was to add music facilities to a new gym the community was levying taxes to build. A junior at Hillsboro High School, Phyllis played the clarinet in the band that practiced in a room above the fire hall on the opposite side of town. The band members would either walk to the practice room or, in the winter, pile into someone's car. Phyllis was driving a car full of band members to practice when she lost control on the icy road to the fire hall and crashed through the window of the local bakery. Fortunately, no one was hurt. The following night the school board was to vote on the bond issue. Phyllis went to the meeting and explained how music, as well as sports, was important to the students and the school board should provide music facilities in the new gym building. Everyone at the meeting knew that Phyllis Larson had broken the bakery window the day before while trying to get to the band's practice room. She won her point with three-quarters of the vote.

Phyllis has strong feelings about the need not only to vote, but to vote responsibly. She was appalled when a man once told her he drank with the candidates to see how many beers they could hold. The man with the best-looking face in the morning got his vote. "That's not responsible voting," she said. "That is why we sometimes end up with people who are not responsible or intelligent or serious enough about the job they are going to be doing for us. Voting is very serious. It is nothing to make a joke about. As voters we must educate ourselves about the candidates." When each of her three sons reached voting age and was preparing to cast his first votes, Phyllis baked a cake and held a family celebration. "When they got to be of voting age, that was a big night," she said.

It was not until 1973 when one son said, "Mom, why don't you run for office?" that Phyllis Onsgard considered becoming a candidate herself. She had been active in the Republican Party and had served as vice-president of the Minnesota Republican Women when she decided to run for the fourth ward seat on the Moorhead City Council. The incumbent was a well-known local radio announcer. Phyllis campaigned door-to-door, called on members of the business community who were uncertain about supporting a woman, and enlisted the help of her friends from the largest church in town. When the ballots were counted, Phyllis had won by 500 votes. She was the second woman to serve on the Moorhead City Council and the first woman to be elected on her own. (The first woman to serve filled out the remainder of her deceased husband's term.)

A major challenge to her independence came when the city council was asked to vote on the location of an Anheuser-Busch malting plant in Moorhead. A decision of this nature required the unanimous vote of all eight members of the council. Though Phyllis was Republican and pro-business she did some research on her own and learned that the malting process used large quantities of water, which was discarded after its use. When she asked the public service commission about the impact the increased water usage would have on the water treatment plant, she was told it would exceed the present plant's capacity, and a new one would have to be built. The cost of the new water treatment plant would be billed to the tax-payers. Phyllis figured what the cost of a new water treatment plant would be to each Moorhead resident and asked the Anheuser-Busch officials if they couldn't recycle their water. The company chemist replied that recycling was not possible.

When the vote was called on the Anheuser-Busch malting plant, Phyllis was the only member of the city council to vote "no." Moorhead business interests were shocked and offended. "I can't believe you," one man said to her. "You call yourself a Republican and say you are for business, yet you turned down a new business for Moorhead!"

"I'm not turning down business for Moorhead," she replied, "I'm thinking about the citizens of Moorhead who cannot afford to have their taxes raised for a new water plant. I want Anheuser-Busch to send back their chemists and tell me they can't use that water over again."

While criticism of her vote mounted, Onsgard visited a competing beer malting plant in Jamestown, North Dakota, and asked to see how the plant manager handled the water. Company officials took her to the top of the tank where she could see for herself that this plant recycled its water. When she reported the facts she had learned to the Moorhead newspaper, her critics quieted down. The city council called the company back for further discussion and the Anheuser-Busch chemists admitted they could recycle the used water after all. A new vote was scheduled, and this time Phyllis voted with the majority. "Today that plant uses the water three times," Phyllis reported, "and the company is doing just fine. I am for business, but it's got to be business that helps everyone. Business can sometimes get away with a lot of things. I think you have to watch that." Phyllis served on the Moorhead City Council from 1974 until March 1977 when she resigned to join the staff of Congressman Arlen Stangland.

Phyllis was giving a piano lesson the day Stangland rang her doorbell and asked her to run his campaign for the congressional seat from the seventh district. Reluctantly she told him she couldn't do it because

Moorhead City Council Member
Phyllis Onsgard

she was on the city council and the mayor was also running. "I've got to work with the mayor," she explained. A week later her phone rang at midnight. Arlen and Senator Cal Larson from Fergus Falls were on the phone. Cal was speaking. "We need you to come run this campaign, Phyllis," he said. "Arlen is just not an organizer." Phyllis knew he was right. A few days before she and her husband had gone to a meeting for Arlen and his organization had been chaotic. At that point, Phyllis gave in. Resigning her city council seat, she took over Arlen's campaign, helping him win the Republican endorsement over eight other candidates. When he was elected to Congress, Phyllis continued to work for him as his district manager.

Phyllis says that "women in government need to have a religious-like work ethic to succeed." When she first went on the city council, some of the men had tried to put her down. "You have to work," she says. "If you are an elected official, you had better not be scared of work or research. You better not be scared of listening. You must sit down with people who are knowledgeable about the questions you are going to be voting on. Don't just vote blind."

Phyllis believes that women have a problem in that they often show reluctance to support other women. "Women don't stick together very well. They are sometimes jealous of another woman more than men would probably be. Many still believe they have to vote like their husbands. We owe our country. Each one of us has to give something back. If we can give of our time and talents that's what I think we should do."

Representative Lona Minne Schreiber was reared by her Finnish grandparents in Hibbing—the heart of Minnesota's Iron Range. Her parents were divorced, and Lona and her mother lived with Lona's maternal grandparents. The grandparents, immigrants from Finland, were the decisive influences in the young Lona's life. Finnish was spoken in their home, and much of their life style was decidedly "old country." Lona remembers how her grandmother drank her egg coffee.

"My grandmother would have a sugar lump in her hand. She would break off a piece of that sugar lump, tuck it in the corner of her mouth, pour her coffee into her saucer and sip it through the filter of that sugar lump." Lona was sent to school wearing long cotton stockings when the other girls wore anklets. Her grandmother kept her hair in braids far longer than was considered the fashion. Lona's lunch, consisting of thick slices of homemade bread, was wrapped in white butcher paper and tied with string while the other children had lunches of white, store-bought bread, wrapped in waxed paper and carried in paper bags. The differences between herself and her classmates were not lost on Lona.

She describes herself as having been a willful, contrary child upon whom, at the same time, her grandparents doted. For part of her childhood, she was the only grandchild in her family and was given special attention by her grandparents and by a childless aunt who lived in Grand Rapids, a community about thirty miles away. Lona remembers with fondness her many visits to her aunt's home on a lake, and she still has books that her aunt gave her. Perhaps as a result of feeling herself to be "a little bit different," Lona, early in life, became aware of the many ethnic and religious variations among the residents of the Minnesota Iron Range. While she did not consider herself one of the poor children from across the tracks ("we weren't project kids—people on social services") neither did she view her family as part of the professional, management class in the community. The social distinctions between those who worked in the mines and those who supervised that work were acute. "Up on the Iron Range all of the people made their living in the mines, and the superintendent of the mines and the people in management generally came from out East."

Lona's experiences in the rural countryside began in 1951 when she was an eight-year-old third-grader and began spending summers with a childless couple who lived on a nearby farm. Though she was given a myriad of heavy chores to do, she enjoyed living at the farm because it was here that she gained her first real sense of family. The couple "felt like real parents," she remembers. "There was a real kind of home there with a man and wife." Lona worked long hours on the farm as a child, driving the tractors and milking the cows. Though it was hard work, she found that she enjoyed the responsibility. Her farm family also gave her opportunities for experiences in the wider community that her grandparents had been unwilling or unable to do. Her grandmother would never eat in a restaurant, but the farm couple took her out to cafes and showed her how to order a meal. They also taught her to drive a car.

By the time Lona was in the fifth grade, she was occasionally taking care of thirty head of dairy cattle all by herself. From time to time she would be left alone over a three-day weekend with the task of milking all thirty cows morning and night. Not knowing anything different, the eleven-year old did not object to the load of work and responsibility but, looking back on the experience, she says with remarkable understatement that it was "a little too much for a youngster."

Lona never knew her biological father, and her mother refused to tell her about him. The first father she can remember was Jimmy Dunne, whom her mother married when Lona was about a year old. The marriage lasted four years. "He was Irish-Catholic and we were Finnish and Lutheran, but I loved him dearly," she says. Her mother remarried again when Lona was eleven. This man, like his predecessor, was an alcoholic who had been married before, and this man had a two-year-old daughter. The new living arrangement was not a good one for Lona, who was a developing adolescent. "We moved in and started this blended family, and it was icky, really icky. The house was small and we didn't have a lot of money, and we were kind of piled up on top of each other."

It took Lona only a short time to realize that she could not continue to live with her mother and stepfather. "I don't want to live here," she said to herself. "I don't belong here. I'm not loved here. I'm not protected here." In a remarkable example of taking control of her life, Lona packed up her clothes, left her mother and stepfather's house and moved in with her grandparents. After she had moved back to her grandparents' home, Lona no longer felt like a little girl. She had almost no contact with her mother, though they continued to live in the same town.

Being on her own as a teenager forced Lona to develop her own moral compass. "I had so many struggles to try to define in my mind what was right and what was wrong, to know if I were a good girl or a bad girl, what was appropriate behavior, not appropriate behavior; shameful behavior and not shameful behavior. . . . All those struggles I had to do by myself."

Lona's self-definition was strongly influenced both by her education and by her grandparents. Most of the children in the Hibbing school system were from blue-collar, mining families. Lona has high praise for the experiences she had as a young member of that community. She considers herself fortunate to have received her education from "that Iron Range system of fine buildings and good schools. We had school nurses, school doctors, dentists, and wonderful educational opportunities. There was a full-time art consultant and a music consultant. All the books and pencils and everything were furnished to us. I even took piano, tap-dancing, and ballet lessons."

Lona's success in school was nurtured by her grandparents, who instilled a respect for learning in their granddaughter. "My grandmother read a lot. We had to wash our hands before we could read a book. And we'd never, never write in a book. When I was taking college courses, I would see people using markers in books. I still can't do that. I can't mark up a book." Lona was proud that her grandparents were literate. "Finns," she pointed out, "had to be literate before they could be confirmed. Of all the immigrants, the Finns were one of the few groups that could read and write."

Despite the fact that her home life was unsettled throughout much of her childhood, Lona was a good student who stayed on the honor roll, went to church on her own, and worked at Bridgeman's to earn spending money. She loved to read — she remembers reading *The Robe* in seventh grade—and excelled in her English classes. "The only problem I had in school was I felt a little different because my mother was divorced, so I didn't have a dad there. But I had a grandma and a grandpa. My grandfather's nephew from Finland also lived with us and worked in the mines." Looking back at her childhood, Lona says, "My grade school years were calm, happy, good, predictable and safe. My teenage years were not. It took me my adult years to sort and settle and grow and learn. I realize now that living is a continual learning process."

It was Lona's grandparents who provided what measure of safety and stability she had in her early life. They were also role models of civic activity. "My grandfather was very active in our community. He established an historical society, of which he served as president for a long time. He belonged to the Odd Fellows and achieved one of their highest ranks. I remember him practicing and practicing in his broken English the creeds and articles that he had to know. Grandfather was a go-between for the local and state politicians. His English was good enough and he was politically astute, so politicians would come and talk to him in English, and he would communicate what they said back to the Finnish miners. He was also a writer. He wrote a weekly article in the statewide Finnish newspaper."

Lona's grandfather's status with the local politicians helped the family navigate the complex politics of the region. Social welfare on the Iron Range involved something called "units," which were political privileges identified not with either political party but with local governmental entities, such as villages and townships. Because of the fluctuations in the mining industry, minors would frequently be laid off and the units of government became the social safety net. Village and township supervisors would hand out units to supporters of various candidates. If those candidates won, the units could be turned in for slips entitling the bearer to five days of work doing public service, such as clearing snow from the roads. The units helped workers find employment to tide them over when they were laid off from the mines.

"You had to belong to the right unit and support the winning candidate. It was very important to pay attention to politics so you could make it through when there wasn't any food," she explained. (The importance of politics in their lives was demonstrated by the fact that Lona's grandmother would get all dressed up in her best dress to go to the polls and vote.)

The first public office Lona Schreiber held was that of Hibbing Municipal Clerk, a non-partisan position. When friends asked her if she was interested, she replied "yes" because she needed a job, not realizing that she would have to be elected to get the job. Up to that point, she had never identified herself with a political party, had never attended a precinct caucus, and if she thought about politics at all, fancied herself an independent voter. However, despite her novice political status, in 1972, she won the election and served as town clerk until 1978.

Lona's new position put her in contact with the political machine on the Iron Range, and she found herself attending meetings and seminars where state legislators spoke on local and state issues. This gave her an opportunity to observe her own legislator, John Spanish, and she was not impressed: "He was way over his head with the technical aspects of legislating," she remembers. "I was embarrassed to have him representing me. Nobody dared challenge him because he was the incumbent. John was a consummate politician. He would go to all of the funerals. He'd be out in front of the post office shaking hands, and he'd call little old ladies at eleven o'clock at night from St. Paul to ask their opinion of the tax bill. People were impressed by that." Lona was not.

When Spanish's term expired and he was up for reelection, Lona decided to run against him. "I had to declare my party preference, and I didn't know what to do. One person advised me, "'You can't run as a Republican on the Range,' he said. 'They don't have Republicans on the Range.' So I ran as a Democrat. I ran pro-choice, and the fellow I had to beat was pro-life. I was branded as a bra-burner. I was witnessed against by the religious people. The charismatic movement in the churches was very strong then, and they witnessed against me during that campaign. They said that a wife and mother does not go into politics. If she goes to St. Paul, what is her family going to do? My youngest was eleven years old, so it wasn't like they were babies, but even so, it was unusual."

Lona won the primary by 125 votes, which was tantamount to winning the election. She was the first and, to date, the only woman to be elected to the Minnesota House from the Iron Range, serving from 1978 to 1988. Before her election, Lona had made only one visit to the capitol in her life. As she drove to St. Paul the day before she was going to be sworn in, she thought to herself, "I don't know my way around. I don't even know how to drive down to the cities, but if John Spanish can figure this out, I can figure it out too."

Life on the Iron Range had always been profoundly affected by conditions in the mines. Residents were never free from feelings of uncertainty. Will there be a layoff this winter? Is there going to be a shutdown? Everyone was dependent on what happened in the iron industry. Decisions made in the East, far from Minnesota, had a strong impact on the community Lona represented. Because of her roots on the Iron Range, Lona was always a staunch supporter of labor. "I have these memories," she recalls. "If it hadn't been for organized labor there wouldn't have been worker protection. Workers had to bring their own tools to the mines. If they worked underground, they even had to buy their own candles. In the early days there wasn't worker's compensation or unemployment compensation. When there were terrible accidents in the mines, the workers' families weren't taken care of. Some of the people on the Range believe there is a class system, that there is a difference between the mining big shots and the miners and that the minors are not good enough to mingle with the professionals—the doctors and lawyers. They think they are just peons down there. When I was elected to office, for some reason I didn't have those class insecurities. I could talk to the doctors' group as easily as I could talk to the local storeowners."

Unlike many women legislators who went onto the Education and Health and Human Services Committees, Lona asked for and received appointment to the Tax Committee. She believed her past experience as a town clerk gave her special insights into taxing policy. Very few women served on this committee, but she enjoyed it and ended up spending her entire ten-year career in the legislature working on tax-related matters.

As soon as she had found her way to her Capitol office, Lona took on the concerns of her constituents. She had not been in office long when one of them called to report that her insurance company was denying coverage for reconstructive surgery after a mastectomy on the basis that the surgery was purely cosmetic. The surgeon who had operated on the woman for cancer had chosen to delay the reconstruction procedure, and when the bill for that surgery was presented to the insurance company, it refused to pay.

When Lona investigated, she found that insurance companies would pay for the reconnection of vasectomies and for the reconstruction of jaws, but not of breasts. Convinced that this was an example of gender bias ("men had jaws, but they did not have breasts") Lona sponsored legislation requiring insurance coverage for reconstructive breast surgery due to diseases such as cancer and also for the repairing of birth defects. It was an uphill battle as the insurance industry resisted any attempts to mandate this coverage. For good measure, Lona tossed insurance coverage for mammograms into the bill as well.

Another campaign took her three years to accomplish, but she eventually succeeded in passing legislation governing the actions of rural cooperatives. People living in rural areas who wanted electricity on their farms had to become members of an electrical co-op. The cards that were sent out to prospective members had a single space that was labeled "Husband's signature." The husbands signed the cards, sent them in and the power was turned on. When electric rates began to go up, some women members tried to attend the meetings of their co-op, only to be turned away because it was their husbands who had signed the membership cards. For a time, even the men who had signed the cards were not allowed to attend their own co-op meetings. Though it took her several years of frustrating effort, Lona was eventually able to open up the co-op meetings to all of the members, whether it was the man in the family who had signed the membership card or not.

Another long-term effort involved 1,700 lake lots scattered throughout Minnesota. The lots were classified as school trust lands and, beginning around the turn of the century, had been leased on a long-term basis to individuals. The revenue from this land was to be deposited in the School Trust Account for the education of Minnesota children. Tenants built cabins on the lots but were not allowed to make physical changes to the property with the result that most of these parcels had non-existent or substandard sewage systems.

When Lona investigated, she found that very little of the lease payment money was going into the School Trust Account. Instead, most was being used for administrative purposes within the Department of Natural Resources (DNR). She also discovered that selling the properties and depositing the money directly into the trust account for investment would bring a far larger return.

The chairman of the House Environment Committee adamantly opposed Lona's bill, and the DNR immediately set up road blocks. However, leaseholders all over the state contacted their legislators and after three years of effort, Lona's bill passed. As far as she is concerned, it was a win-win situation for the School Trust Account, the environment, the state, and the individual leaseholders.

On another occasion, while serving as chair of the House Property Tax Division, Lona learned that a woman member of a private golf club, though she had paid full membership fees, was being asked to leave the course at prime golfing times because those hours were reserved for men only. Golf courses enjoy a lower property tax classification because they are thought to add an esthetic value to the community, even though the courses are often located in high tax areas. Lona, and most members of her committee, believed that the tax benefit was intended for the equal enjoyment of everyone. In a bi-partisan vote, the committee passed language prohibiting the practice of excluding women members during prime golfing hours. (The bill had to be revisited a number of times through the years, however, as some golf organizations resisted the directive.)

Within her all-male delegation from the Iron Range, Lona caused some gender-based discomfort—not because the men were prejudiced against her, but because they were not sure how to relate to her. For example: during the delegation's frequent closed-door meetings with union representatives, the men often resorted to profanity. Then, seeing Lona sitting there, they would "fall all over themselves apologizing." Though they never discriminated against her, their discomfiture at her presence was apparent to Lona.

Overall, Lona enjoys strong feelings of satisfaction over her political career. "When I look back on my political career, I hope there's one or two young women who were influenced by my presence," she says. "Women's views on issues and solutions are necessary for government. Too many women don't become involved

State Representative
Lona Minne Schreiber

because they think they don't know enough. There isn't any special class that teaches you. You just have to step in and do it. I celebrate my heritage and my ethnic background. I'm mindful of some of the values of that generation. When you are in government or politics, you have to have a good, keen sense of and appreciation for history so you won't repeat mistakes. You have to know what the history was to find your solutions.

"I gave the commencement speech at Hibbing High School—the first woman to ever do that. It's a big, wonderful, prestigious school, a national historical facility, and they graduate very large classes. It was the largest group of people I've ever addressed. I hope there was one young woman sitting in that audience who said, 'I saw a woman politician and I want to be like her. I want to get involved in government. I don't want to just lick envelopes. I want to be able to participate and pass legislation.' Being in politics was very honorable. I'm proud of the time I served."

ca4so

"Convictions no doubt have to be modified or expanded to meet changing conditions but to be a reliable political leader sooner or later your anchor must hold fast where other men's drag." —Margot Asquith

County government in the United States takes its basic form from similar units established by the original thirteen colonies. The organization of these units was based on local government institutions that the settlers of the New World had brought over from England. Colonists who pushed from the eastern seaboard into the Northwest Territory brought these political systems with them, systems that were then used as models for county government in the Middle-Western states. That part of Minnesota lying between the Mississippi and the St. Croix Rivers was in the original Northwest Territory and was part of the Wisconsin Territory. Stillwater was once part of St. Croix County, Wisconsin.

When Minnesota became a territory in 1849, the land between the two rivers was reallocated, and the new territorial governor, Alexander Ramsey, proclaimed that the same laws as those existing in Wisconsin would govern the new Minnesota Territory. The first Minnesota counties were Benton, Isanti, Ramsey, Wabasha, and Washington. Fifty-seven of the present eighty-seven counties were established during the territorial period that ended in 1857.

Although in 1981 only sixteen of the 447 county commissioners in Minnesota were women, by the year 2000 that number had risen to sixty-six. No one knows how many women served in the early 1970s, when both Diane Ahrens, and later Ruby Hunt, became commissioners of Ramsey County, because no one thought to record the gender of holders of that office, the assumption being they would all be male.

"County government was and, in many cases, still is a men's club," observed Molly Woehrlin, former Rice County Commissioner. "In the 1980s, women county commissioners were given a hard time by the men if they tried to get together and share experiences. When we had our dinners at conventions, we didn't print it in the program because some women felt too intimidated. Men were threatened by the very fact we were meeting. If a meal was involved, the women would be afraid to submit the bill."

County boards have traditionally had the lowest representation of women of any elected group, including school boards, city councils, and the legislature. The seats were often held for life by retired farmers, and it was considered not "Minnesota nice" for anyone to run against an incumbent. The threat presented by the few women who managed to get elected to their male counterparts was most deeply felt in rural counties. One woman, who took her seat as a new member of a county board, found the man she had defeated standing threateningly behind her chair at her first meeting. Another had the experience of male fellow commissioners refusing to speak to her because she had defeated a man for her position.

Two women who became exemplars of successful county governance are Ruby Hunt and Diane Ahrens. Though they did not take their seats on the Ramsey County Board the same year, they worked together there for over a decade and retired at the same time. Not always agreeing, they nevertheless worked as a team and exerted political influence far beyond the boundaries of their political office.

Known to her colleagues as a strong individual, Ruby says that, as a child, it would never have occurred to her to challenge authority. In looking back at her school experience in St. Paul, Ruby remembers that she was a shy young girl who tried hard to be a good student. "I guess because I was an only child, I liked to read, but I didn't read anything in much depth. I didn't get a lot of encouragement because my father was an immigrant from the Ukraine and my mother was born on a farm, and neither one of them had a lot of education. I think I was fairly good at everything. I did well because I paid attention and tried."

Ruby's father was an iron worker for the railroad and was able to work steadily until the arrival of the Great Depression. Then, when work became scarce, he took a series of odd jobs to provide for his family. Ruby's mother took in boarders. "I had to sleep in the front room, which wasn't really a bedroom, so that we could have the borders sleep in our second bedroom," Ruby remembers. She believes that in high school she was "a nondescript kind of person who was not very popular," though she had a group of girl friends with whom she hung out. In actual fact, Ruby was an excellent student, valedictorian of her Monroe High School class of 280 graduates. Today Ruby makes light of the achievement. "Monroe wasn't a very competitive kind of high school situation," she said. "It wasn't hard to be the valedictorian. I can't look on that as any great accomplishment. However, I think the people in the neighborhood were pretty impressed. My mother and father thought being the valedictorian was nice, but they weren't about to encourage me to go to college. That wasn't part of their lifestyle."

Ruby graduated from high school at the beginning of World War II when opportunities were becoming available for talented young people to continue their education. Unfortunately, though she had been the top scholar of her class, none of Ruby's teachers or school counselors suggested that she investigate opportunities to go on to college. Lacking both parental support and outside encouragement, she took the government examination for a clerk-typist position. Based on her test score, the Federal Bureau of Investigation offered her a position in Washington, D.C., as a clerk stenographer. The Bureau had finished its background check of her, sending investigators as far as Odessa, Minnesota, to question residents of her mother's home community, and Ruby was about to leave for Washington, when a former math teacher learned of her plans and discouraged her from going to work for the Bureau. As a result, Ruby turned down the job, took another examination and was hired, again as a clerk stenographer, by the Corp of Engineers to go to the Panama Canal Zone. Thus, at the age of nineteen, Hunt left home to work for four years in Panama where she would meet her husband.

The PTA and the League of Women Voters, the two organizations that appear on the resumes of many Minnesota woman in politics, propelled Ruby onto St. Paul's political stage. She was a young mother and full-time homemaker when one of her neighbors, Josephine Bonnie, began talking to her about the League. "She said it was a wonderful nonpartisan organization and you could learn a lot about politics." Though her friend never joined, Ruby became a member in 1954. Her leadership potential was immediately recognized, and before long, Hunt found herself president of both the PTA and the League.

Ruby's rapid move up through the ranks of the PTA led to her appointment as PTA lobbyist at the state level. In 1963 the PTA was supporting legislation that would keep drivers under eighteen from getting a driver's license until they had taken and passed a certified driver education course. Both the Minnesota School Board Association and the Minnesota Education Association were opposed to the measure. Though the bill had two prominent authors, Robert Dunlap, chairman of the House Education Committee, and John Zwach, majority leader of the Senate, it was not going anywhere. Sensing that timing might determine the fate of the bill, Ruby went to the Capitol one morning at 7:00 A.M. and happened to encounter Zwach in the hall. She stopped him and asked him to hold a hearing on the bill. "Will this bill apply to private and parochial school students as well as public school kids?" he asked her. Ruby assured him that it would.

That morning the bill was brought up before the Education Committee, and Ruby was given the opportunity to speak in favor of it. Peter Popovich and Bud Gallop, paid lobbyists for the Minnesota School Board Association and the Minnesota Education Association, spoke against it. Despite the eloquence of the opposition, the bill passed and is still in force today. "That is something I feel very proud of," Ruby says with satisfaction.

Ruby was relentless when her civic values were challenged. In the late 1950s, the St. Paul Chamber of Commerce, along with several major corporations, planned a conservative rally that, to Ruby and her fellow members of the League of Women Voters, had all the trappings of a meeting of the John Birch Society — an organization known for its racist, right-wing positions. The more they learned about the promoters of the proposed rally, the more convinced they became that they should do something to stop it. Since the League was non-partisan and non-political, the women who were members had to be very careful how they went about opposing the gathering.

Under Ruby's leadership, they sought out support from the community. One of those who supported the women was G. Theodore Mitau, a political science professor at Macalester College, and another, a local university president. With the help of friends from B'nai Brith, the League members exposed the fact that the organizers of the rally were indeed allied with ultra-right-wing extremists. League members quietly spread the word and were so successful that the rally fizzled because so few people signed up to attend. "No one would go to this thing," Ruby remembers. "There's a saying: 'There's no secret in politics.' Even though we were not speaking out as members of the League, because we couldn't do that, all these other people were speaking out for us. I learned that you can really make things happen by communicating with the right people."

Ruby's leadership positions in the PTA and the League of Women Voters put her in a position to influence a far-reaching community decision: the adoption of a new city charter that would change St. Paul's form of government and separate the governance of the school system from that of the city. The old 1914 city charter was four inches thick and filled with administrative details. It provided for a weak mayor, who sat as a voting member of the council, and six council members, who served as heads of departments—to which they were appointed by the mayor. An unusual post was that of an elected comptroller who created the budget and was also in charge of civil service, an extraordinarily powerful position. The comptroller got help preparing the budget from an organization called the Municipal Research Bureau, financed by local business interests. (It was often said that St. Paul's annual budget was prepared on the third floor of the St. Paul Athletic Club.)

The League of Women voters took a position in support of the Charter, and Hunt argued the League's position before the Charter Commission. Adelaide Enright, a member of the commission, was so impressed by Ruby's arguments that she resigned her seat and convinced the district judges, who made the appointments, to appoint Ruby in her place. The maneuver was successful and, from her position on the Charter Commission, Ruby was able to play a leadership role in eventually convincing the voters to approve the new charter for the City of St. Paul.

Passage was not easy. Though most civic organizations, including business and labor, supported the proposal, two colorful political figures, Rosalie Butler and Charlie McCarty, opposed it. Rosalie went to every public meeting and got equal time with the charter advocates. The populist style of Charlie and Rosalie prevailed, and the first time the charter was presented to the voters it went down to defeat.

At the next city election, Charlie McCarty was elected mayor, and Rosalie won a seat on the city council. Lou McKenna ran for comptroller on a platform to abolish the office. He won, which set the stage for a second charter vote. Charlie appointed Rosalie to head the city finance department, but she soon learned that, with a comptroller in charge of the budget, there was little she could do about the city finances.

A second vote on the new charter was held at the general election in 1970. Because the charter had been so soundly defeated the first time it had been presented to the voters, nobody was willing to be named chair of the campaign. Finally Phil Stringer, a member of the charter commission and a respected attorney, agreed to be named treasurer and have his name appear on the required disclaimers. This time, in a quiet campaign with no vocal opposition (Charlie McCarty had changed his mind and now supported the charter), the charter passed.

Under the charter, which took effect in 1972, the mayor was the chief executive of the city and no longer voted with the city council. When an election for the seventh city council seat was announced, friends urged Ruby to run. "You should run for that city council seat," they said, "so you can implement the charter. Otherwise, it would be like giving up your baby for adoption."

Ruby ran and in 1972 was elected to the St. Paul City Council. She was the third woman to win a seat. The second, Rosalie Butler, at first welcomed the newcomer, but the two soon found they had major differences. Rosalie was using her position as president of the city council to gear up to run for mayor against the incumbent. Though a member of the DFL Party, Rosalie continually challenged her fellow Democrats. Many people felt that someone should stop Rosalie Butler because of her tactics, but no one would challenge her until Ruby decided it was her job. "If there had been someone else who would have been in a position to do it, I would have been only too happy to have supported them, but I was the only one. I've never shirked my responsibility, but I've never gone out looking for big challenges either." In the coup that followed, organized by her fellow city council members, Rosalie Butler was unseated and Ruby became president of the St. Paul City Council.

On many occasions Ruby did not follow the majority. For example, it was customary for the city council members to ride in open convertibles at parades in the city. This bothered Ruby, so, when Rosalie Butler urged Ruby to ride in a convertible, she instead got out her bicycle, put a sign reading RUBY HUNT CITY COUNCIL on it, and peddled her bike in the parades. Despite their public differences and Ruby's unseating of Rosalie, the two joined to support County Commissioner Joe

Danna against a conservative woman candidate. Ruby designed a newspaper ad with her picture on one side and Rosalie's on the other. In the middle of the ad was a picture of Joe with the slogan, "On This We Agree."

When the People Mover (an overhead rail system) was proposed for downtown St. Paul in 1979, Ruby was the only elected official in the city to oppose it. "I sensed that there was no real support for this other than boosterism on the part of the Chamber of Commerce." Since the only way to defeat the measure would be by referendum, Ruby got her friends in the legislature to introduce a law that said the citizens of St. Paul would get to vote on the People Mover. "The people didn't want it, the businesses downtown didn't want it, the Commercial State Bank and the people at West Publishing didn't want it. It was just a juggernaut," she said. "The Chamber of Commerce had hired all kinds of people to promote this thing. They talked the city council and the mayor into thinking it was a good deal for St. Paul. I found all kinds of people that didn't want it and they gave us all the money we needed to put on the campaign." When the matter was put to a vote, the People Mover was defeated. "I saw to it that we defeated that People Mover," Ruby recalls happily. Regardless of the merits (or lack of them) of the People Mover system, the defeat of the proposal was proof that Ruby Hunt had mastered the art of political persuasion.

Then there was the matter of the five swimming pools. In 1974 a group of citizens in the West Seventh Street area began lobbying the city of St. Paul to build a swimming pool in their neighborhood. The only pool to which they had access at that time was the Highland Park pool, and the West Seventh neighborhood wanted one of its own. When the group brought their request to the city council, the council voted "no." The neighborhood group then carried their request to the state. The senator representing their district was Nick Coleman, one of the most influential senators in Minnesota. "Whatever Nick Coleman wanted up there, he got," Ruby remembers. Coleman introduced a bill to provide a swimming pool for the West Seventh Street neighborhood but when the other St. Paul senators saw it, they said they wanted pools for their neighborhoods too. There were five senators, so the bill gave the city of St. Paul permission to levy funds to construct five swimming pools, one in each senatorial district. When the legislation came to the St. Paul City Council, the council had to approve it. Though it was a highly unpopular thing to vote against swimming pools, Ruby introduced a resolution that, in effect, said to the state legislature, "Thanks, but no thanks. We cannot afford five outdoor swimming pools in the city of St. Paul."

In July, 1973, an invitation from the University of Minnesota athletic director Paul Giel to St. Paul Mayor Lawrence Cohen to play golf in a celebrity tournament landed Ruby on the front pages of the Twin Cities newspapers. Cohen did not play golf and suggested that Ruby, president of the St. Paul City Council who shot in the low eighties, go in his place. Giel refused to invite Ruby because she was a woman. "We don't have anything against women," Giel was quoted as saying. "Some of our best volunteers [meaning 'workers'] are women." Giel tried to bluster his way past the community's outcry and portray himself as, somehow, a victim. "Here we're trying to do something that is right and proper, and at the eleventh hour they take it upon themselves to substitute a woman," he grumbled. In the midst of the furor, Ruby said she would play if invited but would not protest if she were not. The tournament went off without Ruby, but she got the last word, offering to host a foursome of Giel and two other male golfers to golf and lunch. The discussion at the luncheon would be "on the future of women's athletics." She also suggested that each of them make a contribution to the Women's Athletic Department at the University of Minnesota.

Ruby believes her biggest contribution while on the St. Paul City Council was making the transition from the old commission form of government to the new with the professionalizing of the departments. At first there was great reluctance on the part of the incumbents to give up being the heads of their departments. Now they had to be strictly legislators and many found it difficult. They kept slipping back into their old roles, and Ruby kept watch on them to make sure they behaved as lawmakers.

Ruby found she even had to watch the mayor, Larry Cohen. Though he was diligent in seeing to it that the charter was followed, Cohen appointed Joe Carchedi to be license inspector. "Carchedi had been the 'bag-man' under the old regime who went around collecting political contributions from the bar owners." The charter stated that the license inspector could not be appointed but must be hired under the classified service. The Civil Service Commission set up a process for applicants and invited people to take the examination. Joe applied, took the test, and, to everyone's amazement, received the top score. He kept his job, this time as a classified civil servant, which set the tone for the administration.

Ruby served on the St. Paul City Council until 1982 when, at Diane Ahren's urging, she resigned to run for the Ramsey County Board. Diane, elected to the board in 1974, had been battling three hold-overs, Joe Danna, John Finley, and Lou McKinna, from the old time DFL political machine that went back to the Karl Rolvaag days. The three dominated the seven-person board of Ramsey County Commissioners and made no secret of their desire to defeat Diane. Twice the three found people to run against Diane, and twice she defeated her opponents.

Then the trio convinced Ron Mattox, a downtown bar owner, to be Diane's opponent. During all the years they had served on the county board Danna, Finley, and McKinna had had essentially free rides. They were incumbents who never had any strong opposition and so had been reelected over and over again. The three decided to put all of their political muscle behind Mattox to defeat Diane. But then Ruby decided to run for Danna's seat. With Rudy's entry into the race, the trio found they had to divide their forces to defend both Mattox and Danna.

Mattox and Danna lost and Ruby Hunt and Diane Ahrens began their long and beneficial collaboration on the Ramsey County Board. Among the campaigns they waged together was a successful one to eliminate smoking from all Ramsey County offices and institutions except for the jail. The campaign was difficult with Commissioners John Finley and Warren Schaber opposed to their efforts.

At one point in her political career, Ruby thought seriously about running for mayor of St. Paul. Many supporters, including Rep. Kathleen Vellenga, urged her to make the run. She probably would have gone for it

Ramsey County Commissioner
Ruby Hunt

if she had not already encouraged Ray Faricy to run and had pledged him her support. "I just felt I couldn't turn around and say to Ray, 'Hey, I've decided to run myself.' Ray hadn't known that I was thinking about the mayor's position." (Faricy ended up losing.) When she looks back on it now, Ruby wishes she had campaigned for mayor. "Being mayor is a terrible job," she says, "but I think back then I could have handled it."

The seeds of Ruby's political career may have been planted by her father when he walked her, as a child of eleven, past the coffin of Floyd B. Olsen, a governor of Minnesota. He later took her to the steps of the capitol when Wendell Wilke campaigned there for president. Of her political style she says, "Though I never avoided the responsibility for speaking up and being held accountable for what I said, I tried to see if there was a group consensus. The League of Women Voters is always great on consensus. If you have a consensus among folks who want to make something happen, you're a lot better off than if you go it alone." She paused and then added, "I've always had a philosophy that I should live a life that's pleasing to God and helpful to my fellow man."

Despite her political success, Ruby describes herself as "never being very cocky as an individual. I never thought of myself as important but worked with other people. I did that in the League and in the PTA. I think my strongest role was the ability to get other people of like mind to band together and feel committed to make something happen."

As a child, Ramsey County Commissioner Diane Ahrens lived in an apartment in Washington, D.C., across from Meridian Park, which she describes as having been "very beautiful with cascading waterfalls." Though her family was not Catholic, she attended a Roman Catholic school around the corner from her home. "The education I got at that point was a fairly formal, rigid one. I remember that the playground was all asphalt—it was an inner city, very-confined kind of play-ground."

When she was nine years old and in the fifth grade, Diane's parents moved to Silver Spring, Maryland, where she entered the public school. "Here the atmosphere was very different. There was much more open-ness and freedom in the public system. I could walk home even though the elementary school was a mile away. I always had friends to walk with, there was a drug store that we passed, and we always got an ice cream cone, which was great. The boys would sometimes throw snowballs at us as we made our way. I enjoyed that school very much. In a psychological sense, I began to blossom a bit with the freedom and friends that I had. I began to feel more independent, more self-confident and more pleased with myself."

Diane's neighborhood playmates were twin boys who insisted she play cowboys and Indians with them on their terms, which meant Diane always had to play the Indian. Diane's father worked at the Washington Bureau of the *Cincinnati Inquirer* newspaper. On occasion he would take her with him to his office where she enjoyed "fooling around, as kids will do."

When she reached high school age, Diane decided to attend the secondary school in Washington, D.C., rather than the nearby one in Maryland. In the 1950s, the Maryland suburban schools were not considered to be very good, while the Washington, D.C., schools were excellent. There was reciprocity between the D.C. district and Maryland, so Diane could attend a District of Columbia public high school without paying tuition. Though getting to the school was highly inconvenient for the students, about eighty percent of her class transferred into the Washington, D.C., high school. "I had to take a bus and transfer to a street car. Then it was a six-block walk to the school. But it was a very good school. Academically, it was terrific. Everyone just knew that this D.C. high school was on a higher academic plain than were the Maryland Schools."

Though she attended the D.C. high school, Diane maintained her social relationships with her Maryland friends. She found the D.C. students to be "artificially sophisticated. I didn't want anything to do with the boys in the city. They were trying to be grown up too soon, just not very natural. I think they were kind of a fast crowd, and I sensed that fastness, and I didn't like it, so I stayed away."

Because her mother was employed outside of their home as the branch manager of the Western Union in Washington, D.C., Diane spent her childhood summers with either an aunt in Florida or her grandmother in Georgia. "My grandmother was very loving, but she had clear rules that you didn't break. She was my mother's mother, a very strong-willed woman who insisted that the family be a close one—and we still are. When we have a wedding, everybody goes; when we have a funeral, everybody goes. What was acceptable and what was not acceptable was very clear. She instilled in me the importance of integrity and honesty and character. She also fostered a religious conviction although she, herself, was not active in the church.

"I trooped off to Sunday morning services and Sunday evening services and mid-week services. The church was Methodist, and the preaching was pretty evangelical. I learned that it was very important to be religious and to take Christianity seriously. My aunt in Florida was the same although she was much more active in the church than was my grandmother.

"These experiences fostered an appreciation for the importance of religion in my life and value system. When I went back home to Maryland in the winter I joined the Methodist Youth Choir, which was my introduction to liturgical music and religious pageantry—something I would not have gotten anywhere else. I did this on my own because my parents didn't go to church."

Diane's grandmother's house in Georgia had a big porch furnished with wicker rocking chairs and large pillows. "Because it was so beastly hot (there was no air conditioning at that time) we'd sit out there in the morning when it was cool. After the big meal at noon we would take a rest and then return to the porch in the evening. I was often in her lap. That's the kind of person she was. I could just get in her lap when I was small. And then all the neighbors would come over, and they would sit and gossip. It was a great feeling."

Diane remembers that she was "not terribly adventuresome as a young girl. I was somewhat insecure and anxious to please. Caution was instilled in me because of the mores of growing up in the South back when I did. There were certain things that women did, and there were certain things they didn't do. It was still very much the old South. In a moral sense you were very careful about how you behaved, very proper and demure. Promiscuity, as we called it, was absolutely forbidden. One of the things you learn in the South is that you may have steel inside but you don't show it. Instead you learn to pretend to a kind of insecurity even though inside you might be very secure or even opinionated and rigid. Steel magnolias. My grandmother was a steel magnolia.

"In the 1930s and 1940s, it was a totally segregated society. I accepted that—that was the norm—that was the way it was, and as far as everybody down there was concerned, that was the way it would always be. At the same time, I became quite close to the black people who worked in my grandmother's home. I got a sense of how they approached life and felt about things. I think that part of it deepened my appreciation so that I could relate to black people in a way that I could not have later on if I hadn't had that close personal experience — even though it was highly prejudicial."

Diane made the Freshman Honor Society during her first year at the University of Maryland, which was significant as many students flunked out after the first semester. This brought her recognition. Before long, Diane found herself the president of most of the organizations to which she belonged, and, when she ran for a class office, she was elected. Fellow students found that she was responsible and would follow through on obligations and tasks she undertook

Diane's sensitivity to the appropriate role of religion in life put her in conflict with members of her sorority at the University of Maryland. "There was one Sunday a year when we were all supposed to troop together to the Episcopal church up the street and be recognized, and I refused to do that. 'This is a sham,' I said, 'and an improper use of religion.' I told them I wasn't going to take part in this. My roommate was the president of the sorority, and she was really mad at me. I didn't try to mobilize support for this church thing as I knew it was a losing proposition. There wasn't anybody to mobilize. There was just me. The other girls didn't care, and they would do whatever they were told to do."

While at the University of Maryland, Diane became friends with Dean of Women Adele Stamp. Stamp was a strong woman whom many observers believed ran the university "because the president was so terrible and so weak." He was a politician, and his qualification to be a university president was that he had been a football coach. "His name was Harry Byrd, but everyone called him 'Curly Byrd.' The university president would never cross Adele Stamp."

One of the campus organizations in which Diane was active was the Wesley Foundation, the Methodist Youth Group. In 1952, during her senior year, the faculty advisor to the Wesley Foundation arranged for a delegation of students from the University of Maryland to hold a weekend retreat with Wesley members at Moorhead State College, an all black institution. Diane, as an active member of Wesley, signed up for the trip, not dreaming that she was about to experience a profound confrontation that would change her life.

When the group arrived on the Moorhead State campus, their leader ushered them into the student dining hall where they were to have dinner with the other students. Diane looked about her at the black students and realized that, for the first time in her life, she was expected to sit down at a table with black students and dine with them. She was profoundly shocked. She had never related to a black person except on a servant level. All her life she had attended segregated schools. The University of Maryland was segregated. Every member of her family, all of whom she loved dearly, were from the Deep South and believed racial segregation to be as much a law of nature as sunlight. "I had absorbed all of the things a child would absorb from people she loved, both the good things and the bad things," she remembered. "Their attitudes were never questioned. My whole life in the South I was taught all kinds of 'you mustn'ts.' You mustn't do this and you mustn't do that. One of the mustn'ts was—you don't eat at the same table with black people."

Though Diane sat down at the table with the other students, she found that she could not eat. Instead, she became physically ill. She was nauseated. After the dinner, she went to the dormitory room where she and another girl from the University of Maryland were to share a room with two Moorhead students. The black girls had given up the top bunk in their room for the two visiting students and were sleeping together on the bottom bunk. Diane and her friend were to sleep on the top bunk. Though Diane climbed up to her bed, she could not sleep. She lay awake all night sick and miserable.

The next morning, though she went to the dining room for breakfast, again she was unable to eat. When it became time for her to go to the first discussion group of the day, Diane found that she was having more physical problems. The culture shock was so great that she was, literally, unable to hold her head up! Her chin resting on her chest, Diane went in search of the campus minister who had driven them down to Moorhead.

"I can't stay here," she told the minister. "I am sick. I can't eat or sleep and now I can't even hold my head up." Diane no longer remembers if she told the minister the reason for her feelings. Whether she confessed to him or not, she suspects that he guessed her problem. "I absolutely understand," he told her. "I will take you home right now." The minister left the retreat and drove Diane back to the University of Maryland.

"Prejudice," Diane says, "is an armor people put on. Prejudice envelops your whole being. It is not just a mental or emotional thing; it is physical as well. It just consumes you and you don't even know it is there unless you have a confrontation." Diane's experience at Moorhead State College was the first chink in the armor of her prejudice. More cracks were soon to come.

Diane had been intellectually stimulated by a few good professors at the University of Maryland, and she decided to continue her education with graduate studies in religion. The best schools of religion on the East Coast at that time, she believed, were Union Theological Seminary in New York and Yale Divinity School. Though she felt naïve and unsophisticated (her travels had been limited to journeys between Washington, D.C., and Georgia), she decided to apply at Yale. "What do I have to lose?" she asked herself. She was late in applying, and when she went to New Haven for her interview the interviewer was not encouraging. Yale at that time had a quota on women (ten percent of the student body) and the man interviewing her reproached her, saying, "If we take you, we will displace a male." Diane went home believing she had no chance of being admitted to Yale. But she was.

One of the first social events for the new students at Yale Divinity School was a tea dance. Diane went to the dance to meet her fellow students and was sitting against the wall watching when a young man came up to her and asked her to dance. The young man was black. Diane remembers that her whole life flashed before her. Her family and all of the "you mustn'ts" she had learned throughout her childhood flooded into her mind. Then she said to herself, "Well gal, it's time to show your mettle. You had better get with the program." Diane stood up, accepted the young man's invitation to dance, and floated off across the dance floor with him. As she danced, Diane says that she felt a great weight lift off her body. "The burden I had been carrying just went away. My partner was just as nice as any other guy there. It was just like a . . . I call it a redemption. Prejudice is sinful, and in order to get rid of that sin, there has to be some sort of redemption. It is God driven— because that is what redemption is all about. Whatever meaning anybody wants to read into it, that was my epiphany."

Diane was helped in her transformation by the Yale culture where discrimination of any kind was absolutely not acceptable. She ended up helping to tutor her young dance partner. The son of a well-known North Carolina minister, he was a highly intelligent young man who had had a poor education in the south. All of the students were struggling to keep up with the demands made by the Yale curriculum, but it was doubly hard for him because of his former inferior schooling. The tutoring was successful, and the young man went on to become the minister of one of the largest United Church of Christ congregations in the United States.

After she graduated from Yale, Diane visited her friend's father's church in Greensboro, North Carolina. Diane had discovered an intimate, emotional connection, a personal tie with the worship in black congregations. Greenboro was the home of North Carolina A & M, an all-black technical college, and the church was the university church. "It was so interesting to go to that church," she remembers. "The 'Ameners' were in the front pews while the university faculty sat toward the rear, very quietly, their hands folded, throughout the service. The minister was so skilled that he could preach to both audiences, appealing equally to the 'Ameners' in the front and the university faculty in the back."

Diane's family found her change in attitude on racial matters both odd and disturbing. While they were proud of her for succeeding at Yale, they also felt she had made a mistake going to "that northern place" and letting it change her. When she and her husband Ray were planning their wedding, they invited several of their black student friends to their Washington, D.C., wedding. When her family learned of their plans, a favorite uncle, whom she dearly loved, called her long distance (a rare thing to do in those days) to protest. "How could you do this to the family?" he asked. "I was breaking a profound social code," Diane explained, "doing something absolutely unheard of in our family." Despite the family concerns, their wedding went off as Diane and Ray had planned it.

When Diane was growing up in Maryland, her parents and their friends had discussed politics. Both the newspaper Diane's father worked for and the Western Union office where her mother was employed were close to the political action of Washington. In the 1950s, senators communicated with their constituents by telegram and were in the telegraph office on a regular basis. Diane remembers that "everybody had opinions. They held very opinionated conversations, cynical and terribly critical. My parents were Democrats although they were Southern Democrats so it is not the same as up here. There was very little praise and lots of criticism. Roosevelt was the only president I knew when I was growing up."

Though her parents and their friends discussed politics at length, Diane did not become interested until she was married and she and her husband moved to Wichita, Kansas, where she joined the League of Women Voters. True to her past experiences, Diane was soon chair of several league committees and active in the Civil Rights Movement. There were not very many Democrats in Wichita, and one Saturday morning the Chairman of the Democratic Central Committee came to the Ahrens house to ask if Diane would run for Congress against Garner Shriver. Garner Shriver had been in Congress for twenty-five years and was the superintendent of the Sunday School of the biggest Methodist church in Wichita. Diane knew enough about politics by this time to decline the invitation to run against Shriver, but her interest continued to grow. When she and her husband moved to St. Paul in 1967, she joined the local League of Women Voters and was soon a member of the league board.

One of Diane's first encounters with local officials occurred when she looked out her living room window on Osceola Street to see a city truck about to dump a load of asphalt on the street. Osceola is one of the few remaining streets in St. Paul to still have its original paving stones in place, and the residents are very protective of their antique street pavers. When Diane saw the asphalt truck, she abandoned her two-year-old son and raced out into the street in the rain.

"Get this truck out of here," she told the driver. "We don't want these stones covered up with asphalt." "Lady," the driver replied, "I've got my orders. You'll have to call the supervisor at the asphalt department." Diane went inside and called her neighbors, most of them women at home with small children. Within a few minutes, calls began to jam the phone line of the superintendent of public works. The truck with its load of asphalt was recalled, and Diane later got a call from a laughing city council member, Ruby Hunt, and her aide, Fran Boyden. They reported that the St. Paul Public Works Street Committee had met and declared that if the residents of that block of Osceola ever wanted their street repaired, they would have to do it themselves.

In 1974 the Minnesota legislature redistricted the county boards, the members of which had previously run at large. After the redistricting, Diane's district of Ramsey County did not have an incumbent, and she inquired about running. A fellow league member, Sid Faricy, told her that all the party regulars were lined up behind Stuart Wells, a popular and well-financed Democrat. Everyone believed that Wells had the party endorsement all sewed up. Despite the discouraging news, Diane decided to run anyway. Three hundred and fifty people showed up at Central High School in St. Paul for the Ramsey County District 4 endorsing convention. Seven candidates were running, and, as the balloting went on through the evening, Diane began gaining support while Wells began losing his. Some candidates dropped out, and voters began to shift their support to the surviving candidates. Jack Adams, a local labor leader who was supporting Diane, came up to where she was standing in the back of the auditorium and told her, "Go walk down the aisle and show those legs."

At 11:00 P.M., Diane was still in the running, and she began to fear that her supporters would tire and go home. George Latimer, calling the County Board a "two-bit Tammany Hall," stayed as did several rows of members of the League of Women Voters. "The league is not supposed to get involved in elections and officially they didn't. But they were all sitting out there, so prim and proper. It was wonderful to have them support me. They were very dependable supporters, and that's how I got elected, because I had leaguers who would work for me."

Getting herself elected to the Ramsey County Board was only half of the battle. The board had been run as a source of patronage by the commissioners. Soon after Diane took office, they voted to hire as an executive one of their friends who was totally unqualified to be an administrator. Another hire they wanted to make was a position called "clerk of the works," whose duties were to supervise all the building projects in the county. The individual proposed had no engineering experience and knew little about construction. His only qualification was his friendship with the incumbent county commissioners. Diane was outraged, but she was only one vote out of the six commissioners.

There was a remedy. An act, called the Optional Forms of Government Act, could be invoked by the submission of a petition, carrying 8,000 signatures, requesting the district judge to appoint a commission to recommend an appropriate form of county administration.

The meeting at which the county commissioners voted to hire their cronies as administrators and clerks was packed with spectators, and when the results of the vote were announced the 300 people in the audience booed loudly. Then a representative from the League of Women Voters stood up and announced that she had 5,000 signatures on a petition for the Optional Forms Act and would soon have the remaining 3,000 required to put it on the ballot. In the shocked silence that followed, Diane moved to set the Optional Forms Act in process. Her fellow commissioners were so unnerved by the boos and the large number of league members in the room that they voted for it. The study took two years to complete, but when it was finished a professional staff was hired to manage the business of Ramsey County.

As her fellow commissioners learned (some to their sorrow), Diane was tenacious and fought hard for what she believed. Her great concern was for human services. Diane served as a Ramsey County Commissioner for five four-year terms, from 1974 until 1994. By the time she had retired, she had become widely known as the conscience of the County Board.

The role model for Diane's life was, she believes, her grandmother, the southern woman with steel in her character. Though she deplores the racist attitudes she learned from her grandmother's family, she also credits them for giving her the close interaction with blacks that she experienced in the South. "Unlike many people in the North who were active in the civil rights movement because of issues of justice, I felt like I knew something about blacks as individuals. We could connect with each other in a genuine way. I had an appreciation and love that others who had not been reared in the

Ramsey County Commissioner
Diane Ahrens

southern culture perhaps did not have." Diane's grandmother also taught her to never give up. "The thing I learned about myself when I got into politics was the necessity of persevering," she said. "You just have to keep at it. It's a kind of flexible rigidity. Just because you were defeated on something once, you don't quit. You have to keep on coming back."

Though county government dealt exclusively with local issues, the commissioners had not been unaffected by what was happening on the national scene. Civil Rights for minorities and the passage, by the Supreme Court, of *Roe v. Wade* dominated political discussion through the 1970s. The court decided in 1972 that women, as part of their constitutional right to privacy, may choose to abort a pregnancy in the first trimester. (Although abortion had been legal in most of the United States until after the Civil War, the Roe decision seemed to many to be a radical break with the past.)

The decision was denounced by religious groups, especially Catholics, Mormons, and Fundamentalist Protestants who felt that safe, legal abortions would lead to widespread promiscuity, undermine family cohesion and create social chaos. Sown by frustration and harvested by conservative politicians, animosity toward feminists and their social agenda became a dominant theme of the 1970s.

ᘉ5ᘔ

"Women are young at politics, but they are old at suffering; soon they will learn that through politics they can prevent some kinds of suffering."
— Nancy Astor

In one of their publications, the editors of *Ms Magazine* declared the seventies to be the Decade of Women. In almost every area, from business to politics to sports, women made gains. In 1979, for the first time in United States history, there were more women than men in colleges and universities. Between 1972 and 1983, the proportion of women in state legislatures tripled to an unprecedented twenty-eight percent. In Minnesota the percentage of women in the legislature went from a half of one percent at the beginning of the decade to 11.9 percent in 1980. Americans sent record numbers of women to Congress in the 1970s including Pat Schroeder and Elizabeth Holtzman — and the FBI hired its first female agent.

Despite impressive gains of the 1970s, at the beginning of the 1980s women still faced obstacles to equality. Cooking, cleaning, and child care were still considered "women's work," and the economic gap between the sexes was still wide. One of the biggest problems facing women was the feminization of poverty. Between 1964 and 1974, the divorce rate in the United States had doubled, and more women than ever before were trying to make it on their own. Divorced women and unwed mothers were faced with the fact that women still earned, on average, less than half of what men made.

Women were not struggling for economic freedom alone. They were also fighting for the power to make decisions that affected their own bodies. Abortion remained a central issue. Few feminists argued that abortion was a good thing, but they insisted women had the intellectual capacity and emotional compassion to determine for themselves whether to terminate a pregnancy. Fundamentalist opponents of abortion condemned not only the procedure itself but feminism, liberalism, relativism, secular humanism—any philosophy without reference or adherence to absolutes. "Pro-life" for such people meant not just a stance against abortion, but an attempt to affirm traditional limits and boundaries to the family and to the state. The position was a turning away from what many saw as social progress to what others believed to be an earlier, simpler and safer time in America's past.

Conservative politicians and televangelists quickly grasped the centrality of the abortion issue in the minds of these Americans and used opposition to abortion to construct a powerful political coalition. That coalition would seize Congress in 1978 and the presidency in 1980. Abortion, as a code word for one's position on social change, came to hold as central a position in the philosophy of conservatives as it did in the political theory of feminists.

Three women whose young adult years encompassed the decade of the 1970s were Ann Wynia, Dee Long, and Pam Neary. One grew up in the West, one in the South, and one was from Minnesota. Their experiences reflected the dizzying change that was taking place in American life.

As a child, Ann Wynia lived in Coleman, Texas, a town of 7,000 people. Her family lived a mile or two out of town and, in the summer, she would take her two younger brothers and walk a mile to a creek where they would spend the entire day exploring the creek banks, building fires, and cooking minnows. "There was a kind of blissful unawareness of all the dangers lurking out there and of the meanness in the world," she recalls.

The public schools of Coleman, where Ann started school, had originally been segregated three ways: whites in one school, Hispanics in another, and blacks in a third. By the time Ann was in elementary school the Hispanic and white children had been moved into the same building, but the two groups of children seldom related to each other. Ann remembers that there was an Hispanic girl in her fourth grade who was incredibly shy and, as a result, was ignored by the other children in the class. At first Ann treated the girl with the same disdain as her friends.

Then something changed Wynia's mind. "This girl was one of the most ignored, lonely kinds of little kids there was," Wynia remembers.

"She never said anything. I don't know if she didn't speak English or if she was just frightened. I decided that we should be nice to her, so I organized my friends to bring food from home—things like canned goods—and give them to her as if she were starving. The girl's older sister was in the fifth grade, and she was really puzzled. She wanted to know why we had done this. Our awkward actions were the product of our segregated lifestyle. The only way we knew to express any kind of outreach to people of a different ethnic background was to act the lady-bountiful role."

The segregation of blacks from whites in Texas in the 1950s extended beyond schools and included youth organizations such as the Girl Scouts. Until the civil rights legislation of the 1960s, the Girl Scouts was an all-white organization. Wynia's mother decided that the black girls in Coleman should also have the opportunity to participate in scouting and since they were not allowed to join the white troops, she organized a black Girl Scout troop. Although acceptable to the community, problems arose when city-wide events were organized and the black and white troops met together to conduct joint activities. Wynia remembers that these combined activities were incredibly controversial. Some people took their daughters out of scouting because they objected to even that minimal degree of integration. Ann's mother, however, was passionate in her support of the black scout troop and, despite the community turmoil over the matter, she prevailed.

As a child, Ann Wynia was also part of a church community. "The Baptist Church was a very important part of our family's life. We went to church Sunday morning and Sunday night and Wednesday nights, and I had Girl's Auxiliary on Monday afternoons. If I never go to church again, I'm still going to hit an average of one hour a week," she claims. Ann was fortunate that her parents let her read during the church services. She would check books out of the church library every Sunday and would go through a book or more each week. Both of her parents were deeply involved in the life of the church, occasionally getting themselves into difficulty with other members because of the activist roles they took in the community.

One Wednesday night a month was set aside by the church for a pot-luck supper to which everyone was expected to bring a dish to share. One member of the church was a crusty old bachelor who, though he came to the dinners, never brought a contribution. That fact did not go unobserved, and one Wednesday night someone asked, "Well, George. What did you bring?" Before he could answer Wynia's mother spoke up. "He's eating with us. I brought enough for him." Later she commented to her family, "How could anybody say something like that? That was so mean."

Ann remembers with appreciation the good times she experienced in her Texas church. "Even though I have rejected much of the religious teachings associated with the Baptist Church, I still value the sense of being part of the group and accomplishing something—working with other people and the great joy of companionship. Even memorizing Bible verses were good times."

Ann's parents served as role models of political action for their children. Ann's mother was active in the Daughters of the American Revolution (DAR) organization and was president of her local society. Early in her tenure, she came into conflict with a local county commissioner named Ira Galloway who had pushed through a plan to demolish the old historic courthouse in Coleman and build a modern building in its place. This was an unfortunate decision because Texas is noted for its ornate and historic courthouses—many of which have been listed on state and national historic registers—and the one in Coleman was a beautiful example of old courthouse architecture.

As a result of Ira Galloway's efforts, the lovely old courthouse of Coleman, Texas, was torn down and an ugly 1950s flat building was put in its place. Also removed when the courthouse was torn down was a stone monument identifying Coleman as a layover on one of the original cattle herding trails. The DAR had been involved in putting up the original monument and when the new courthouse was built they discovered, to their dismay, that the stone had disappeared. Wynia's mother and the DAR organization of Coleman were convinced that the county commissioner was responsible for the mysterious disappearance of the stone marker because they had made his life so miserable over the tearing down of the old historic courthouse.

Ann's family spent many Sunday afternoons driving over the countryside looking for the lost stone. Eventually her mother learned that Ira Galloway had, indeed, ordered the contractor to take the stone and drop it in the bottom of a nearby lake. It had been a deliberate action on his part. Wynia's mother was so incensed by this deed that she organized her supporters and, at the next election, they defeated Galloway. A replacement monument was carved and put up on the lawn of the new courthouse with Wynia's mother presiding over the ceremony. "It was perceived as a great triumph for my mother that she had busted this guy," Ann remembers.

When Ann Wynia was in the fifth grade, her father became chairman of the Democratic Party for Coleman County, Texas. The big event in those pre-TV days was election night. A platform would be put up on the street by the newspaper office and as all the precincts around the county reported their tallies, Wynia's father would stand on the platform and write down the results. "The mood was very festive, and there was always a lot of excitement. It was like a fair in some respects. I felt a sense of pride that my dad was in charge of all that."

One of Ann's father's responsibilities was to prepare the ballot booklets. Texas had a long ballot, and the names of all the candidates in the county had to be hand written in the booklets. This was a time consuming job, so Ann, as a fifth and sixth grader, was hired by her father to write the candidates' names on the ballots. It would take her several days to complete the job, and when she was finished, she knew by heart the names of all the candidates. One name that stayed in her mind was that of the only woman, Sarah T. Hughes, who was running for the Texas Supreme Court. Ann asked her mother about Hughes. Her mother explained that she was not going to vote for Sarah T. Hughes for the Texas Supreme Court because she felt that Hughes was doing a good job on the Texas Court of Appeals. Ann thought no more about Hughes until the assassination of John F. Kennedy. Then she recognized Sarah T. Hughes as the judge who swore in Lyndon B. Johnson as president.

As a nine-year old in 1952, Ann remembers listening to both the Democratic and Republican conventions on the radio. "In those days they played them both all day long on the radio. There was only one radio station in town. I heard Eisenhower saying, 'I will go to Korea.'" Politics permeated Ann's parents lives. She clearly remembers their discussion in 1954 when the Supreme Court rendered the *Brown v. Board of Education* decision. Ann's parents were big fans of Ralph Yarborough, one of the most liberal individuals to hold statewide office in Texas. They supported him for governor through two campaigns, both of which he lost, before being elected to the United States Senate. Ann and her brothers were active passing out bumper stickers for Yarborough.

Overall, Ann's elementary school experience in the small town of Coleman was a happy one. Despite her experience handwriting ballots, she was a good student in every subject area but handwriting. She was asked to do special handwriting practice, but she says that she never overcame the problem. Looking back on her childhood, she thinks that she was bright and adventurous. Because her mother worked outside of their home, she had less supervision than some children. She played a lot with her brothers, who were four and six years younger than she was. She says that she was responsible enough "that I never got us into serious trouble."

After Ann completed grade nine, her family moved from Coleman to Arlington, a city of 60,000. Coming in as a sophomore to the large city high school and having registered late, Ann, the good student, was put into classes for slow learners. She was shocked to find her fellow students "goofing off, shooting spitballs. They were not the kind of people I had typically been friends with."

Because Ann had to ride the bus home immediately after school, she found it difficult to find time to socialize with other girls her own age. "I got down on myself in high school and felt very socially isolated much of the time. The other girls would get together every afternoon after school to read movie magazines and talk and do all those things that girls do. I never got to do that because I had to get on the bus and go home. At the time, I felt I was losing out, but as an adult, I think I was incredibly lucky because I used that time to read and get into really big science experiments. I had an incredible bug collection. This sounds nerdy but, in some respects, these were more meaningful activities than reading movie magazines. But it always made me feel a little bit outside—not as clued in as the other girls. That's stuck with me as an adult. Now I'm so old I don't care. I realize that I'm not like a lot of other women, and I just don't care. I'm really happy with who I am."

Ann's singular happy memory of high school came when she was placed in a speech class. As a young girl feeling "incredibly shy," she found her first speech to be "a horrible experience." But she had a teacher who saw the potential in the shy student and worked with her. By the end of the year, Ann was competing in speech competitions and feeling a measure of success. Then she was selected to be the business manager for the school annual, a position that gave her an opportunity to work with a group of her fellow students.

Ann attended the University of Texas at Arlington and immediately became involved in campus politics. Though she was elected to offices in her women's social club, she soon got the clear sense that she would never get to run for a major school office herself. If she wanted to be involved in politics, the best she could hope for would be to find and marry some man who wanted to run for public office. Then, vicariously, through his work, she could experience working on public policy. "I did not perceive that politics was an option for girls. Sometimes I blame it on being a female in the South. It was so ingrained to be good little girls, not to cause trouble, to smile and look pretty and not make a fuss."

For two years, Ann was president of her sorority and active in student government. "I would have been president of student government except I let a man persuade me to drop out so he could run and win. In retrospect, I realize that had I decided to run, he could never have beaten me. I was still not internalizing the fact that women can do anything they want. Instead, I continued to allow society to impose restraints on my aspirations."

When Ann was a senior at the University of Texas in the early 1960s, though the school had integrated when she was a sophomore, she became concerned about the school mascot, "Johnny Reb" and "Dixie," the school song. The violence in Little Rock and the Civil Rights marches in Birmingham had taken place, and Ann grew increasingly uneasy over all the "confederacy kind of stuff" at the University of Texas. Being action oriented she organized, and led, an effort on campus to get the school mascot changed. She did not do anything radical to try to bring about change such as burn the Confederate flag or stage a protest to shut down classes. Instead, she and her friends worked within the system appealing to people's minds as well as their hearts. The issue was placed on the school ballot and eventually lost, but not before it had generated a great deal of discussion, as well as some abuse, directed personally toward Ann. Fortunately, she had the support of her friends. Her best friend had been elected "Miss Dixie Bell," and the two of them, along with their friends, in private belittled the name and the assumptions behind the beauty queen concept.

Years later, Ann was attending a ceremony honoring the University of Texas's outstanding alumnus in education when the honoree suddenly turned to Ann and said, "I remember you. I was only a freshman when you were a senior, but I so admired what you tried to do about the rebel theme. That was such an important lesson to me to see that happen." As they talked he added, "You know, I sent you money. I'm a member of EMILY's (Early Money Is Like Yeast: It makes the dough rise) list." The man had had no idea they had been fellow students when he had sent in a campaign contribution for women candidates.

Not until she was living in Minnesota and witnessing the beginning of the women's movement and the organization of the women's political caucus did it occur to Ann that she could be a candidate for political office. "It gave me permission for some of the hidden aspirations that I had." In college, Ann and a woman friend had read *The Feminine Mystique* and while they were impressed with the message, they could not see how it would play out in their lives. "The first breaking loose from the expectation of what girls did was the decision we both made to go to graduate school. We decided we would not spend our senior year in college looking for someone to marry. We weren't just going to get married."

Ann's irrational feelings that she should not be running for political office continued even when she ran for a seat in the Minnesota House of Representatives in 1976. She voiced her concerns to a friend that she was not qualified to be a representative, that running was a terrible mistake, that she did not know enough to do the job well. The friend laughed at her and said, "Wait until you see your colleagues." The feelings of inferiority did not completely leave Ann until she was serving in the legislature. Once there, she finally got the sense that she was doing well. "I may not be as smart as everybody here," she told herself, "but gender is certainly not the criteria that determines IQ."

There was great excitement among the women in the legislature in 1976 as they saw their numbers increase from five to eleven. Ann quickly discovered just how indebted the new members were to the pioneering legislative class of 1972—to Joan Growe, Linda Berglin, Phyllis Kahn, Mary Forsythe, and Helen McMillan—who had established high standards of achievement for women. These early members of the legislature had also defined women's expectations for the male members of the legislature, that women were to be treated with respect and with a serious regard for their abilities.

One of the committees to which Ann was assigned by the speaker, Martin Sabo, was Financial Institutions and Service. Ann joked that she was the perfect individual for that committee because, like most Minnesotans, she had insurance policies whose fine print she had never read and bank accounts that she struggled to keep in balance. She would bring the perspective of the consumer to the committee. She soon discovered that the committee was dominated by men, all of whom had connections with the banking and insurance industries. When she went to the first meeting of the committee at the Capitol, she found the room packed with spectators. She could see only three women: Marge Lang and her assistant who were clerks to the chairman, Bernie Brinkman, and one young woman in the audience. Everyone else in the crowd of seventy-five or more was male.

The committee meeting was spent having each of the lobbyists stand and introduce himself and who he represented so the committee members would know from whom they would later be hearing. The lone young woman introduced herself as the lobbyist from MPERG, a student group at the university. One man in the room, who looked different from the others, did not introduce himself. He had longer hair and a hippy look about him. Ann could not resist, and at a break she asked him who he was. "I'm Walter Sawicki, representing a consumer group," he told her, "and, furthermore, I voted for you."

"Thank goodness," Ann thought. "There is somebody here who represents a perspective similar to my own."

That was Ann's introduction to how different it was to be a women in the legislative setting. She subsequently came to enjoy the work of the committee and, during her first term, introduced a controversial bill to eliminate gender distinctions in the rating system for insurance. The matter was a serious policy issue that was explored by Federal Human Rights Commission hearings in Washington, D.C. When she first introduced the bill in Minnesota, however, many members of her committee thought she was either joking, or it was just one of those silly ideas put forward by a woman.

Ann kept working on the issue and gradually gained support. Though he did not agree with the bill, Brinkman, who was a fair man, agreed to give it a hearing and sent it to a sub-committee. Even Ann was shocked when the sub-committee recommended passage of her bill and sent it on to the full committee. However, Ann's surprise was nothing to that felt by the insurance industry. Overnight, insurance companies began flying what were probably their only female actuaries to St.

Paul to speak against the bill. Ann had never seen so many women suddenly appear before the Financial Institutions and Insurance Committee. "Clearly the insurance industry figured out that they had better have some women arguing against this. They needed women's voices as well as men's." Ann's bill did not pass, but she was pleased by the fact that, within a few months, every major insurance organization and bank had at least one female lobbyist. Her efforts had significantly increased the employment opportunities for women as lobbyists in the field of insurance.

Ann's greatest legislative accomplishment was the passage in 1987 of the Children's Health Care Plan that guaranteed basic health care for all children under the age of five. The legislation had been in the planning stages since 1984, when the Children's Defense Fund had paid Louann Nyberg to work in Minnesota, developing legislation and public policy around the issue of children's health. The Democrats were in the minority in 1987, but when they came back into the majority, Ann was asked to chair the Appropriations Division of the Health and Human Services Committee. She immediately began working with Nyberg, introducing the bill and working it through the legislative process. "How can anyone be against insuring that children get access to basic health services?" she asked. The children to be helped were not the very poor, who were assisted by other programs, but the children of the working poor whose parents did not have health care benefits.

To fund the program, parents paid a twenty-five dollars a year in insurance payment and Ann put a five-cent tax on cigarettes. In 1987 any suggestion to raise taxes caused concern—even a five-cent tax on cigarettes. Then the pro-life lobby became concerned believing the bill was some secret way to sneak in payments for abortions. The abortion rumor had started because the bill would pay for prenatal care for pregnant women. Ann met with the concerned committee members and convinced them that the Children's Health Plan bill had nothing to do with abortion.

Ann had managed to get the bill into what looked like a good solid position when Easter break came and members went home to their districts. However, when Ann's DFL caucus returned, "they were up in arms." A tax rebellion was underway in some districts, and members were told they had to cut all of their spending bills. As chair of the Health and Human Services Committee, Ann was given the task of cutting a major chunk out of her budget. She had few options. When cutting the budget, it was easier to keep existing programs on which people were depending than to fund new ones, that did not yet have a constituency.

Ann still remembers her pain as she offered up the Children's Health Plan to the budget-cutting knife. Then, to her joy, she discovered that she had done such a good job of explaining to her fellow legislators why this bill was important that her cut was met with dismay and protests. Legislators had been convinced of the bill's importance. Though she took it out of the House agenda in order to meet her budget target, the members of the conference committee put it back in, and the Children's Health Plan was passed in 1987.

There were many less exciting moments. As Majority Leader, Ann had to work hard passing such legislation as making milk the state drink or blueberry the state muffin. "Those bills weren't bad," she commented, "but they were a waste of time. They were not going to make a difference in people's lives." Senator Larry Pogemiller brought a fossil from the Science Museum of Minnesota into the House with the idea of making it the "state fossil." He was passing the fossil around when one of the members dropped it, breaking off a piece. "You think, 'Oh my word! Why are we all here?'"

Ann decided those were things she did not want to spend her time on, so when Governor Perpich offered her the opportunity to run the Department of Human Services in 1989, she took it. Many people were shocked that she would give up the position of Majority Leader of the House, and she admits it was not an easy thing to do. She knew it was a big risk. There was no guarantee that Perpich would be reelected in 1990, and at that time he had not even said if he were going to run for reelection. "The thought of going to an agency and being able to devote one-hundred percent of my time and energy to a set of issues and to advancing causes that were core to what I really cared about—that was too much to pass up." Life, she said, is full of risk and she has no regrets about her decision. "The year and a half I spent at the department was one of the hardest jobs I have ever had, trying to stretch resources to meet incredibly painful human needs."

As Commissioner of Human Services, Ann was able to celebrate the first birthday of the Children's Health Plan. She and Rudy Perpich traveled around the state visiting children's health clinics with birthday cakes as a way of getting families to sign up for the plan. "The letters the department received from parents about what the program meant in their children's lives were some of the most wonderful I have ever read," she said.

In 1993-1994 Ann decided to run for the United States Senate. Under most scenarios, leaving the legislature would have been the end of Wynia's career as an elected official; however, several events in the early 1990s conspired to change her mind. Among them was the treatment afforded Anita Hill by the United States Senate, the election of 1992, which saw a dramatic increase in the number of women serving in the Congress, and a spirit in Minnesota that seemed to be saying, "It's time we sent a woman to Congress." As Ann reviewed her experience it seemed that she was as qualified to run as were the two other women, both close personal friends, who had also declared their candidacy. One was Senator Linda Berglin, Ann's role model when she had entered the legislature, and the other was Dee Long, then Speaker of the House, who Ann considered to be one of the smartest women in the legislature.

Ann decided there was nothing wrong with having a strong field of women candidates. "The best way to elect a woman is to make sure that we are all challenged in the nomination and endorsement process so that the strongest candidate wins," she said. Ann was not sure she would get the nomination but she believed they all would be the stronger for competing. "Nobody was going to be advantaged by having a free ride to the nomination."

In June of 1993, Ann took an unpaid leave from the teaching job she had taken after leaving her commissioner's position, and devoted a full year to work on the race prior to the endorsement. She knew that she could not ask others for money and support for her Senate race if she was not putting everything she had into it as well. "I was not going to do this as a little diversion from weeding the garden," she remarked. "It is incredibly daunting to run. One does not run for the U.S. Senate from Minnesota without raising and spending at least three million dollars." She remembers waking up in the middle of the night thinking, "Three million dollars! How can I do this? My husband and I are both teachers without any personal wealth." Then she reminded herself that other people before her had figured out how to raise money.

"I'm a smart person, I know how to solve problems," she told herself. She went about the challenge methodically, developing plans for fund raising, plans for reaching the delegates. She talked to people and got information from the library. In September of 1993, she hired a campaign manager and organized a staff of volunteers. Every day she had a goal. "Today I must get on the phone and raise $10,000. I spent many days at my kitchen table on the phone asking people for their support. It was very hard." One couple stands out in her mind. Early in her campaign she went to see Ken and Judy Dayton. They listened to her talk, and then Judy said, "I know who my candidate is." Then Ken smiled, shook Ann's hand and added, "Yes, she is mine, too."

Ann won the primary against Tom Foley and went on to face Rod Grams in the general election, where she lost. Opposing Grams in the IR primary had been Joanell Drystad. "If it had been a race between Joanell and me, I would have been personally disappointed to lose — you can't spend a year of your life on something and not be disappointed when you don't succeed — but I could have looked at the winner and said 'she will speak with integrity and voice concern for some of the issues I care about.' It would have been easier if I had lost to a candidate for whom I had some respect." Ann was disappointed when Joanell endorsed Grams and did a TV ad for him. "I would never have done that to her," Ann said. "That is the way it went."

As Ann learned personally through her own defeat, 1994 was probably the worst election in fifty years to be running for office as a Democrat. Timing is everything in politics. One has to go back to the 1920s to find a similar turnover in party control. She also does not attribute her loss to being a woman even though she ran into gender-based overt hostility in parts of greater Minnesota. She balances that off against the tremendous surge of enthusiasm that her being a woman brought to the race. "That was one of the assets I brought to the race. That is why I think we did as well as we did."

Shortly after her defeat, Ann received a phone call from a seventh-grade student who had followed her campaign as a class project and wanted to interview her. "Talking with this little girl, Chelsea, and getting a sense of what it meant for her to have a woman run for U.S. Senate and her own aspirations of what she was going to do, made me feel so good. I like to think there are lots of other Chelseas out there who were similarly inspired. Every time a woman runs, she creates a half-dozen more women to run in the future. Eventually we are going to start winning some of these races."

Ann believes that one area where women in politics may have a greater problem than men is in accepting defeat. She thinks women sometimes internalize defeat more than men and are more likely to take a defeat personally. That presents the challenge of keeping women in the game because politics has so many defeats. Ann learned the lesson of defeat in 1984 when she decided to run for Speaker of the House. To be elected she had to get the support of her caucus, which she thought she could do since, between 1982 and 1984, she had been an assistant majority leader in the House and was the first women to have served as Speaker Pro-Tem.

The first time Ann was called up by the Speaker there had been a hushed silence in the chamber. "My word, what is he doing?" the members thought. But Ann had been studying. The chief clerk had given her lessons, and she had a good sense of how to run a meeting. Ann had been serving as Speaker Pro-Tem for a month or more when the Speaker, Harry Sieben, returned. Ann stepped down, and as she did so, George Mann, one of the more senior members of the House and a highly respected member of the caucus, came up to her in all innocence and said, "You know, you do pretty good up there for a woman."

Ann knew George meant it as a most sincere compliment. A variety of people encouraged Ann to run for Speaker when Sieben retired. So in 1984, she got into the race. There were a number of other strong candidates, including Fred Norton—who ultimately won. Ann lost badly. It was a painful loss because she had worked hard, traveled all over the state, called on people, only to be rejected by her peers. She realized that she had probably interpreted some comments as being supportive when they were not.

Something else happened in 1984; her party lost the majority in the election, so, instead of electing a speaker, they elected a Minority Leader. Ann decided that if she could not be elected Minority Leader, she would run for another office. She became one of the assistants to Fred Norton and continued to work hard in her caucus. She now says it was the smartest thing she ever did because it showed her peers she could accept defeat and stay in the game.

In 1986, the DFL got the majority back. Ann became a committee chairperson and Fred, after one year as Speaker, accepted an appointment to the appellate court. The person who was the Majority Leader decided to run for Speaker, and Ann decided to run again for Majority

Leader. In 1987, she was elected Majority Leader with strong support. "That would never have happened if, in 1984, I had not shown people I could accept defeat and stay in the game," Ann says.

"The challenge for women is to see a defeat, not as something personal, but as the normal part of the political process—a situation they can hope to change. This may be why women sometimes seek solutions that have more winners than a lot of unhappy losers. This is one of the strengths women bring to the political process that has not been successfully communicated to the public. While much of the public is dissatisfied with the stereotypical political style of bluff and bluster, they have not yet perceived the difference women can bring to the process."

Ann Wynia served seven terms in the Minnesota House of Representatives, from 1976 through 1990, before she ran for the United States Senate. Politics, for her, evokes the sense of community and affiliation that she first experienced as a child, in her church and in her small Texas community. "There's a kind of joy in being able to take care of other people when they need help," she says. "And a grateful joy of knowing that they're going to be there for you. One of the joys of participation in the DFL Party was this sense of friends, this willingness to participate in one's joys and sorrows. That's always been, to me, one of the most rewarding things about politics, what I like about friends and neighborhood politics. I loved my campaigns for the legislature when we would get a dozen people sitting around the dining room table slapping on stickers. There was the involvement of older people who could only do those kinds of activities.

"Much of my Senate campaign was pure misery because there was no sense of connection to other people. It was as though I were an automaton trying to perform for a newspaper reporter so that somehow, something would get reported. I give politicians, who have figured out how to create that aura of community through these third-party intermediaries, a lot of credit. I don't think I ever figured it out and I know I never felt it. That's why I think in some ways I'm not suited for this modern political world. My upbringing, which was largely devoid of television, was very much enmeshed in real life relationships."

Ann realizes that when she is a member of an organization she rather quickly cuts to the chase: "Okay, so what are we doing and how are we going to do it?" She says that people who ask those questions often

State Representative Ann Wynia

become the ones who end up accepting the responsibility to see that something gets done and are the ones who are generally called the leaders. There are others who are the social leaders, who make everyone laugh. Ann remembered a recent canoe trip. "There was one woman in the group who was wonderful, she made us laugh all the time. But I would never let her choose the route. I was the one who figured out how to use the compass and how to get us where we were going. I just assume that kind of role. But if the whole group had been composed of people like me, we wouldn't have had any fun. I think it is probably my sense of organization and purpose combined with a certain kind of intellectual ability to solve problems that results in my assuming leadership positions in organizations."

Ann still loves adventure and travel. On that canoe trip in the Boundary Waters the group made fourteen portages, the longest a third of a mile. "Hauling that canoe back and forth gave us a great sense of accomplishment. It was a joy to know that we were doing it well." Ann also loves traveling by herself. She has camped alone in the San Juan Islands and traveled by herself in Argentina. Her husband, Gary, had gone to Argentina to do some research, and she joined him there as soon as her term as Commissioner of Human Services had ended. Gary had to return early, and, when Ann could not get a flight home for a couple of weeks, she took off and traveled in the remote area of northern Argentina by herself. "I just had a wonderful time. I love the sense of exploration, of freedom, of seeing new things, of negotiating in a foreign language. It was very satisfying, that I was able to be in those areas where nobody spoke English. And I could take care of myself."

◄♦►

As a child, Dee Long, first woman to hold the position of Speaker of the House, along with her older brother, were pranksters. Her parents were permissive, and Dee describes herself as having been mischievous, bright, and not well disciplined. "I was the ring leader in pranks," she remembers. "My brother and I put tacks on teachers' chairs, that sort of thing. Other kids were involved, but I was the ring leader."

Dee's parents had been married for several years before they had their children (her mother was thirty-nine when she was born) which, Dee believes may have resulted in their being "extremely permissive." She recalls that "my brother and I were known as very wild children. There was almost a conscious effort that we should be allowed to run free."

Dee's father believed in giving his children a variety of experiences so they would not be afraid of anything. When they were young he took them up in small airplanes and set them on the front seats of roller coasters. "He held me and we laughed," Dee remembers. "That sort of thing, heights and speed, has never bothered me, and I'm grateful for it." When Dee and her brother were seven and ten years old, respectively, their parents dropped them off with an uncle and aunt in Chicago for a visit. The uncle and aunt lived in an apartment, and the youngsters raced around to such an extent that, after their visit, the couple declared they would never have children of their own. (They did not!) Dee admits that, during the visit, she and her brother were "both probably a little on the hyperactive side—maybe more than a little." After a few days, the uncle and aunt put the two children, by themselves, on a train for the nine-hour trip to Red Oak, a small town near Shenandoah, Iowa, to stay with Dee's grandparents. Dee remembers that she and her brother fought all the way. When they arrived in Shenandoah, Dee says they were so dirty and grungy, their relatives were almost embarrassed to claim them.

While in Red Oak, Dee was recruited by her family to circumvent a neighborhood feud. Dee's grandfather owned stock in the local utility company that was involved in a controversial buy-out, and the issue had divided the community. Neighbors had taken sides, and among those opposing the stockholders in the utility were two sisters, who made and sold the best local ice cream. They made the ice cream in their home and refused to sell their product to anyone on the other side of the utility issue. Dee's aunts, uncles, and cousins, who were visiting the grandparents, wanted that ice cream and decided to send the seven-year-old Dee to purchase it. If questioned, she would say only that she was visiting from Minneapolis and was not to divulge her family relationships. "If they ask you what your name is, say it is Anderson," she was told. Dee was delighted with her assignment and marched up to the door to make the purchase. To her disappointment, the sisters sold her the ice cream without question and never asked her anything about her family.

Though they squabbled at times, Dee and her brother were mutually supportive. When Dee was in the second grade and rode her bicycle to school, she had to pass a house where a family with numerous children lived. The family name was Hamilton, and the children were both older and younger than Dee and her brother. One of the boys in the family would hide in the bushes until Dee rode by. Then he would jump out and push her off her bike. This happened several times, with Dee coming home from school with cuts and bruises. Though Dee's mother called the principal, it was her older brother who solved the problem. He went over to the boy's house and beat him up. Dee is not sure if her brother fought more than one boy, but an understanding was reached among them, and Dee was no longer ambushed on her way to school.

Years later, when Dee's brother was in a bar in New York, he began chatting with the man next to him who had stopped in for a drink. The man said he was from Minneapolis. He turned out to be one of the Hamilton boys, now a member of a New York law firm. Dee was amazed to hear the story. "I thought they would all have wound up in jail given the way they were as kids."

Dee was a good student in school, attending first Northwestern University with a major in psychology. She went on to graduate school at the University of Minnesota, completing all the requirements for a Ph.D. in experimental psychology except for the dissertation.

Both of Dee's parents were involved in a variety of politically-oriented activities. Dee's mother was active in the Sierra Club and served for fourteen years on PTA boards. Though a Republican, Dee's father took her to see and hear Harry Truman when he spoke from the back of a train in Minneapolis. On election nights, he would take his children to party headquarters, both the Democrats at the Leamington Hotel and the Republicans at the Curtis, to watch the results being posted on the big blackboards as they were called in from the precincts.

Dee was riding in the car with her father in Minneapolis one afternoon, when they saw a white driver run a stop sign and crash into a car driven by a black man. When the police arrived, the policeman began to berate the black driver, even though he had not been at fault. Dee's father did not stand idly by. "My father, who never lacked motivation to jump in, got on the cop's case. The cop got mad at my dad and threatened to run him in too." As it happened, Dee's father was a friend of the then mayor of Minneapolis, P. Kenneth Peterson. Their families had known each other for years. When Dee's father reported the incident to the mayor, the mayor replied, "Well, that guy will be back on the beat." The incident impressed Dee and planted the concept in her mind that "when you see a wrong done, you have to do something about it." Dee says this sense of fairness characterized both of her parents, though her mother was more gentle in her approach. "If my father saw something he didn't like, he would be fairly confrontational and tell people off. He had this belief that people should be treated decently and with justice."

The problem of civil rights in America came home to Dee's mother when a woman's group in which she was involved brought a black singer to Minnesota for a concert. They had booked a room for the soloist at the Nicollet Hotel in Minneapolis only to learn the hotel would not accept the singer because of her race. This was the first time Dee's mother really became aware of the discrimination faced by minority groups and, her sense of justice aroused, she became active in civil rights causes.

The Civil Rights Movement and, later, protests against the Vietnam War were the agents that propelled Dee into politics. As she explained, "I was walking past the Armory one day on the University of Minnesota campus and a friend was there picketing. She said, 'Take a sign.' I did. We helped raise money for people who were going into the South to register voters." Neither party was as supportive as she thought it should be of civil rights and the Vietnam protests, but the Democrats, she believed, were closer to her own beliefs than were the Republicans so, despite her family's Republican background, she registered as a Democrat.

Dee attended her first caucus in 1966 where she met the nuns from St. Stephen's Catholic Church. The nuns were strongly opposed to the war in Vietnam and were listening to Gene McCarthy, who had not yet announced his decision to run for the presidency. The nuns asked Dee

Speaker Dee Long (left) and Secretary of State Joan Growe (right) at Dee's swearing in as first woman Speaker of the Minnesota House of Representatives. (Photo courtesy Joan Growe.)

if she wanted to be a delegate. Dee replied that she did not know. The nuns were not to be deterred. "We'll help you," they told her, and Dee became a delegate.

By 1972, Dee was an experienced local precinct worker. She and her husband worked in Earl Craig's senate campaign against Hubert Humphrey. Dee's husband had been at Kenyon College with Craig and she found politics to be a great deal of fun. "Earl used to throw great parties." By 1974 Dee was the precinct chair, organizing and getting to know people. She was sitting at the Minneapolis city convention when a neighbor of her's, JoAnne Thurbeck, mentioned that she was thinking of running for the library board. "If you do, I will manage your campaign," Dee said. The neighbor was endorsed and won. Then in 1976, Dee managed Robert Tenneson's successful reelection campaign for the state senate. In 1977 Thurbeck ran for the Minneapolis City Council and again Dee managed her campaign. Dee had about convinced herself that she liked working behind the scenes instead of as a candidate when Tom Berg, from Dee's district 60A, decided not to run for reelection to his house seat so he could run for Attorney General. His position was open. Another candidate, Margaret Macneale, had been campaigning for over a year, telling people she was running for Tom Berg's seat. That did not sit well with Berg who had not yet made his decision at the time Macneale began to promote her candidacy. Berg gave his support to Dee and in the ensuing endorsement battle, Dee Long won on the third ballot.

Dee also won in the general election. "I came in with a tied house, sixty-seven to sixty-seven," she remembers. "It was weird. They couldn't agree on anything. We didn't even have office space for a while. Don Moe's aide was leaving, and he let me use his office."

The legislature in those days had what Dee called "the aura of a college campus. It was a much less serious place than it is now." The legislature was in session on April 1, and Dee and some colleagues decided, for an April Fool's joke, that someone should introduce an amendment that would make the state capitol and its grounds an extension of the Minnesota Zoo. The new zoo was very much in the news in those days. At that time, if a member introduced an amendment there was never any record made of it if the amendment was not formally offered. Bob Vanasek, who preceded Dee as Speaker of the House, was one of the ring leaders of the prank. They found a member who was willing to have the amendment passed out and who would rise to speak to it. All that remained was to find a zoo animal to testify. One of the group knew of a disc-jockey who had a gorilla suit, and for thirty dollars the man agreed to wear it on the floor of the Minnesota House.

The night before this was all to take place, Dee and her husband went out for the evening, and the baby sitter allowed their children to make a huge amount of popcorn. "Why don't you take this to the office and get rid of it," her husband suggested. Dee took the stale popcorn to the capitol and gave it to the gorilla. As the amendment was being discussed in the House of Representatives, the gorilla burst into the back of the chamber and began throwing popcorn at the house members. Ray Faricy was in the chair presiding. The gorilla ran up to the chairman on the podium and tried to pick him up. Faricy was larger than the gorilla and in the struggle, Faricy fell backwards, his head hit the Abraham Lincoln portrait and the painting began to swing back and forth on the wall. "The painting is going to fall and be wrecked," Dee thought in a bit of a panic. "We are really going to be in hot water." Fortunately, the Lincoln portrait did not fall, order was restored in the house chamber, and the gorilla was escorted out. Dee admits that some of the members disapproved of the escapade, but she adds that the rest of them had a good time.

Dee feels there is not much mentoring of new members of the legislature, in part, because everyone is too busy. She says that no one mentored her, though Ann Wynia gave her some good advice, telling her to "get on some committees that are not the traditional women's committees of education, environment, health and human services." She also advised Dee that even when she wanted to get home at the end of the day to be with her family, to stay around the capitol and go out to dinner with the rural members, especially the women. Despite their full schedules, and the fact that "there is not as much comraderie among the women of the two parties as there was at one point," women still do support each other. When Dee carried the bill to have insurance coverage mandated for bone marrow treatment for breast cancer, the women members of the legislature came to the committee where the bill was being heard and sat in a group on the front row.

Dee became Majority Leader of the Minnesota House of Representatives in June of 1989 and was elected Speaker in January of 1992. Connie Levi and Ann Wynia had been majority leaders before her. Running for Speaker was the obvious next step, and Dee won handily on the first ballot. Immediately, she began to institute reforms, some of which were strongly resisted, particularly by the old timers who felt they were losing power. One of Dee's reforms was to reduce the number of committees. While this resulted in savings on staff, some members who had hoped to become committee chairs, were disappointed.

The second reform was to merge the Policy and Fiscal Responsibilities committees. In the past the members of the Appropriations Committee, who tended to be the most senior members of the legislature, made all the decisions. It made no difference what the Policy Committee had decided. Merging the two committees, as Dee explained, "allowed every member to have some input in the matter of state spending. We tried to bring the two things together. It ruffled a lot of feathers. The men were upset, but the women were not."

Dee's first major crisis as Speaker came about under the pretext of a telephone scandal. Each member of the legislature had a telephone access number to the long-distance system—a number that was expected to be kept in strictest confidence and used only by members of the legislature for official business. It became apparent that someone was abusing the legislative telephone system. The misuse of the system grew to such an extent that one day it crashed. It was later discovered that Rep. Allan Welle had given the access number to his teenage son who had apparently passed it around. Dee informed the leadership of both parties of what had happened and concentrated her efforts on modifying the phone system so the problem could not occur again. Believing that it was an administrative matter, she never held a press conference to inform the media of what had happened.

The telephone situation presented an opportunity for legislators who were unhappy with the Dee Long reforms to attack her. One of them got a friend to go to the press with the story that there was a telephone scandal cover-up. For a time, the press activity resembled a feeding frenzy. A reporter from the *Star Tribune* came to Dee's office to question her about the phone records. One of the records listed a telephone call to a hotel in Italy made from Dee's phone. "I never made a call to Italy," Dee protested. She later learned that one of her fellow representatives had been a professional hockey player in Italy. Dee asked that member if he had ever stayed in that particular Italian hotel. "Yeah," he replied. "That is where I lived." It turned out that another house member had called the hockey player in Italy from Dee's phone, to talk him into coming home and running for legislative office.

Dee is still angry about one of the reporter's remarks to her during the interview and wishes she had thrown him out of her office. He asked her about a call made from her phone to Cape Cod. "That was to the Legislative Leaders Foundation," she replied. "I am on the board." "Oh," said the reporter with a leer. "We thought maybe you had a little thing going with a Senator out there."

Dee says that she learned a lot about how to handle the press from the experience, though it was a hard way to learn. "We did not have any PR advisors helping us out at that point. I got blindsided. So it made for a very messy session." A short time afterwards Dee, along with other legislators, attended the NCSL (National Conference of State Legislators) convention in San Diego, California. She, with other lawmakers, went out a few days early to play golf, and she was photographed on the course by a Channel 5 news team. Male attendees were also playing golf, but their pictures weren't taken. The picture of Dee playing golf before the conference began was shown on the TV screens in Minnesota with a voice over saying that she was playing golf while other legislators were attending the sessions. The golf shot was immediately followed on the TV screen with a picture of Representative Alice Hausman and Senator Ellen Anderson listening to a speaker at the conference. What the TV announcer did not say was that the conference speaker Hausman and Anderson were photographed listening to was Dee Long herself, and that the pictures of Dee playing golf had been taken days before the convention began.

"I had played golf before the conference ever started," Dee explained. "And I was out there early paying all my own expenses. But that didn't matter. By then I thought, 'I don't have to put my caucus through any more of this. I don't have to put my family through any more of this.' So I resigned." Dee resigned her position as Speaker of the House in August 1993, to be effective in September.

Dee considers herself to be "one of the least introspective people I've ever met. So in terms of, do I say things to myself? No. I experience, react, and don't spend a lot of time thinking about why. I think people in our society tend to be overly introspective in terms of thinking about themselves." Throughout her political career, Dee had never felt that there was a double standard between men and women. But, when the phone and golf issues came up, everything changed. "But this time I did. Being in leadership you are out there. Should I have stayed and fought? Maybe. Was there sexism? You betcha. It was blatant. They were out to get me. I am not trying to say that I did not make mistakes, I did. We all do."

Other legislators besides Dee were photographed at that NCSL conference. One legislator was shown leaving with his family for a trip to Mexico, and another was photographed coming out of an X-rated movie. Only the pictures of Dee playing golf, however, were rerun over several days of newscasts. One of the lasting tragedies of the whole affair, according to Hausman, is that, because of the adverse publicity given Dee Long, few members of the Minnesota Legislature attend the NCSL conference, one of the major conferences in the country that educates lawmakers and brings them together.

Dee Long's district in Minneapolis has been represented by women longer than any other district in Minnesota. The first representative was Mabeth Paige, followed by Sally Luther, Dee Long, and Margaret Anderson Kelliher. In 1996 Dee ran for reelection in her district. The fight was a messy one. She was opposed by Betsy Whitbeck, who was a Republican but ran as an Independent so she would not have to abide by the spending limits. "She got a ruling from the Ethical Practices Board about this," Dee said. "Because I had accepted public financing, I was limited to spending about $21,000 and she spent about $55,000. Steve Sviggam came and spoke at her endorsing convention. She was getting all this help from the Republican Party. It was just a fraud in the way the law was drafted. Some Republicans told me they had never voted for me before, and they probably wouldn't again. But they did this time because they were so angry about this." The campaign was a tough one. Dee says that Irv Anderson, Speaker of the House at the time, gave her no encouragement in her bid for reelection. Despite the problems, Dee was reelected, and, as soon as she was in office, she got the law regarding spending limits and definitions of independents changed. She was also active in the campaign to elect Phil Carruthers Speaker of the House and in defeating Anderson in 1996. Dee chose not to run for reelection to the house in 1998.

"The average person out there neither knows nor cares much about the political system," Dee believes. "Those of us actively working in politics somehow think we're the center of the universe and nothing

State Representative Dee Long

could be further from the truth. Most people find us irrelevant to their lives." She is not sure if she would do it all over again. "One of the things that saddens me when I talk to women who are thinking about running for public office is when they say, 'I don't want to put my family through that,' and I realize that they are not necessarily off base. The whole golf episode was very hard on my family, especially my daughter. I am not sure if there are not still scars there. I was asked once if I had it to do all over again, would I run. I don't know if I would."

When Representative Pam Neary was asked to describe herself as a young girl she answered, "competitive." She has, she says, "been competitive my entire life. If there was a spelling test, I had to get all the words right. If there was a timed math test, I had to finish first. If we were playing softball, I had to hit the ball furthest. If we were in a race, I had to win it regardless of gender. I was just very competitive." Until her younger sister was born, Pam was the only girl and youngest child in a family with three older brothers living in Oak Creek, Colorado. From an early age, Pam became convinced that the world revolved around her. When she was three years old her brother took her to school with him for "show and tell." Another brother, who was four years old at the time, was supposed to memorize some lines for a Sunday School Easter performance. The boy was horribly shy and had trouble learning his lines. Pam, though a year younger, had no such problem and when it came time for the Easter program, she got on the stage in her brother's place and spoke his lines. "I was never reluctant to be in the spotlight," Pam remembers.

When Pam was in first grade, her mother said, "We need another person in softball. You have to come out and play." Her brothers would pitch just as fast to a six-year-old girl as they would to their eleven-year-old buddies. Pam was determined to meet them on their own grounds. "I'm gifted athletically, so I could do that," she says.

Pam's kindergarten teacher coached a gymnastics club for elementary school children. While still in kindergarten, Pam was determined to be admitted to the club. On her own, from first through the fifth grade, she walked to school an hour early in the morning and stayed an hour after school so she could participate in gymnastics. As she looks back on what motivated her, she now believes it was less the goal of perfection in gymnastics than the desire to be noticed. While she enjoyed being the best, Pam believes she relished the recognition even more. "I think that stayed with me," she says. "I always liked the aspect of being unique — of being singled out."

In elementary school, Pam was elected to the student council. When she reached junior high, because there were no athletic outlets for girls, she ran for cheerleader. She credits the cheerleading experience with enabling her to feel comfortable before large crowds of people. Pam has good verbal skills in part, she believes, because she came from a dysfunctional family where there was a great deal of shouting and arguing. "We had a house that was usually in an uproar," she explains. "There were five kids, and my parents didn't get along at times, and my mother would start hollering." Because of that, she was not as frightened of conflict as were girls coming from less riotous homes. Pam was often the one to orchestrate the internal affairs within the family. "Let's all vote on what movie we get to see tonight," she would suggest, or "Can we go to the drive-in tonight?" If the answer was "no," she would counter with "Why not?" "Well, the house hasn't been cleaned." Upon hearing that, Pam would organize everyone to clean the house. Her family debated issues daily, including where to go on frequent picnicking and camping weekends in the Colorado mountains, and though she lost as well as won some of the contests, she learned early in life that she had the ability to influence outcomes.

The dysfunctional nature of Pam's home centered on her father's drinking. He was a social alcoholic who did not drink during the day but went on occasional binges. He never drank at home but would come home drunk. Though he was verbally abusive to Pam's mother when he drank, he never swore at the children. Fortunately, Pam had some good friends, who had more normal families where the parents did not fight all of the time. As a result, she understood that the situation in her own family was not the way most people lived their lives.

Despite the conflict between her parents, Pam has wonderful memories of growing up. On the weekends, her family would clean the house and then, with a picnic lunch, take off for the mountains. The family did a lot of camping together, and her parents enjoyed playing games. Pam says that her dad was a very funny man. Her friends wanted to come to the house so they could play with her father. Her father's drinking made him unreliable. She could not count on his being home on the weekends when he said he would. She never knew if he would go to the Elks Club or come home to be with his family.

The father's alcoholism had graver effects on his sons, all of whom had problems with alcohol or drugs at some time in their lives. Pam's brothers connected with youth who came from families even more dysfunctional than their own, and their house became a refuge for many of their friends. Pam often woke up in the morning to find a youth who had come home with one of her brothers sleeping on the couch. Though she got along with her brothers and their friends, she was not close to them. "They ran in a different crowd than I did," she explains. She also realizes that she was treated differently by her parents than were her brothers and younger sister. "My father loved to brag about my accomplishments," she says. "To this day, I think he carries a picture of me in his wallet. I was the apple of my father's eye and I knew it."

Pam's community centered around the school and the church. Most of her good friends went to her church and, despite their constant whining about it, attended regularly. Pam sang in the church choir and believes the experience had a stronger influence on her than she thought at the time. She and her brothers regularly played in a park nine blocks from their home and thought nothing of it until a ninth-grade girl whom Pam knew was abducted, raped, and murdered. For the first time, she understood that girls needed to be fearful, and she was angry at how frightened she had become. Despite the tragedy, her neighborhood was one where the adults looked out for children and intervened in their behavior. Pam remembers a neighbor calling out to them, "Quit walking in the road. Get on the sidewalk." It was that kind of community.

As with many other women in political life, Pam excelled in school to the point that she intimidated some of her friends. She was in high school in the early 1970s, graduating in 1973, which were the years when many aspects of high school life were rapidly changing. Dress codes were being modified, attendance rules reviewed. As a member of the student council, Pam was involved with the administration in working through changes in the governance of her school. "From our perspective, as students, big changes were happening. Being able to wear pants instead of dresses was a major thing to us. In high school, they changed the smoking codes, a big deal, something we thought was worth fighting for, and we did." Pam was fortunate her teachers were willing to negotiate and encouraged their students to debate issues with them.

Individual teachers made strong impressions on Pam. Her cheerleading sponsor emphasized the cheerleader's role, as being a model of what the school stood for, and the girls took their responsibility seriously. Her English teacher pushed his students to justify everything they did, making them defend their ideas and explain the books they read. Though some students panicked at the pressure, Pam flourished in the demanding environment. She liked discovering that the way she thought about issues was not always good enough.

The intellectual rigor of courses such as her English class contrasted with the behavior she saw in other groups on her high school campus such as Young Life. Here Pam found herself envying the ability of those girls to be sweet all of the time, continually smoothing the rough waters. While she admired these traits, they also irritated her, and she wondered that the women never seemed to have any passion in their lives. As for herself, she was uneasy with the fact that she seemed to be a magnet for controversy. People had learned that if they could engage Pam in an argument she would probably take it to the wall. It took time, but eventually Pam learned that not every battle was worth the cost.

Pam's first experience with politics came about when she was in the fifth grade and she was assigned the Vietnam War as a debate topic. Though she knew nothing about the conflict, she chose the side that was opposing the war. When she did her research and made her speech, she was surprised to discover how virulent other students' opinions were on the subject. They were expressing their parents' opinions, of course, but the experience led Pam to go on to learn about

Communism. She was thirteen when Robert Kennedy and Martin Luther King, Jr., were shot, and she was shocked at the events, avidly reading the newspaper stories with far greater interest than did the other members of her family. The deaths made public service seem like a noble occupation to her. "Politics was something that these people clearly thought was worth the risk of dying over." She was disturbed to find that her country was going through difficult times and that public affairs had literally come to mean life and death for many people. She objected to the status quo and, like many young people, saw its acceptance as a generational issue. Though she now realizes it was the egocentric perspective of an adolescent, she can vividly remember believing that people over thirty had no understanding of the true state of national affairs.

Pam was impressed by the Kennedy family. What some people called "driving ambition" in the Kennedys, she saw as their dedication to do good. Despite the deaths in their family they continued to be active in politics and she was deeply affected by their commitment to public service. There seemed to be a sense of social fairness in the Kennedys that motivated them, a sensibility that Pam also felt. Though Pam lived in a fairly wealthy district, her own family did not have a lot of money. She had an acute awareness that they were considered poor at the time. There was a social hierarchy, based on economics, that did not make any sense to her. Just because someone else had more money than someone else did not make them better than she was or smarter or more capable. Pam's perception was that she was equal to everyone; that everyone was at the same level. While circumstances or choices may create distinctions between individuals, she believed that there was nothing inherently different about people. That fundamental sense of equality is what drew her to the Kennedys. To Pam, they seemed to be a wealthy family that was concerned about people who were not wealthy. "That was an intriguing thing to me," she remembers.

One of Pam's mother's practices created a strong sense of the gift of giving in her daughter. She insisted that the children make gifts for each other at Christmas. The gifts could not be purchased at a store, they had to be handmade. Though the custom may have been related to the fact that the family did not have much money, it provided family members with the opportunity to give part of themselves in the gift. "It was not just any gift," Pam explained. "It was sitting down and figuring out what each person would like and then figuring out how we could make it." The custom began when the children were very small and could only make cookies. That was important because "they were just their cookies." Pam credits her mother with helping her understand the art of giving, how giving is more than the item being given and should be a giving of oneself. She believes that her concept of sharing may have come from the gift-making experience in her home, and she has continued the tradition with her own daughter. Because she liked to cook as a child, instead of making one big cake, she would make two smaller ones and take one of them to the neighbors, saying, "I knew you were busy today. Why don't you take this cake?"

Pam's mother's example was reflected in many of her daughter's activities. Pam was the one who collected money for UNICEF or, when she was in the ninth grade, volunteered to tutor in the poor inner-city schools. Pam was the one who wanted the Girl Scouts to use the cookie money they had earned to give a party for the poor children at a local nursery. When the other girls would not agree with her suggestions, she would negotiate. "Okay," she would say, "if we don't want to give it all, why don't we buy one gift and give it to the nursery school?" Early in her life, Pam learned the skill of negotiation, that if you can't get it all, getting part of what you want is better than nothing, that compromise and negotiation are always the better route to take. Without realizing quite what she was doing, Pam was setting priorities in the organizations to which she belonged. She was also not reluctant to use shame to get what she wanted. "How can you go home and eat a big dinner tonight knowing. . . ."

Pam's mother was a strong-minded individual. Though she spent most of her adult life as a homemaker, she worked outside her home for two years, breaking into a male-dominated area by becoming the first woman letter carrier in the Denver area. She also became a union officer and Pam remembers union meetings in their basement, the air blue with smoke from the men's cigars. Pam's mother eventually sued the federal government over gender discrimination. She had scored extremely high on the civil service test yet was consistently passed over for promotion by her boss who gave as his excuse, "You're not the primary breadwinner in your family. You don't need this job as much." Pam says that her early memories of her mother standing up for what was right were very defining for her.

Despite her admiration for her mother, Pam had a not-untypical, hostile adolescent relationship with her parent during high school. Looking back now, she wonders how her mother ever survived those years. Pam's mother was interested in her daughter's life and when Pam became a cheerleader wanted to attend the games. Pam, however, objected. "I just thought, 'I'm doing fine on my own.' I'll come home to eat."

When she went to Fort Lewis College in Durango, Colorado, Pam had a political science professor who became a mentor for her and helped her develop her political and personal philosophy. She had started out as a biology major but was so impressed by her political science professor that she undertook a double major — adding political science to her program. Her professor taught his students that active engagement with government was critical for a democracy. Students who took his courses were required to become involved in a campaign. While he did not discourage viewpoints different from his own, he made his students justify and understand the ramifications of their ideas. The students were required to justify their answers to his questions. "Why do you think that?" he would ask. Or "Where did you get that idea?" Students learned to understand the weaknesses in their logic and thinking. "And that's what politics was to him," Pam remembers. "It was this great debate about issues in which we had to go out and get practical experience about how people engage those issues in the real world through a campaign." The professor taught her that she had no right to complain if she was not engaged, that engagement is essential to determining one's own future. "You have to be involved," Pam says. "It is more than responsibility, it is an obligation. That's something that has always been a part of me. I don't wait for the world to offer the tray — I go pick out the food for myself."

Pam admits that her arguments were not always rational. "I was quite emotional in my thinking and I thought that was perfectly justifiable and I wouldn't let my professor back me off on that. But it did make me understand that if you could build an argument, whether it was an emotional one or a rational one, that it was a useful way of getting your message across and winning the argument. I think righteous indignation can be a powerful tool."

Pam wrote her undergraduate thesis in political science on women in the Colorado legislature. She was intrigued to note the number of women who ran for office for the simple reason that someone else had asked them to. The women themselves, had not initiated the effort. Pam was surprised at this finding and realized that she would not have waited to be asked but would have decided to run for office on her own. "It wasn't a matter of hoping that someone would say, 'Gee, would you do this?' before taking action."

Pam credits the fact that she would never have waited to be asked to participate in politics to the male values she absorbed through participation in sports. "Competitiveness wasn't common for women my age because we didn't have that outlet. I had it through gymnastics and from the state-wide softball team I was drafted onto in junior high. The team was made up of girls and it was on a very competitive level. We worked our way up through the ranks. When you are on competitive teams you're in competition with not only other teams but internally with other women who want to play. You learn that that's an okay thing to do. So I had those kinds of experiences that a lot of women my age and older didn't get that nurtured in me the ability to say, 'You don't have to be invited to participate. You can do it on your own terms.'"

Despite her self-confidence, while in college, Pam fell into a destructive relationship with a verbally abusive young man who, she now believes, may have reflected her father. She was with him for two years during which he shredded her self-confidence, insisting that she give up every aspect of herself that she liked. "I thought that's what you did in relationships," she explains. With the help of friends, she was able to get out and she now feels it was a valuable lesson on what not to do; demonstrating that when you give yourself up, you don't have anything left. The experience taught her to set limits on what she would do to accomplish something she wanted. She realized that not everyone whom she met would like her and that that was all right.

Pam's first encounter with an anti-intellectual bias toward women came when she was in college. She began to get negative feedback from fellow students and some adults about how smart she was in class. "Guys don't like that" she was told. She had never before had an adult tell her that competition wasn't ladylike or not good. All the adults she had previously known had always told her to do her best. Now, at college, she was getting different signals and she did not have adults around her telling her to disregard these negative attitudes. It was a major shock to learn that smart women were not always popular.

Eventually she realized that she needed to choose the people whose opinions she valued, listen to them and not worry about the rest. "I found that I like me, which is a really useful thing to have as a politician."

Pam began her career in banking and went from that career to work for women's organizations. She was the first lobbyist for the National Organization for Women in Minnesota where, she says, she learned not to be competitive with women. She was elected to the Minnesota House of Representatives in 1992 and served until 1994. She believes that women have a different perspective on public life from men, although many women eventually—perhaps in self defense—evolve a male model for themselves. One of the things she says that women have going for them in politics is an intuitive sisterhood, an understanding that, regardless of party differences, they will get support from other women. "You understand that you're a female in a pretty male world and one whose rules you didn't write and one whose rules you wouldn't have written had you had the opportunity. So you need to have that kind of sisterhood which I think intimidates some of the men over there."

State Representative Pam Neary

Pam believes that women, more than men, are apt to look at policy from the perspective of how it will affect relationships or families rather than what it means for a business. People outside the legislature may not be as aware of these differences between the female and male legislators. "The battles that get fought on the inside are colossal," she says, "compared to what you see from the outside." The conflicts, she says, did not overly disturb her.

Pam's philosophy is that life is meant to be lived with gusto. "My worst nightmare is to become unengaged. I don't like being boring. I like being unique, kind of different. My favorite poem is about the road not taken. I think I am the kind of person who has to learn through bumps, not the smooth road. That's just who I am. People who opt to take the smooth road are not very brave or don't know what they're missing. Following your passions isn't always the easiest thing to do but it certainly satisfied me more than doing otherwise."

Pam has found that her most productive work alliances have been with people who are different from herself—people who have a more measured, analytical approach to problems. "My enthusiasm, impulsiveness, and impatience will bring them along in a way they don't often go and their more rational, slower approach slows me down so that we become a very compatible team."

ଓଷ6ଛ

"Like art, political action gives shape and expression to the things we fear as well as to those we desire. It is a creative process, drawing on the power to imagine as well as to act." —Madeleine Kunin

A woman whose childhood reflected the pre-Civil War values of a free Kansas grew up to be the unlikely jurist to sweep aside the barrier to women in Minnesota's highest court. Profoundly shaped by the Civil Rights Movement and the euphoria that swept the country following the end of World War II, Rosalie Wahl moved to Minnesota to live an idealistic dream of community. She and her husband came to the state full of hope, inspired by the oratory of Hubert Humphrey and needed to be optimistic because her early life had been marked by a series of deeply personal losses.

Rosalie was the great-granddaughter of Scotch-Irish pioneers who had migrated west into Kansas after stops in Pennsylvania, Ohio, and Iowa. Farmers, they settled on the Walnut River in Chautauqua County in southeastern Kansas, forming a tiny community called Gordon—a village that no longer exists. Rosalie was the third of four children. Her older sisters were Mary, six years her senior, and Jeanette, four years older. Her brother, Billy, was two years younger.

Tragedy struck the family when Rosalie was a few months beyond her third birthday. Her mother suddenly became ill and died. No one knows the cause of her death though Rosalie suspects that her mother, who was only thirty-two when she died, may have been simply worn out. The family had earlier been quarantined with scarlet fever. In those years, a notice was nailed to the front door of the house and everyone, including Rosalie's father, was prohibited from entering. Rosalie's mother, already exhausted, had had to manage alone.

Fortunately for the children, their mother had been the eldest of six and her parents, brothers and sisters lived on nearby farms. After their mother's death, Rosalie, her brother, and sisters were surrounded by aunts, uncles, and cousins and the children moved in with their maternal grandparents while their father left to work on the oil pipelines in the region. Within a year her father had remarried a girl not more than sixteen or seventeen years old who had little education and even less desire to rear four stepchildren. For a brief time, the year Rosalie was in first grade, she and her sisters with their father and step-mother lived together in the town of Towanda. The arrangement was not a happy one. Rosalie remembers that "my sister Jeanette and I had to wash all these piles of dishes, and we would talk about when we would get to go back to grandma's when school was out. And that would be wonderful."

The next year, as a second-grader, she and her younger brother, Billy, lived with her grandparents. Rosalie was considered big enough to walk the mile from her grandparents' home to the one-room Birch Creek School. Country schools in those days were open for only eight months of the year because the rural children were needed to help in the fields. The Birch Creek School let out in April, and in May of that year, 1932, another tragedy struck. One evening, Rosalie, her little brother, and their grandfather were riding in a horse-drawn wagon across a meadow and creek. To get to their house, they had to cross a railroad track that ran around the side of a hill. Rosalie's job was to get down from the wagon, open the gate for the horses, and close it after the wagon had passed. Rosalie had opened one gate and closed it and had opened the second gate on the other side of the tracks when she became aware that a train was coming. The engineer on the train never blew his whistle. Rosalie's grandfather drove his wagon onto the tracks and was hit by the train. Both he and little Billy were killed instantly only a few feet from the terrified seven-year-old. Mercifully, her only conscious memory of the event itself is of her grandfather's shout of "Whoa" and of the team of horses racing past her.

The accident happened in full view of her grandparents' house, about a quarter of a mile across the meadow. Rosalie's Aunt Sarah, her mother's sister, was visiting. Both her grandmother and her Aunt Sarah witnessed the accident and ran to the scene. Rosalie's only other memory of the tragedy is of later riding in a car across the meadow with her head buried in her Aunt Sarah's lap.

Following the accident the entire family gathered to decide what to do. Rosalie's father came and she can remember her grandmother saying, "You won't take Rosalie from me, will you?" and her father's answer of "No, I won't." With her husband dead, Rosalie's grandmother could not manage the farm so the family decided to sell off the livestock and equipment and move the grandmother and Rosalie into what they called "the old stone house." The sale was held in 1933, at the depth of the Depression. Rosalie remembers that her grandmother's cows were sold for ten dollars each. There was no social security and there were no benefits for the widow. The railroad took no responsibility for the accident. One of Rosalie's uncles went to see a lawyer but the lawyer would not do anything to help them unless they gave him an advance payment of one hundred dollars. "It might as well have been a million," Rosalie remembers.

The old stone house into which Rosalie and her grandmother moved was about a quarter of a mile from the farm home and had been built in the 1870s by Rosalie's great-grandfather when he had come as one of the first settlers to Chautauqua County. Before 1872, Chautauqua County had been Indian Territory. The house, a small rectangle, had been built from stone quarried on the homestead and resembled the small crofter's cottages of Ireland and Scotland that her grandfather may have remembered from his youth. The walls were two feet thick and straight, there was no electricity, and water was hauled up from a cistern. The house was heated with two wood stoves, one in the living room and one in the kitchen. Rosalie says that she "learned all about the kinds of wood you need to start a fire quickly in the kitchen so you could cook your breakfast and the kind of wood to put in at night so there would still be coals glowing in the morning."

Rosalie's grandmother was an unusual woman. She had lived in Indian Territory in Oklahoma until she was ten years old and did not receive any formal education until her family moved into Kansas. She loved school and went through the eight grades available to her, spending three years in the eighth grade because that was the only schooling she could get. Rosalie says that "my grandmother couldn't go to high school and she always wanted to go." She made sure that her own six children completed high school. She and her husband had to pay twelve dollars annual tuition for each child which was a great deal of money for farmers to pay in those years. Rosalie's mother had graduated from high school in 1914 and then gone on for additional education at a normal school.

Chautauqua County in Kansas is a rolling country of streams and woods. There are both timber and open pastures for grazing. Rosalie and her grandmother lived mainly off the land. They had one cow, which Rosalie milked every morning before she walked to school and again every evening. The first year they lived together, she and her grandmother planted the garden. Thereafter, the care of the garden and all of the other outside chores were Rosalie's responsibility. She planted and cultivated, took care of the chickens and the cow, hauled water, cut weeds, and, every fall, helped her grandmother can the modest harvest from their garden. "My grandmother got a pressure cooker. I remember sitting there in the afternoons watching the gauge on the cooker. It was hot as hell in the summer in Kansas and I had to sit there and watch the gauge on the canner."

Their early years in the old stone house were also the years of the dust bowl. Rosalie remembers dust blowing so thick she could not see. Their cistern ran dry and Rosalie had to draw water from a well some distance away in a pasture. The water was so full of sediment that they had to let it settle three times before drinking it. "I don't know why we didn't die," she marvels. When the ponds all dried up there was no water for their milk cow or for her uncle's cattle. Rosalie helped her uncle and cousins drive their cattle to the river, more than two miles away, so the animals could get water to drink.

Though Rosalie grew up in a solitary situation, she does not remember being lonesome. She played with her cousin Delores, who was three years younger. The two girls would always be thinking of work they could do because they could be together if they were working. They picked blackberries together and helped hang out the laundry. Rosalie's grandmother would put a big copper boiler on the cook stove and boil the sheets. Rosalie's job was to hang them out to dry. "I have a wonderful memory of how sweet the sheets smelled on the line," she recalls. On Saturdays, her job was to clean all the kerosene lamps, fill them, trim the wicks, wash the chimneys, and put them all back.

Though electricity did not come to Birch Creek until Rosalie went away to college, they did have a cooperative farm telephone. Everyone was on the same line and every party could (and usually did) listen in. As Rosalie says, "It had its good and bad parts. When you had an emergency and needed help, it was useful. Everybody on the line knew your business. Later on, when I was growing up and had a boyfriend, it was terrible to have him call and everybody on the line know it."

Rosalie loved her one-room Birch Creek School. The parents were proud that Birch Creek always had a teacher who had had at least one year of college. The school had fewer than a dozen pupils and one year the only pupils were Rosalie and her four cousins. Toward the end of that year another family, the Ledbetters, moved into the school district from Arkansas. As soon as the Ledbetter children began to attend the school, the other children got sick. "We all got the measles, pink eye, and the itch," Rosalie remembers. "The last day of school was always a big occasion. We would have a program and everyone would come and bring good things for dinner and play ball all afternoon until the cows needed to be milked. It was a great time. The year the Ledbetters came all the Birch Creek kids were home sick. Only the Ledbetters were there."

The county seat of Chautauqua County was Sedan, a town about twenty miles away from Birch Creek. Sedan was where the county fair was held every fall. The county fair was a major event and everyone participated. Rosalie remembers that "if you were in the 4-H Club, which I was, you took everything up there to the fair. The schools had floats in the parade. That was where all the contests were." The year Rosalie was in second grade, her school float portrayed John Smith, Pocahontas, and the Indians. Rosalie was one of the Indians. When they made up her face someone forgot to put cold crème under the brown paint on her skin and, for a time, the paint would not come off.

The fair also featured athletic contests. Every school entered the track and field contests and Birch Creek School entered every student in the events. One year Rosalie was to compete in the foot race. She thought she was pretty fast and was dressed up for the event in a new blue cambric shirt. However, she lost the race. "That was the first time I realized a lot of people in this world could do things better than I could and were faster than I was. It was a good lesson," she recalls.

As a child, Rosalie longed for the kind of primary family other children had, with a father and a mother. She loved her father, missed him and wanted to see him more often. Though he tried to maintain contact with Rosalie, he traveled in his work as an oil pumping station manager and, as she says, "wasn't much of a writer." She later learned that her father was quite inventive and had obtained several patents on his oil industry inventions. Despite the lack of contact with her father, Rosalie always felt surrounded by love and a broader family. "There just wasn't anybody that was mine," she remembers. While her grandmother did not talk a lot, Rosalie always felt that she was "a neat person. Coming home from school, I would open the door and call for her. Until I heard her answer, I never felt quite sure that everything was Okay."

Despite the fact they were very poor, Rosalie says that she never felt poor. Part of it was due to the fact that they raised much of their own food. As a child, Rosalie loved the out-of-doors. She had an outgoing personality and a cheerful disposition. Though she might go to bed at night thinking she could die, "by the morning things would look pretty good. My joy does not jump quite so high anymore."

Election days were festive in Chautauqua County. The Methodist Church, to which Rosalie and her family belonged, had a bazaar on election day in a room above the post office. The women earned money for the church by serving meals to the people who came into town to vote. Though her grandmother always voted, Rosalie wasn't aware of how she felt about the issues. Most people did not talk about politics. No one ever asked how anyone had voted. Voting was considered one's private, personal business. Besides, almost everyone in Kansas was a Republican. "You had to be born a Democrat for it to be all right to be a Democrat," she remembers. "That is tied historically to the fact that Kansas came into the Union as a free state—Bloody Kansas. Kansans were still very aware of it, and, to them, the Democratic Party was the party of slavery."

When it came time for Rosalie to attend high school, she moved into the town of Caney, about four miles from Birch Creek, living with a relative of her grandfather's and going home on weekends. For the last two years she was in high school, her grandmother moved into Caney into a tiny apartment and they stayed together. All of the other high school students had been together through elementary school and knew each other. "So I knew what it felt like to be an outsider and to be treated like one." Though she eventually gained the other students' acceptance and became part of the group, she never forgot what it felt like to be excluded and ignored.

Rosalie's Aunt Sarah also played a large role in her life. Sarah was a nurse in a Kansas City hospital and, every month, sent twenty-five dollars to her mother, Rosalie's grandmother, and an extra two dollars for Rosalie so she would have some money of her own. When Rosalie started high school in the town of Caney, Sarah decided that the young girl needed to learn to manage money, and she sent her eight dollars a month to buy books and clothes. Sarah, herself, did not earn much money. "But she had this knowledge of right and wrong and what your priorities should be," Rosalie says. "Grandma and I were her priorities and so she sent us money. Aunt Sarah has always been there for me, all of my life." From an early age Rosalie learned to be independent. She felt responsible for her grandmother and knew that her grandmother both needed and relied on her. "My aunt Sarah told me she did not worry about grandma because I was there. That made me feel pretty good."

Despite the fact that Caney High School did not have any school counselors and few students, particularly girls, were encouraged to go on to college, by the time she was a senior, Rosalie knew that she wanted to attend the journalism school at the University of Kansas. She had studied under an English teacher for three years who inspired Rosalie to go on with her education and to take journalism. Aunt Sarah also believed that every woman should be able to support herself and urged Rosalie to attend the State College in Emporia where she had taken her nurse's training. Rosalie would hear nothing of it. Her mind was set that the only place she could go was the University of Kansas at Lawrence.

The final showdown took place at the old stone house when Aunt Sarah came to visit in 1942. "We had this big ruckus about it, and I remember stamping out to the barn, which had been built of old weathered lumber, and staring at the back of it. I can still see the grain of that wood. I was saying to myself, 'I've just got to go. I've got to go.' As much as I loved Birch Creek, I knew I had to leave. I couldn't stay. There wasn't anything more here for me. I had the knowledge that I had to go."

Aunt Sarah capitulated. She told Rosalie to go ahead and register at the University of Kansas, and in an act of remarkable understanding and generosity, Sarah put her niece on her checking account and gave her a book of checks. Rosalie applied to the University of Kansas and was admitted. She took the train to Lawrence and, when she arrived at the depot, hired a taxi to take her to the university, located on one of the only hills in eastern Kansas, known as Mt. Oread. Unfortunately, the taxi driver, too, was new and neither of them knew where the hill with the university was located.

Rosalie's political education began at the University of Kansas. Her new friends challenged the ideas she had brought to the university from her conservative background. Through them she learned that by waiting tables at Corbin Hall, she could earn her room and board. She joined the YWCA and gradually began to absorb its principles. Her main interest, in addition to her education, however, was her relationship with a young man from Caney High School with whom she had fallen deeply in love. Because his parents were from Tonkawa, Oklahoma, Elden Peck had gone to college there. During Rosalie's freshman year at KU, Elden would hitch-hike up to visit her on campus, and when she went back to Birch Creek he would join her there. Rosalie loved Elden's family and longed to become a part of it.

In 1942, Elden joined the Air Force and, before he left for boot camp, Rosalie spent a few days with him at his parents' home in Tahlequah where they became engaged. The following year, in 1943, Elden was severely injured in a training accident. When Rosalie received the news, she left immediately by train for South Carolina. Her sister lent her one hundred dollars for the ticket, and Aunt Sarah met her train in Kansas City where, because Rosalie did not have one, she gave her her winter coat. The trains in wartime were jammed and slow. Rosalie will never forget that long ride through the South, staring through the train windows at the red clay fields of Georgia. When she finally arrived at the air base, she learned that Elden had died the hour before.

Rosalie returned from South Carolina with Elden's parents, and after his funeral in Oklahoma, she returned home. At the end of her first year in college, Rosalie, disheartened and dispirited, decided to stay home in Birch Creek. It was a soul-searching time. She says that "if the Methodist Church had had a religious order, I would probably have stomped off and joined it. I had always been pulled between the two parts of me—one was the mystical side, and the other the practical, socially-involved side—and I was torn between the two poles."

Temporarily unable to regain her enthusiasm for the university, Rosalie took summer classes at Pittsburg, Kansas, for a temporary teaching license and accepted the position of teacher at her old Birch Creek School. She had eleven pupils in eight grades. Though she enjoyed teaching, by the end of the school year, she again knew her own mind and was ready to return to Lawrence. This time she decided that whatever she did with her life, it had to be something that would help other people. Though she had originally planned to go into journalism, she now changed her major to sociology.

The campus Rosalie returned to was a yeasty environment of ideas and idealism. The war was ending and students believed it was possible to create a better world. When Franklin Roosevelt ran for a fourth term, Rosalie—though not yet old enough to vote and a Republican by birth—decided that if she could she would vote for him. She resumed her work with the YWCA whose crusading campus secretary put ideas into the students' heads that they thought were their own. Peace and justice issues placed high on their agenda. Though the University of Kansas was racially integrated, black students still could not live in dormitories with whites or sit on the main floor of the Lawrence movie theater. Campus cafes had discrimination policies, as did the university swimming pool.

Because there were no interracial accommodations at the University of Kansas, Rosalie and her friends decided to establish the first interracial women's cooperative on campus. Called Henley House, it was home for five white and five black women, Rosalie among them. Their first year in Henley, their neighbor, who for some reason owned the auger that fed coal into the furnace of the house, removed it out of pique at having black women living next door. All that winter, the women of Henley House had to shovel their own coal to keep their furnace filled.

Though she had not majored in journalism, Rosalie became the editorial page editor of the student newspaper, the Daily Kansan. On VE day, the newspaper succeeded in scooping the Lawrence daily newspaper, and the jubilant students stood in the rain on Massachusetts Avenue (Lawrence's main street) handing out newspapers.

By 1946, Rosalie was a senior and again in love, this time with the son of the dean of the medical school, Russ Wahl. Russ had served with the Seventy-fifth Infantry in the Battle of the Bulge and shared Rosalie's social convictions. They were married in August of 1946. While Russ completed his final two years at the university, Rosalie worked as the executive secretary of the Lawrence League for the Practice of Democracy organizing sit-ins and demonstrations.

The Lawrence friends of the Wahls were idealistic young couples who were interested in developing what were called at the time "intentional communities." "We wanted to build an intentional community, establish an economic base, and live according to the principles we believed in," Rosalie explained. "Lots of intentional communities were being formed and we knew about all of them. That is why we came to Minnesota." One of the couples in their group had come to Minnesota to work with an American Friends Service project with co-ops and had purchased a tract of land. The group had also been influenced by a speech given in Lawrence by Hubert Humphrey, then mayor of Minneapolis. Humphrey's speech inspired them, embodying as it did the principles they wanted to live by, and when the opportunity came to move to Minnesota, they took it.

Rosalie remembers that they arrived in Minnesota, in February of 1949, in the middle of the night, when the temperature was seven degrees below zero. All of their possessions, and a baby, were packed in the old car they had driven from Kansas. The only housing that was livable on the co-op was the basement of a house. Two families with young children lived together that winter in the basement. Although permanent homes were later constructed, the intentional community was never able to get off the ground and, in 1955, Russ and Rosalie bought property for themselves in Lake Elmo. Other members of the original cooperative moved near them.

In 1962, with four children in school and eighteen years after she had graduated from the University of Kansas, Rosalie began to look for ways to help support her family. "I never thought about becoming a lawyer," she says. Then she went to a dinner for Joe Karth and sat next to Mary Lou Klaus, a lawyer, who also had children. "I was impressed by the fact that a woman with children could do something like that." There were only two law schools in Minnesota at the time, the University of Minnesota and William Mitchell College of Law. Classes at Mitchell were offered at night and that meant Rosalie could be at home when her children came home from school. She applied to William Mitchell, was accepted, and before long she was putting dinner on the table for her family at a quarter after six every evening, then rushing out of the door for classes and study.

During her second year of law school, her fifth child, a daughter, was born and, from that time, Rosalie felt as if she had a tiger by the tail and could not let go. She enjoyed law school and felt that her studies were like a giant jigsaw puzzle in which pieces that she did not know were missing would suddenly appear and then fall into place. She realized that she was "tired of sitting outside doors waiting while the men on the inside made decisions." It seemed to her that it would be easier to be on the inside. Rosalie graduated from William Mitchell Law School in 1967, the same year that her daughter Sarah graduated from high school.

Because she felt she needed to be home part time for her youngest child, Rosalie took a job in the Public Defenders Office, which had been established just the year before. She began writing briefs and arguing cases before the Supreme Court, getting experience she could not have gotten in any other way. The Public Defenders Office was in the basement of Fraser Hall of the University of Minnesota Law School. One day someone sent technicians down to the basement offices to measure the air and discovered the people working there were getting only about a third of the oxygen they should have had. "We wondered why we were always getting sleepy."

In the early 1970s, the Minnesota Supreme Court decided under its rule-making power that anyone who was going to be charged with a misdemeanor, or had any possibility of being sentenced to jail, had the right to a lawyer. Since there were not enough lawyers to manage the cases that would be affected by this ruling, the two law schools in the Twin Cities set up clinical programs to handle the large number of clients and also to give students experience. In 1973, William Mitchell asked Rosalie to set up a clinical program for criminal cases and to work with the students.

During the decade of the seventies, the Women's Movement in Minnesota was taking off. The Women's Political Caucus, the DFL Feminist Caucus, IR Feminist Caucus, and NOW had all been organized and were becoming active. Their members believed that the reason the governor was not appointing more females to commissions and agencies was simply because he had not been told who the accomplished women were. All these organizations had to do, they told themselves, was just inform him. Consequently, the female lawyers decided to make a list of women available for appointment. They put together a questionnaire and sent it out to all the women lawyers in the state of Minnesota, asking, among other questions, if the lawyer would be willing to accept a judicial appointment.

Rosalie kept the questionnaire for two years before filling it out. She was interested in the judicial appointment question but was not sure how to answer it. She had never practiced before a woman judge. The only woman judge in Minnesota at the time was Sue Sedgwick, and Rosalie had never appeared before her. The only judges Rosalie had seen had been men, and, to her, they all appeared to have been poured from the same mold. If being a judge changed people as much as it seemed to have changed the male judges she observed, it was more important to her, she decided, to go on being who she was. In retrospect, she says that until she got on the Supreme Court she did not know how large a part judicial appointments play in the lives of male lawyers. "Some will spend their entire legal careers trying to position themselves so they will get appointed to the District Court or the Supreme Court. It had never crossed my mind. I had never considered the possibility."

Judge Joe Summers, however, was an exception and he changed her mind about seeking a judicial appointment. "He was wonderful in the court room. Judges control the atmosphere in their courtroom. Joe was always so friendly with the people who appeared before him. Some judges treated people like dirt—especially the public defender clients. Joe did not do that. He would greet the defendants when they came in and would talk to them as if they were people. I could see that Joe Summers was very much a person and was a very good judge. Slowly I got the idea that being a judge was possible." Rosalie decided to fill out the questionnaire and send it in.

Governor Rudy Perpich was the speaker at the DFL Feminist Caucus dinner at the Minneapolis Women's Club in February of 1977. During his speech he said, "When there is a vacancy on the Supreme Court, I will appoint a woman." Gwen Jones, a reporter for the *Minneapolis Star Tribune*, featured the Perpich statement in a major story in the newspaper. Within a few months, it became apparent that a vacancy on the Supreme Court would be coming up and again Jones ran a story in the *Tribune* reminding Perpich of his pledge.

The women's organizations began sending their lists of candidates for the Supreme Court to the governor's office. Rosalie's name was on all of the lists, and her friends began talking her up. Initially eighteen women candidates were identified. The list was cut to seven, then five, then three, and, finally, to two. Rosalie's name was still there. When the list had been cut down to three, Rosalie received a call to come to the capitol and talk with the governor. It was her first meeting with Governor Perpich and she was surprised to see how tall he was. She chatted briefly with him alone, and then she met with his advisory council.

A massive women's meeting was scheduled to be held in St. Cloud the weekend of June 6, 1977. Rosalie and her daughter, Sarah, were planning to attend. On Thursday they drove to a motel on the outskirts of St. Cloud and had just entered their room when the phone rang. It was Ray Bohn, Governor Perpich's appointment's secretary, calling to see where she was. "No, the governor has not yet made a decision," Bohn told her. Rosalie was exasperated. Though she was polite to Bohn, she remembers thinking to herself, "If the governor does not know by now who he is going to appoint, he can just take his appointment and stick it!"

An hour later the call came. Friends and students of Rosalie had gathered in her motel room and, when the news of her appointment came, they piled into cars and drove in a caravan to the gymnasium where the Minnesota Women's Meeting was in session. Joan Growe was presiding and, when she heard the news, she interrupted the proceeding to announce that Esther Tomlianovich was being appointed to the District Court and that Rosalie Wahl would be the first woman to be appointed to the Minnesota Supreme Court.

Four thousand women were in the gymnasium and when they heard the news they leaped to their feet, shouting and cheering. As Rosalie said, "The audience went wild." The appointment of Rosalie Wahl to the Supreme Court was a major milestone for women in Minnesota. (Rosalie would go on to successfully defend her appointment through three elections until her mandatory retirement at age seventy. Her first challenge came the year following her appointment. She faced three opponents, two seated judges and an attorney general, the first time in Minnesota history that a seated Supreme Court judge had that much opposition.) When the room quieted, Rosalie spoke to the crowd saying,

"I am remembering tonight all those generations of women who have gone before us. Women had to obey the laws but they had no part in making them and could not vote for those who did. Hairpins, wedding rings, cook stoves, offspring — all belonged to the husband.

"Women could not speak in public. When Prudence Crandell's School for Young Ladies of Color was attacked and closed in her

Minnesota Supreme Court Justice
Rosalie Wahl

Connecticut village, she had to have a man speak for her in the town meeting.

"When the first Women's Rights convention was held at Seneca Falls in 1848, no woman had ever presided over a convention. Lucretia Mott's husband, James, was called on for this service.

"I am remembering that remarkable Quaker, Susan B. Anthony, who met Elizabeth Cady Stanton at the Second Women's Rights Convention in 1852—a meeting called by many men who were present a 'mob meeting of unsexed females' who were 'stepping out of their sphere in defiance of laws both human and divine.' Called 'freaks of nature' they knew scorn, fury, hardship, adventure, agonizing disappointment.

"I am remembering Mary Peek's grandmother, Kari Anderson, as a young woman in Norway, refusing to marry the man chosen by her father, asking for her dowry, coming to the New World alone, knowing no English. As an old woman of seventy-eight years, she was the first woman in line to vote at the first election after the ratification of the Nineteenth Amendment.

"I am remembering Sojourner Truth and all those brave, unnamed, unremembered women who gave so much that we might have the freedom and opportunity that is ours. Men are not the enemy. Men are our brothers, our sons, our husbands, our fathers, our friends.

"The enemy is fear, fear that by being all of what we are, by realizing our full potential, we will somehow jeopardize what little security we have attained for ourselves and our children. A good many years ago, when my then four children were in school and I had gone with some trepidation to law school to prepare myself to help share the economic burden of supporting those children, a poem came to me which expressed my feelings at that time of what it meant to be a woman:

Foot in nest
Wing in sky
Bound by each
Hover I.

"Now I know it is not necessary to hover. Now I know it is possible to soar."

Three years after Rosalie Wahl was appointed to the Minnesota Supreme Court, the most colorful, flamboyant and, frankly outrageous, person to hold office in Minneapolis took her seat on the Minneapolis City Council. The child of wealthy, alcoholic parents and an alcoholic herself by the time she was a teenager, Barbara Carlson shared her addictions and her passions with her bemused — and at times enthralled — constituents. Barbara's first marriage was to Arne Carlson who, after their divorce, became governor of Minnesota. Though each remarried, the two maintained cordial relations, at least for the press, and Barbara caused a media sensation when she attempted to interview the governor on television (as she did other guests) from her hot tub.

Barbara Carlson was her parents' first child and the first grandchild in her family. By her own account, she was spoiled by her grandparents and was used to getting everything she wanted. "I assumed that I was going to be the leader, to be number one, and I assumed that I was going to get all the attention. Those assumptions are not necessarily the best basis on which to raise a child but that is certainly how I was raised. I came from a very dysfunctional family. My parents were both alcoholics, so they were out all the time, and I was raised by a series of maids and au pairs."

Despite the absence of her parents from major periods of her life, Barbara remembers her early childhood as having been mainly a happy time with many friends and activities, in part because of the close relationship she had with her grandparents. They provided the all-important system of support for the precocious little girl. She describes her childhood self as being "extremely curious, outspoken, difficult, ambitious and lots of fun. I was always the ring-leader, the president. I have two younger brothers, one who is two years younger and another that's ten years younger. George, the brother who is two years younger than I, was always the quiet child, the perfect child, and I was always the outrageous child, the kid that got in trouble all of the time."

Barbara was close to her father. "I adored the fact that he was charming and attractive, a great raconteur and fabulous story teller and a lovable drunk. He would take me out for dinner and I would act as his escort. When I was ten, my mother became sick with the birth of my brother. From the time I was ten until I was eighteen, I was my father's escort—sort of a surrogate wife. I think that's a form of abuse, of child abuse. My mother would go to bed. She was in her bed a lot, very addicted to morphine and to all drugs."

Barbara's relationship with her mother was a difficult one. "I really didn't like my mother from the moment I was born," she says. "We always had a difficult relationship. I was much fonder of my grandmother." Three older women were influential in Barbara's early life: her father's mother, Mamie; her mother's mother, Nana; and a friend of Nana's, Isabelle Miller, who lived in South Dakota. Of her grandmother Mamie, Barbara says, "She was the quintessential grandmother, a girl raised with all men. She wasn't pretty, had a limp and married the man of her dreams. She had the money. I could do no wrong. I was her perfect child. She fed me, she nurtured me, she played bridge while I fell asleep on the sofa. I was a very, very spoiled child."

Nana's friend, Isabelle, also made a strong impression on the young Barbara. "Isabelle was the most delightful, outrageous woman that I've ever met. She died at ninety-five and the last four years of her life she taped her eyelids up with scotch tape so she could see. She still drank martinis, smoked and she drove her car. I just loved her joy of life. I adored her. She was my Auntie Mame."

Barbara's most powerful and comforting childhood memories are those of family gatherings with her uncles and cousins, especially at Thanksgiving and Christmas. On Saturday nights she would go with her grandparents to the home of her great aunt and uncle where the adults would spend the evening playing cards. "I can remember the cards," Barbara says. "The shuffling of cards is a very soothing sound. I was somewhere in the room, normally on the sofa, and they'd be playing cards and talking and having a good time, but it was not boisterous. It was very secure. Family is security for me, even though my father and mother were both raging drunks."

Though Barbara began her school career as an A student, her antics soon got her into trouble. As she explains it, "I was never thin, I was never beautiful, I was never the best in anything, and so I think that I used my personality, my outrageousness, even as a child." Over time, Barbara's "outrageousness" grew worse, a series of maids quit, her mother became ill, and Barbara was shipped off in the eighth grade to boarding school at Villa Marie Academy. Boarding school had a temporary restraining effect, and after a year there, on the condition that she would behave herself, Barbara was allowed to come home and begin her freshman year at Visitation Convent.

After a year at Visitation, her parents again sent her back to boarding school. Carlson no longer remembers the incident that provoked her removal from Visitation Convent but she does not blame the school for suggesting she go elsewhere. "I was a difficult child. I just remember that I would threaten them and be difficult and demanding and hostile. Nobody wants to live with a controlling child." Despite her behavior problems, Carlson was a straight A student in high school until she began to drink. "Then I would either get straight A's or I would get F's. It came to the point that whatever I was interested in, I would do well in and when I was not interested, I failed." Despite her erratic academic performance, Barbara graduated from high school and entered the University of Minnesota where her downward spiral with alcohol and drugs continued.

"I rarely went to class so when it came time to take my tests I passed some of them but not with flying colors. I was never there. Then I started flunking out. My parents said, 'What is wrong with this child?' and they took me to a psychologist for tests. The test results indicated that there was no reason I was not doing straight A work. Of course, I was just a drunk and also a drug addict. They put me in the hospital. I was in St. Mary's in the psyche ward, I was at the hospital out in Golden Valley, I was at Milwaukee Sanitarium and at Wauwatosa. I had lots of jaunts to the funny-farm which I loved because, instead of booze, they gave me medication. Then I went through treatment in 1975 and have been sober ever since. That's why I'm alive today."

One teacher from Visitation Convent, Sister Mary Regina, was able to reach the rebellious teenager. She saw the potential in the conflicted young woman and convinced Barbara that she could be anything that she wanted to be. "Sister Mary Regina is in her nineties now and has followed my career. She's the most wonderful woman who ever lived." Convent education for girls in the 1950s was still very traditional. Catholic girls were expected to "spend a year or two in college and then get married and have all these beautiful Catholic children." Soon after meeting Barbara, Sister Mary Regina realized that she had a different spirit on her hands, one who would challenge the conventional convent education. Fortunately for Barbara, Sister Mary Regina did not turn her away but instead nurtured the young girl and supported her desire to take risks and follow a non-traditional path in her life.

The first project Barbara undertook that was deeply meaningful to her was starting a chapter of SIDS after she and Arne Carlson's first child died of crib death. Though the two were emotionally estranged at the time, both bereaved parents poured their energy into helping other parents facing the same tragedy. Rather than bringing them together in their marriage, the death of their child only moved them further apart.

Barbara credits her marriage to Arne Carlson with her interest in politics though she did not run for Minneapolis City Council until after her divorce. "I'd been in the real estate business and I was bored with what I was doing. I was just so bored. I was divorced, my kids were living with Arne, I was at loose ends. I used to stand in my shower and say, 'God, what do you want me to do? Would you please send a message down?' God never sent a message so I went through CHART (a Twin Cities organization that helps women determine career goals) and their testing said I would do very well in politics or law. Well, I wasn't going to go back to school to be a lawyer."

A seat on the Minneapolis City Council opened up in 1980, and Barbara ran for it, beating out two other well-qualified people for the Republican endorsement. In her campaign literature she explained to the voters that she had done it all. "I've been married; I've been divorced; I've been an alcoholic; I've been in recovery; I've had lots of money and I have lived on as little as $4,000 a year. I've been taken care of as a wife, I've been totally responsible for two children." Her campaign was successful and Barbara was elected to three terms on the Minneapolis City Council. Her Ward Seven included Elliott Park which, according to Barbara, had one of the lowest incomes in Minneapolis, and Kenwood, one of the wealthiest. Barbara fought many battles for Kenwood. "They were not to my mind the most sympathetic constituents, but they were taking a bath on property taxes." In 1997 she ran, unsuccessfully, for mayor of Minneapolis.

Before making her decision to run for mayor, Barbara consulted with two ministers, a Catholic priest and a Lutheran pastor. She wanted to explain to them that if she were elected mayor, she would find it necessary to cut back many social service programs out of a belief the city was spending too much on welfare programs. She wanted the city services to get back to the basics of police and fire protection. "How am I going to be able to do this," she asked, "when I really believe that we are raised as good Christian people to help others?"

Minneapolis City Coucil Member
Barbara Carlson Anderson

"The Lutheran pastor understood me completely and talked about what I could bring to the job. His only concern was for me as an individual and where I was going to get my solace and support because this was going to be a rigorous, vigorous campaign. I was going to get buffeted and was probably going to be called racist. And then he asked what they could do to support me. 'You know,' he said, 'you are never alone.'" Barbara was so touched she began to cry. When she went to see her old friend, the priest, he asked her, "Why are you here? Are you here for spiritual advice? I'm a very busy man." He told her how helpful her opponent had been to him and criticized her for running for mayor and for being what he called "so strident."

Barbara stormed out of the priest's office and joined the Lutheran Church. "I went to that particular Lutheran Church, crying through the entire service, feeling that it was the most affirming wonderful place. It was Mount Olivet. I thought, my God, if it's good enough for Martin Luther, it's good enough for me." She has continued to attend that church. "I like those Sundays and that hour that I spend in that church, and I like singing those hymns and being surrounded by those people. It makes me feel whole and warm and supported."

As to her personal style, Barbara says she is a screamer. "My mother would cry and scream and go to bed. I'm a great screamer and a ranter and raver, and that means I don't carry grudges very long." She admits that her screaming can decimate her associates and make it difficult for people to be involved with her. She confesses to being insecure about her weight and her age and sometimes wakes up asking herself, "Who the hell do I think I am that I can change this city?"

Other times Barbara reminds herself that she is honest and truthful and a strong communicator. She is a role model for older women and believes that younger women enjoy her because she has been her own, sometimes outrageous, self and has been successful. Barbara says that there are messages for us in life if only we will take the time to listen for them. She believes that her message is to help others, to tell their stories and to say, "We're here for you. You're not alone."

ೞ7ഏ

"What troubles me is not that movie stars run for office, but that they find it easy to get elected. It should be difficult for millionaires, too."
—Shana Alexander

The election of Ronald Reagan in 1980 marked the triumph of social and political conservatism. Reagan's political agenda focused on rolling back many feminists' gains and undoing the liberal consensus that had prevailed since the 1930s, a consensus that reached its highest point during Johnson's Great Society of the 1960s. American business was urged to return to doing what it did best, producing mountains of goods for a society that reveled in mass consumption. Conservatives called for a return to more traditional moral values holding that social justice and civil rights movements had gone too far and it was time to draw the line against them. The gains women had made in the 1960s and 1970s increasingly came under attack from the New Right, and after the Equal Rights Amendment failed to be ratified, the feminist movement fell into a period of disarray.

Advocates for the homeless struggled with little success to gain public support. Those who sought to raise public awareness of the AIDS crisis and to evoke a serious governmental response fought an uphill battle. Members of the Religious Right charged that AIDS was God's way of punishing homosexuals for "perversion." Reagonomics, with its tax-cutting fervor and pro-business bias, fostered a noticeable rise in self-interest. With the emphasis on self came a newfound pleasure in possessions and wealth that fueled the consumer boom of the 1980s. Americans were urged to spend and then spend again, buying everything from gold Rolex watches to large-screen home entertainment centers to hundred-dollar running shoes. No guilt was attached to spending at either the personal or governmental levels and both individual and borrowing on a national scale sent the national debt to previously unthinkable levels. No one seemed to realize (or care) that they were breaking the implied contract that Americans had traditionally honored—that the next generation would be given the potential for a higher standard of living and not burdened with debt.

Women taking elective office in the 1980s had multiple social forces to contend with as well as the peculiarities of local issues. Though they brought their own life experiences to their decision-making, many found they needed to fall back on deeply-held core values in order to contribute to, and at times survive, the political process.

Although a tide of conservatism was rolling over the country in the 1980s, one elected official swam against the tide. She was Representative Karen Clark, the first openly lesbian elected legislator in Minnesota, and the second in the United States. (The first was Elaine Noble from Boston.) Karen was candid about her sexual orientation before she ran for public office and, since 1980, has been continually reelected from her district. She says that every woman knows she has to be twice as good as men to succeed. Being lesbian "probably adds another dimension to the need to do well. You have to be three times as competent to prove yourself. You will not get the respect or credibility unless you go way beyond expectations."

Karen was one of five children of poor sharecroppers in Southwestern Minnesota. Her father farmed on shares, sending two-fifths of any profit the family made to the rich California landlord. The town of Edgerton, where Karen, her sister, and three brothers attended public school, was steeped in the philosophy of the conservative Dutch Reformed religion that also permeated the school system. Karen's family was Catholic and the children, together with their cousins, were the only Catholics in the entire twelve grades of the school. When she was in first grade the other children told her they could not play with her because she was Catholic and a terrible person ("Nuns eat babies!"). "I'd see my brothers beat up. I learned at a very early age to defend myself verbally."

Karen says she survived because she was able to excel in school and had a strong family support system with grandparents, uncles, and cousins "right across the field." Her mother also gave her wise counsel, telling her that the other children who were taunting her did it because they did not know any better, that they were hearing prejudice from their parents, that it was not the children's fault and that Karen should try to make friends with the children. Another message Karen received from her mother was to protect the underdog. While at the time she did not think of her family and siblings as being underdogs, she realizes now that they were; economically, religiously and as the country children in the small consolidated Edgerton school.

Though her family was very poor, Karen says she did not think much about it at the time because of the self-respecting attitude of her parents. Not having nice clothes did make her feel inferior, however, and she was still wearing clothes her mother made for her when she went away to college. "We didn't have things like running water until I was eleven and I remember the first toothpaste we ever bought. We used to just use salt and baking soda." For a time, Karen took piano lessons from a neighbor girl who was paid a small amount for her teaching. Karen was so aware of her family's financial hardship that, though her parents never asked her to stop, on her own she cancelled the piano lessons.

Karen's parents placed a high value on education so Karen, though terribly shy, decided early on that school was a place where it was important to do well. Soon she was the top student in all of her classes. She loved school so much that she went home and taught her little brother, who was two years younger, everything she had learned in class. "When he went to school he could read and write and do everything a second grade student could do. He was also extremely bored and got in trouble because he already knew how to do all those things before he got to school."

The concept of the separation of the church and state had not penetrated very far in Edgerton as evidenced by the fact that the fourth grade teacher made the children stand every morning while she read the Bible to them. Karen refused to stand. She had been taught that this wasn't her Bible so she didn't have to listen to it. "I don't know what else I did. I probably sat there and said my own prayers. But I remember the feeling of being the only one. I learned how to handle it. It was a religious minority experience."

Karen's teacher was kind and did not abuse her for her passive resistance to the Bible reading, but the Dutch Reformed religion was definitely a part of the public system. "It was a public school in which religion was always right under the surface, a form of covert discrimination." The school officials did not know quite what to do about Karen and her younger brother who were among the top students in the school. Her brother was denied being named salutatorian because he was Catholic. "The principal, whose wife was Catholic, called him in and told him. He said, 'You have the grade level, you have everything, you should be salutatorian. But because you're Catholic, the teachers have voted that you're not.'"

During Karen's last years in high school, the National Farmers Organization was working to convince farmers to hold their farm products for higher prices. This was considered a radical thing to do. Karen wanted her father to participate and tried to talk him into it. Her uncle had joined and Karen believed there would be strength in numbers. "In those days unions were big city things that farm people were supposed to be scared of or see as their enemy. I was attracted to the idea of being self-respecting enough to organize." Karen's father would have nothing to do with it. "We farmers are extremely independent," he said. "That's just our failing, but I'm one of them." Karen remembers her family's experience with the National Farmer's Organization as the beginning of her understanding of who runs much of the world.

At the age of thirteen, Karen experienced a religious crisis when she realized that she might not believe in God. The problem frightened her and kept her awake nights. "I don't believe in God! What am I going to do?" After worrying about the problem for a time she wisely decided to defer the decision about God until she went to college. She planned to attend a Catholic school and she decided she could take up the problem of God when she got there. Karen went on to attend the College of St. Teresa in Winona and loved the school. She was introduced to the radical Catholic tradition through people like Daniel Berrigan, who came to speak. She and another woman organized the first peace march in Winona. "I'll never forget walking down the street and the editor of the Winona paper was sitting out there in his military uniform that he had worn in World War II with all his medals on, glaring at us. We marched happily by singing our protest songs."

Though the future legislator found formal public speaking difficult, she discovered that she could speak out on issues. She had learned the value of speaking out as a child in a minority situation in her school and, as an adolescent, argued with her mother. Her younger brother commented that "it was such a relief when I went to college because he didn't have to listen to me and mother argue."

From St. Teresa, Karen went on to earn a B.S. degree in Nursing from the University of Minnesota, and later a Masters Degree in Public Administration from Harvard University. She was in the first class of OB-GYN nurse practitioners to be graduated from Hennepin County General Hospital. Though she worked full-time as a nurse practitioner, Karen was also an organizer, actively organizing the nurses in the hospital in a union. For nurses to be unionized ("Oh my God, aren't you professionals? You can't do that!") was a radical idea in the early 1970s. Throughout the decade, Karen and friends marched in the streets for civil rights, for gay and lesbian rights, and against the Vietnam War. They founded a Women's Health Clinic in Minneapolis that gave out birth control, abortion, and adoption information to unmarried mothers. They also organized a group called the Lesbian Feminists Organizing Committee that took positions on such issues as sexism, racism, classism, and homophobia, as well as campaigning for a broad range of issues including minimum prices for farm products and rent control.

Karen's political activities caught the attention of the Farmer-Labor Association, one of the groups that had come together to form the DFL Party. Concerned that farmer and labor problems were being ignored, the organization asked Karen to run for a Senate seat that might become open in her Minneapolis neighborhood. They wanted her to be their candidate because of her broad base on the issues. "Those issues were not unfamiliar to me," she conceded. "I had worked for every one of them." The incumbent Senator was pro-life and the district was mainly pro-choice. "He never came up past Lake Street," Karen observed. "and ignored this part of town."

Nevertheless, when she was asked to run, Karen was dumbfounded. "I just laughed," she said. "Running for office was absolutely not on my radar screen." In fact, for much of her life, Karen had believed it was futile to work within the political process. As a result of her attitude during those years, she says that now she "really understands young people today who wonder if they should do it."

Once Karen realized that her supporters were serious in their invitation for her to run, she told them they would have to deal with the fact that she was lesbian. "It's part of who I am," she explained. "Politically it will be an issue. Are you sure you want me to be your candidate?" Karen, herself, was not sure she wanted to run. She called a public meeting of the Lesbian Feminists Organizing Committee and put together a panel discussion to help decide if they wanted to participate in the public arena. Karen was the moderator. One side urged partici- pating in electoral politics because that is where the decisions are made that affect lives. The other side said politics would be a diversion and the organization should work in other ways.

Karen decided to run for the Senate and had been preparing her campaign for a year when the incumbent senator resigned. Rep. Linda Berglin, Karen's representative in the legislature, decided to run for the vacant senate seat so Karen changed her plans and ran for Linda's vacated house seat. The musical chairs maneuver was successful and both women were elected.

When she took her seat at the legislature, Karen found herself in a highly homophobic atmosphere. On one of her first days at the Capitol, a St. Paul legislator walked up to her in the corridor and without intro- ducing himself or even saying "Hello," launched a pre-emptive strike. "Don't think you can come up here and pass a gay rights bill," he warned. "My city (St. Paul) voted it down in a referendum and I won't vote for it."

Karen held out her hand. "Hello," she said. "I'm Karen Clark. And what is your name?" That legislator later became one of Karen's strong allies. She credits the change to personal growth on his part but also to the man's ability to read the political climate. Gays and lesbians were getting organized and Karen believes her successful campaign encour- aged others to become involved in electoral politics. Despite her accept- ance on a personal level by her legislative colleagues, Karen later learned that there had been a motion floated to censor her and keep her from taking office. She never saw it but was told about it. "Because I was lesbian, they thought I must be breaking some law. There is no law that says you cannot be a lesbian," she pointed out.

After she was elected, Karen tried to organize a women's caucus among the female legislators. She met with only partial success as some of the women were fearful of offending the male members. "We don't want the men to feel threatened," they said. Even today, Karen says that when four or five women legislators are standing together talking, a man will invariably walk over and say, "Uh-oh, what's going on here?"

Karen has found that a majority of the hard bills in the legislature are put forward by women. "The bills that are really difficult, that are controversial, are often carried by women. Issues that deal with civil rights, child-care, human rights, are carried (not exclusively) by women. You have to have a lot of dedication and know where you are coming from. Disproportionate to their numbers, women carry the tough bills." Karen believes that women display a great deal of courage in supporting their causes. "Look at Alice Hausman and what she was trying to do on nuclear waste storage," she said. "Sometimes we take a lot of abuse for supporting these things. I have shared tears with many women legislators over issues that we felt just berated about. Many times, we are not able to be as effective as we want to be. "

Karen believes that women's value systems tend to be different from many men's, particularly in their ordering of priorities. Fortunately, that is changing. When she first came to the legislature, child-care was a radical idea and was opposed for being anti-family and enabling women to leave their homes. Now many men support funding for child-care. However, the support for such issues is still tenuous. In the mid-1990s, the legislature was asked for bonding money to build a hockey arena in St. Paul. The only sources of bonding funds were from housing and child-care. Karen and others had worked hard to set aside bonding authority for the construction of child-care facilities. "If we are going to spend money for prisons, let's spend some for head-start and early childhood education," she had said. When the legislature threatened to raid the child-care funds to build a hockey arena the women in the legislature rose up in protest. "It was spontaneous combustion." They held a press conference, protested and, working together, were able to keep most (but not all) of the child-care bonding money from being diverted into St. Paul's hockey arena.

One of the toughest bills Karen worked on was called the Worker's Right to Know Law. It passed in 1983 and required companies to reveal to their employees the facts about hazards in the corporate workplace. Passing that legislation taught her a great deal about the power of chemical companies and big business. Two decades later, she worked to pass the Human Rights Amendment on Sexual Orientation to the Minnesota Human Rights Law. Advocates had worked for twenty years for passage of that amendment. The bill had lost by two votes in a committee the year before. When it passed in 1993, the bill was the strongest human rights legislation for sexual orientation in the United States. Sexual orientation was defined to include lesbian, gay, transsexual, and bi-sexual individuals. Transgendered individuals had not been previously covered by any legislation anywhere else in the country and, while not named in the law, the bill is written in such a way that it is clear they are included. There have been several cases since passage of the law where the legislation has been upheld in Minnesota courts. Karen credits the high level of organization—a huge grassroot effort—along with strong support from the unions and the churches for the bill's eventual passage.

Karen is convinced that women make a difference in legislative bodies. "We bring different agendas and different ways of working. I'm not blessing all of our ways; we have women who are just as out of touch as men and use methods that I would not. But for the most part, I find women easier to work with, easier to reach. They are willing to change their opinion, to grow and look at things differently—and to be courageous. Women are just more tuned in to the human side of things. I'm a big fan of women in policy-making positions."

There is a reason women can afford to be courageous in legislatures. According to Karen, women do not have so much to lose. She points out that women do not have the same financial backing that most men do. "I am having a fund raiser in a couple of weeks because I am basically broke," she said. "I don't get the big donations from corporations. The NSP and corporate lobbyists who lost out on the Worker's Right to Know Bill will never donate to me. The corporations fought it. The big drug and chemical companies don't donate to people like me." If she were beholden to corporate interests she would not be able to "go out there and push things," she said. "I am not beholden but it makes it tougher to run.

State Representative Karen Clark

Women need early financial help with their campaigns and often they don't get it."

Karen is working in the legislature for more support for child-care and for affordable housing. She helped pass legislation making corporations responsible to provide the jobs they promised when asking for public subsidies and tax breaks. "If companies don't create the promised jobs, they must pay back part of the subsidy they received. For example, Northwest Airlines promised 4,000 jobs and they delivered 400. Yet they got this huge subsidy from the state. Those kinds of things are not just a gender issue but they make so much difference in Minnesota," she said.

While Rep. Carolyn Rodriguez is a twin, she is the oldest child in her family, having been born six minutes before her brother. Her other sibling is a sister who is six years younger. Their early years were spent in Austin, Texas, where Carolyn's father, an officer in the United States Army, was completing a graduate degree at the university. The only girl of her age in a neighborhood of boys, Carolyn found herself excluded from a boys' group that would not admit girls as members. Unwilling to accept that situation, she challenged the boys, one on one, to fights until she was allowed to join. "That's the only time I ever remember picking a fight with anybody in my entire life," she remembers.

"I was raised by very traditional, very middle-class parents," she said. "They had an excellent, loving marriage and were very close. Mother was a homemaker and my father was the breadwinner and the disciplinarian. It was expected that girls would grow up to be good wives and mothers and if they wanted a career it would be in teaching. Boys would grow up to have a 'real' career. I was never encouraged to do well academically, but I was never discouraged from it either. Academics were always held up as a high expectation for my brother. He was encouraged to be athletic, too, while I never was. It was a kind of role reversal in a way, since I was good in sports, especially tennis and swimming, and he was never particularly good at athletics."

For much of her early childhood, Carolyn was in conflict with her father. "He was very much of a disciplinarian. We were never allowed to call him 'Dad.' It was 'Yes, sir; No, sir' or 'No excuse, sir.' It was a very standoffish relationship, very military. So it was difficult to feel a real connection with him. He had this rule that we had to clean our plates, even if we intensely disliked something. There are still things to this day that I will not eat, not because I dislike them, but because of my memory of them. When I was ten or eleven, I decided that enough was enough and I refused to clean my plate. It was carrot salad—and I still won't eat carrot salad.

"On one occasion, my father made me sit at the table for two or three hours and I still wouldn't eat what was on my plate. Finally, out of sheer desperation, he let the dog into the dining room. The dog had never been allowed in the dining room so it did not want to come in. I think my father had this desperate hope that I would feed the carrots to the dog. But I refused to give my plate to the dog because I had a point to prove. Finally, Father let me leave without finishing my plate." Though Carolyn's father continued to impose his rule, after her rebellion, he allowed his children to have one or two exceptions.

When Carolyn was fifteen, her mother died suddenly and Carolyn took over the care of her younger sister. Her father, devastated by his wife's death, withdrew into himself and his children only saw him at dinner time. With the responsibility for the household, to a large extent, on her shoulders, along with the care of her younger sister, Carolyn quickly learned to compromise with her father. "When my mother died, we had to get along," she explains. "I probably would have been a lot more stubborn for longer had that not happened. But when something like that happens you just have to say, 'All right. I can't be that way anymore. I've got to start taking a more responsible position.'"

Despite the change in Carolyn's attitude toward her father, the children's upbringing continued to have many negative aspects. They never received rewards for being good, but invariably suffered consequences for not doing something they were expected to do. Each child was given a very small allowance, out of which she had to pay for everything she needed, including clothes. Carolyn failed to make her bed one morning. Though she had done everything else she was supposed to do, her father deducted a portion of her allowance for the unmade bed.

In spite of their conflicts, many aspects of Carolyn's relationship with her father were positive. "Even though we fought, he always trusted me completely to do what I had to do. He never gave me a curfew.

Never said, 'You have to do this at this time.' There was always complete trust that we wouldn't do something that we shouldn't do. And he was right. We never did. There were always certain expectations that we would always meet. We would be polite, even if we were arguing. We would not steal. We would not tell a lie. It just never occurred to me to do any of that."

Consequently, Carolyn developed an acute sense of fairness that came out when she was engaged in a high school debate in speech class on the respective merits of Kennedy and Nixon as presidential candidates. Though she does not now recall which man she was supporting in the debate, she remembers that the teacher made remarks that were highly predisposed toward Carolyn's side. The person who argued the opposing position had made his case well, and Carolyn was offended by the teacher's obvious bias—even though it had favored her. At first, she complained about the teacher to her friends. Then realizing that it wasn't fair to be saying something behind the teacher's back that she would not say to her face, she went to the teacher and told her directly that, in her opinion, the teacher had not been fair.

In a related incident, when she was thirteen, Carolyn was shocked to discover that her father harbored racial prejudice. He would say, "If they [African-Americans] would only be patient, things will happen." And Carolyn would retort, "Why should they be patient for one hundred more years?" She invited a black friend from high school to her home without asking her father's permission. She could tell from her father's manner that he was uncomfortable with her friend's presence, but she persisted in the friendship and her father responded by withdrawing. However, when she included her black friend in a birthday slumber party of girl friends, her father objected and refused permission for the girl to attend. Carolyn responded by canceling her party. "It was a way of emphasizing my distress over my dad's decision."

In college, Carolyn became active in the movement for racial integration. Though she never participated in demonstrations, she tutored, signed petitions, and went to restaurants with black friends. When they were refused service, they would walk out together. She remembers how she felt one day at the university when a black male friend came up to her as she was sitting by herself at a booth eating lunch and studying. "Do you mind if I sit with you?" he asked. "No, I don't," she had replied, knowing very well that everyone in the cafeteria would be staring at them. She later went to a football game with the same young man and they became good friends.

The adult in her family to whom Carolyn was closest was her maternal grandmother in San Francisco, the family member who helped provide stability in her life. "Her home was the one place I could go back to that was always the same. Being in the military, we were always moving." Carolyn's grandmother gave the young girl unconditional love but, like her father, insisted on high standards. "We sat down to a formal dinner every night, served in courses. The silverware was always polished. From an early age, we were taught to answer the phone courteously. When grandmother had guests, we were expected to come in, even when we were only five- and six-years old, talk to her guests for a few minutes and then quietly remove ourselves."

Carolyn's grandfather was Catholic but her grandmother was not. The two had not married until she was about twenty-five and he was twenty-eight, because the two families had been deeply opposed to the marriage. "My grandmother was a beautiful woman. While she was whiling away her time before the marriage, she rode the ferry back and forth to Berkeley and was the first woman to get a Master's Degree in mathematics from the University of California at Berkeley. After she married, she became the traditional homemaker, mother, and wife."

The Catholic tradition continued in Carolyn's family through her mother and Carolyn, herself, until she reached her young adult years. Religion was a subject she took very seriously. "My family wasn't Catholic, I was," she says. Then, as a young woman, Carolyn made the decision to leave the church. However, she felt it would not be right to just drift away without an explanation. True to her forthright self and undoubtedly influenced by her father's insistence on taking responsibility for her actions, she made an appointment with her parish priest to explain her decision. The church was St. Austin's Catholic Church of Austin, Texas.

"I don't think there was ever a saint by the name of St. Austin," she said. "I probably was a feminist but I just got to the point where I did not accept the teachings or the authority of priests. When I decided to leave I went in and formally announced to my parish priest that I was leaving and gave him my reasons. He was a wonderful guy, just wonderful. I had great respect for him. I thought that the only fair thing to do would be to go in and thank him for the time he had spent on my behalf and say 'I'm leaving.'" Carolyn's leaving the Catholic Church was somewhat ironic because one of her great, great, grand uncles had been one of the founders of the Paulist Fathers and was considered the black sheep of the family because he had been the only Catholic at that time.

Early in life Carolyn demonstrated a strong sense of self-efficacy, which includes such traits as being strong-willed, stubborn and unafraid of challenge or conflict. When she was in college, a member of her sorority transferred in from another campus and the local group would not accept the young woman because she did not come from a family they deemed to be sufficiently socially prominent. Carolyn resigned from the sorority over the issue. When her sorority declined to accept her resignation, she moved out of the house and into an apartment.

In Carolyn's mind, her sorority's refusal to accept the transferring member "undermined the whole premise of sisterhood. I learned that one can join one of the best sororities and it's not important if it doesn't live up to the standards it claims. It goes back to the fact that you can't deny people certain rights. You can't treat people differently. You have to treat every group equally."

When she was twenty-two, Carolyn went to Spain where she lived for ten years under the Spanish dictatorship. She credits that experience with giving her a greater appreciation for democracy. Early in her stay she met her future husband, a man born and reared in Spain, and became engaged. Though her father did not speak out against her marriage, he was not in favor of it and gave her little assistance. So her grandmother stepped in, bought her a trousseau and sent her back to Spain to be married. "She just trusted that I had chosen a good person. She was ill at the time and knew that she would never see me again. But she made sure I had nice dresses to take back to Spain to get married in."

When Carolyn and her husband were married she did not speak Spanish and he knew very little English. "The first year was really rough because we were learning how to communicate," she remembers. "But we always knew if we worked at it, we'd get there." Her husband, Jesus Rodriguez, became an American citizen in 1991.

Carolyn's husband is a devout Catholic who never misses attending Mass. "My decision [to leave the church] does not mean I can't respect a Catholic or love a Catholic," she explained. "I'm on a board now where three of the board members are nuns. They are the most wonderful people. Their beliefs have nothing to do with my beliefs so very clearly I can respect their beliefs for them. I've never imposed my beliefs on others. I might try to persuade others, but I'm not going to lose respect for someone if they don't agree with me."

Carolyn Rodriguez's career in politics was, to a remarkable extent, an extension of the values that guided her life. Carolyn first ran for office in 1978 as the point person for a group of suburban women who believed that the issues of battered women, pay equity, choice, and child-care were not being addressed. The group banded together, along with some men who believed more women should be represented in the legislature, raised $800 and sent Carolyn into the political battle as a challenger to the status quo. To their surprise, she garnered about thirty-eight percent of the vote. "That convinced us there was potential there," Carolyn said. When she ran again in 1980, she won.

In the political climate of the early eighties, women believed they had to imitate men. Carolyn recalls that Joan Uselmann took her shopping to buy conservative man-tailored suits, blouses with Peter Pan collars, and scarves to be worn in a feminine version of a necktie. When she campaigned, the most common question she received was how she thought she could serve in the legislature and take care of her family at the same time. Carolyn's reply, that she had a strong family and her husband, Jesus, was an equal partner, did not satisfy many of her constituents. "They still thought I should be home with our son — that serving in the legislature was a man's job."

At the time of Carolyn's election concern was growing over the issue of equal pay for equal work. Nina Rothchild was head of the Commission on the Equal Status of Women, and Carolyn was named to the Commission. Together they conducted a study and discovered that every group in which women were the majority of the employees the women were being paid below the scale for men doing the same work. When the study was completed, Carolyn and her associates wrote legislation requesting the legislature to mandate wage equity. When it came time to take the bill to the legislature, despite the fact that Carolyn was the person who had done most of the work on the bill, the bill was given to Wayne Simoneau, a prominent member of the DFL Party with strong labor connections, to sponsor. Carolyn was named a co-sponsor. The bill passed the legislature, establishing the principle that workers should receive equal pay regardless of gender for the same standard of work and responsibility. The bill was not funded the first time through but at the next session of the legislature Carolyn and other supporters, succeeded in getting funding to implement the bill.

Carolyn Rodriguez was elected to two terms in the Minnesota House, serving from 1981 through 1985. When she ran for the fourth time, she was defeated. She is now on the Metropolitan Council and works for a private, non-profit agency helping the disadvantaged improve their living standards

State Representative Carolyn Rodriguez

and, in the process, take responsibility for themselves. In doing so, she continues to maintain her standards. "Some people are not as capable as others. So long as a person is working in a dignified way in a job forty hours a week, I'm willing to tax someone else to give her subsidized housing—make sure she has a decent existence. But I'm not willing to be an enabler. I'm not willing to say, 'Oh you poor thing. No matter what you do, I will keep on helping you.' We had the case of a fifty-year-old woman who was being evicted from her subsidized housing because she refused to be a good neighbor. She played music too loud, did drugs, got drunk, argued, wrecked her place. It is going to be tough on her if she has to go into a shelter. But I don't think it is our responsibility to allow her to endanger others. People are never going to learn unless the lesson is taught."

In reflecting back on her career, Carolyn believes that she "didn't last very long in politics because I wasn't able to compromise my basic beliefs, which is probably not a good thing in politics. I've learned to have a great deal of respect for people who can compromise to a certain extent to achieve more. And I could as long as it didn't attack my core beliefs."

When Carolyn was serving in the legislature, she received a petition from her district with over 3000 signatures asking her to vote against a bill supporting equal rights for gays. "I just couldn't do it. Everyone is equal or else they aren't equal. If you start making exceptions for one group, you could make them for any group—including my group. And I just never made exceptions to that. I never did. I don't ever remember making those kinds of exceptions." Carolyn believes that her stand on this bill was a contributing factor to her defeat when she ran for a third term.

Sen. Pat Piper, born in 1934, was the oldest of nine children. Her family lived in the small town of Delavan, Minnesota, which had a population of 300. Just as she was going into third grade, her father was drafted to serve in the South Pacific during the Second World War. Reacting to the trauma of the times, Pat's mother retreated within herself and refused to perform such simple daily acts as going for the mail or answering the telephone for fear they would bring news of her husband's injury or death. As a result, the young Pat took on responsibilities unusual, even in those times, for a young child. Not only did she bring in the mail and answer the telephone, but at her mother's request she also took on the responsibility for the partial care of three elderly people in the village. Pat did not resent the assignment. Helping care for the older residents gave her a feeling of belonging and contributing to the community.

"One was a lady who was probably eighty at that time. She lived in a tiny little house. I took her her mail, mowed her lawn, read her letters to her and wrote her letters. It was just like going to a dollhouse and being with this little doll-like lady. The others were my great-grandparents who lived in town. My mother had me go over every single night after school. I think maybe my mother thought one less kid at home would be a help and it was also a chance to make sure that great grandma and grandpa were Okay. I always felt that I was pretty grown up. I was just old enough not to be a bratty kid. I'd sit and listen and I was intrigued. All three of these older people, my great-grandparents and this other dear lady, were just like storybook people."

The world of Delavan was made even smaller by World War II. The children of the town had few resources, and their only way to explore the world beyond Delavan was to walk along the railroad tracks. One day

Pat, a third grader, and two friends went for a walk on the tracks. The day was pleasant and they continued walking, picking pussy willows as they went. They went on and on, not paying any attention to the time, until suddenly they found themselves in the neighboring town of Winnebago — possibly ten miles away. The trains ran only twice a day so the children had not been in any danger, but now they had to find a way to get home. They were too tired to walk and it would soon be dark.

Pat's grandmother lived in Winnebago and, though Pat was a little afraid of her, the girls found their way to her house. "She had a car and, when she saw us, my Grandmother Tippitt laughed and laughed at us. She thought it was so funny. She called my mother and said, 'You won't believe what I've got here — three little girls and a big bouquet of pussy willows.'" The children exchanged their gleanings for a ride home. Pat's grandmother kept those pussy willows for years.

As was almost everyone else in the community at the time, Pat's parents were poor. To help her family, Pat worked in the onion fields, detasseled corn, and hired out to do odd jobs in the town. Her big break came when she was in the fourth grade and got what she thought of as her first real job — other than baby-sitting. She was hired by the Delavan Drugstore to scrape gum off the bottom of the booths. Fortunately, the store had only three booths. Pat thought it was a marvelous experience to be able to work for pay.

Pat's family did not own a car. During the war years, gasoline was rationed and very few people in Delavan had automobiles. One who did was an old man who owned a Model T Ford. On one memorable occasion, believing that her children should have the experience of seeing a movie, Pat's mother decided to splurge and hired the man to drive them to Blue Earth to see "Going My Way."

On rainy days, when she couldn't play outdoors, Pat organized her friends to take a census of their town. Using the large paper bags that covered dry cleaning ("we never had anything dry cleaned at our house but others did"), they mapped out every house in the village and recorded the number of people living in each dwelling. Debates would erupt over whether to count individuals away in the service or in college. For several years, Pat and four of her friends kept a running census of their community on dry cleaning bags.

Pat Piper was in the sixth grade when her father returned from service in World War II. He had been gone for three years and had difficulty realizing that his oldest child was as grown up as she was. He treated her as the child she had been when he left and it caused a problem for the resourceful and independent young girl who had been her mother's bulwark during her father's absence. "Can't he understand I'm grown up," she thought. "I'm not a little kid any more." Soon after her father's return, the family moved to Blue Earth.

Since she had been a principal caregiver during much of her father's absence, it was Pat who shepherded her younger brothers and sisters to their first day of elementary school in their new community. Pat was entering the seventh grade in the same building. She walked her brothers and sisters to school, not realizing that the junior high began earlier than did the elementary school. To make it more complicated for the newcomer, the junior high classes were held on the third floor of the elementary school building.

When Pat realized her mistake, she suffered an agony of embarrassment, trying to figure out how to get to the third floor and her classes. Not knowing the building, she walked into a large room to find it full of students. "There was the principal sitting way in the back on a platform. One of the teachers said, 'That was the boys' stairway you came up. The girls' stairway is here.' I was mortified but I pretended that it was all right. How awful I felt. I was embarrassed for a whole year that I had done something so stupid."

When Pat's father returned from the service, he worked as a butter maker. Pat and her brothers and sisters took his lunch to him every day, a distance of eight blocks from their home. They would be given crackers and butter when they delivered the lunch, and in the winter they would suffer from the cold during the sixteen block walk. Though the children would be cold, Pat's mother told them they were never to stop at anyone's house on the trip through town but to come straight home. One bitterly cold winter day, Pat and her little brother disobeyed their mother and stopped to warm up for a few minutes on the return trip at the house of friends. Though Pat explained they could only stay for a minute, the couple insisted she take off her little brother's coat and scarf. After warming up, Pat put her brother's coat back on him and the two children continued on home.

When Pat's mother asked if they had stopped on the way home, Pat replied, "No, we didn't." Pat's mother continued her questioning, finally stating that, despite Pat's denials, she knew they had stopped. Pat was horrified at having been caught in a lie "How did you know?" she asked.

"Look at your brother's coat," her mother replied. The boy's coat was buttoned crookedly, with a button-hole at the top and an extra button at the bottom. "No adult would have buttoned his coat like that," her mother explained. The incident made a lasting impression on Piper.

Pat was a sophomore in high school when she got what she still believes to be one of the best jobs she ever held. There was a dress shop in Blue Earth where all of the girls Pat ran around with wanted to work. One day Miss Paulson, the school principal, announced that there was a job opening at the dress shop. Pat asked the principal about the job because she knew she would have to consult her mother as her mother would not let her take just any job. Miss Paulson asked Pat about ten questions and then said, "That is all I need to know."

When Pat got home from school, her mother told her there had been a telephone call for her and she was supposed to call back. It was from Dorothy Johnson, the owner of the dress shop. When Pat called back Dorothy Johnson told her, "Miss Paulson thinks that you would be excellent. I want to hire you." Then she added, "There's another young girl that I'm going to hire too." Pat asked who it was because she knew that a classmate, Rachel Torres, was very poor and really needed a job. "I'm hiring Rachael Torres," Miss Johnson replied. Pat was thrilled that her friend had also been hired at the store but later she was disappointed because Rachel had to work in the back room while Pat got to work in the front of the store waiting on customers.

"Dorothy Johnson was a powerful influence on me," Pat remembers. "She taught me so many things. Nobody could come in, try on a dress and leave looking dowdy with that dress. We were not to say things to a customer like, 'Oh, that's just perfect,' or 'the color's just great' when it fact, it wasn't. Anyone could bring clothes back because Dorothy said that we want our customers to look really nice. It wasn't so important to say you sold this many items. What was important was that you had this many satisfied customers. She was an amazing, incredible woman."

Dorothy Johnson advertised her dress shop on a weekly radio program connected to the station in Fairmont through the telephone on the wall in her office. One day, she decided that Pat could manage the radio program. She showed Pat the big clock she used to time the program and told her to write the scripts. Pat suggested bringing in popular people from the school, such as the captain of the football team, and putting them on the air to add local interest to the program. That was fine with Dorothy Johnson so long as Pat wrote the script and managed the program. The responsibility for the weekly program was totally hers. Pat brought different individuals from the school to the dress shop and put them on the air, making the introductions and timing the guests by keeping a close watch on the big clock. "A lot of the boys liked me because I was a conduit to publicity for them," she remembers.

Pat was also the editor of her high school newspaper. The advisor, Anna May Dawson, insisted that Pat do everything related to the production of the paper. "I had to go down and argue with the printers. I used to think I shouldn't be doing that—I was only a junior in high school. Miss Dawson was a tremendous influence. She challenged you but was always there if anything fell apart."

"I had a very deep religious faith because that was a part of our family," Pat Piper remembers. "Both sets of grandparents and great-grandparents were very religious. While we had no resident clergy in our little town of Delavan, the things that went on in church were very important and we were always there. At least, I was always there. Sometimes the younger ones didn't go, or my mother couldn't because she was taking care of the children. We would have 'adoration' and that would be for twelve hours. Everybody had a certain period of hours to do and I would be there with my grandmother, probably providing the hours for my family because my mother would be at home with the kids. So I was the family representative."

At an early age, Pat became sensitive to those people who were shunned by others in her town. She became the one who would always talk to the Mexican children. Though her family was "dirt poor," there were others who were poorer than they were. Either from her parents or her religious experience, Pat grasped the concept that everyone was special and, if someone was being ignored, that she should reach out to them.

Pat Piper's first experience with politics came when her father ran for County Treasurer. Though he did not win, Pat thought it was "neat" that he ran, "that he was willing to do something that was pretty public and was a risk." Pat's father belonged to every organization in the community, and he was always downtown. Her mother loved it because when her father came home, he could bring her all the news. There were now nine children in the family and Pat's mother was busy taking care of the house.

Two years after her father ran for County Treasurer, Pat, at age eighteen, left home. A few years later, Pat's mother returned to teaching in the Catholic school. Pat remembers that the priest had called her mother up and said, "'I forgot to tell you that as President of the Rosary Society you are needed to teach third grade.' And she did it. I can't imagine how she did that because she still had six kids at home. She did it for quite a few years and it was exhausting. She would say that she would come home and go to bed and sleep so she could get up and do her homework."

During Pat's first year out of high school, learning that a friend would sell his old car for $600, she took the money out of her savings account and bought the car for her father. "I was so proud of that. My dad was pretty happy about it too. He never showed gratitude as such but I knew he was really pleased. Neither of my parents expressed their emotions very much. They were a little self-contained, but you always knew how they felt. I thought he would pay back the $600 when I needed it, but then, when I was eighteen, I entered the convent. I don't think my father was ever able to save up $600."

Even though Pat had an aunt who was a nun, her decision to enter a convent was a shock to her parents. "I'll give you a wonderful wedding," her mother promised, in an attempt to dissuade her. But Pat was highly motivated by her past religious life and admired the nuns for the good work that they did. The time had come for her to take control of her own life. "So I entered the convent and it was an Okay experience." At first, away from home for the first time, Pat missed her family terribly. Her mother had told her, "Whenever you get lonesome, go to the chapel." As a result, Pat spent a great deal of her time in the convent chapel crying. She was desperately lonely, but her pride would not allow her to admit it. At that time, postulants only went home once every six years. They could write letters but they never made a telephone call unless a family member had died. Pat Piper spent twenty-two years in the convent. "I always had the option all along to drop out. My leaving was very easy. By that time, things had changed dramatically in the church, and I felt that there were many more things that women could do."

During her years in the convent, Piper taught both kindergarten and religion classes for children during "release time" from the public schools. She traveled around the upper Midwest teaching in various communities. One of her posts was at the Chandler Air Force Base near Slayton, where she taught religion to pre-school children in a large gymnasium. At one end of the gym was a bar where the off-duty airmen would come for drinks. The airmen would be drinking at one end of the room while the young nun, in her long habit, would be teaching the children at the other end of the room. Before long, Pat had groups of young men standing around watching and listening as she read stories to the children and jumped around with them in their games. Piper was very conscious of the airmens' presence and subtly tailored her lessons to her adult audience as well as to the children.

In the 1950s, kindergarten was a new concept in the Catholic schools of Minnesota. Piper started a kindergarten in Luverne and spent her summers at Catholic University in Washington, D.C., getting her master's degree in religious education. "I've had these marvelous experiences of trying things that were new and different. Teaching religion was a whole new experience in our religious order. There were a couple of other nuns, much older than I, who had done it, but they had never gone on to get their master's degrees. Nuns probably use the word 'called,' but I never used those words to describe my work. I just loved teaching religion to all different age groups, from kindergarten to the upper grades. These were children released from the public school. I had not attended a Catholic school myself and I felt these public school children were being shortchanged because the kids who went to Catholic school got all the parish money and attention and the others didn't."

Though it took her ten years to complete her graduate degree, the period was productive for Piper. Those were the years of the 1960s race riots and peace marches. Every Sunday, Piper and other nuns would march in support of the Civil Rights Movement. Their Sunday evenings were spent working in the poor black neighborhoods of the Capitol. On one memorable occasion, she met Dr. Martin Luther King, Jr.

When Pat returned to rural Minnesota from her experiences in the nation's capitol, she found that she was in demand as a speaker at the local service clubs and church groups. The churches were always looking for speakers and she got on the circuit early. There was probably not a religious group in her region that did not hear Piper speak, and it was her speaking activities that led to her appointment to a board of the diocese where she discovered that as an administrator she had the power to make changes.

An early project she undertook in Luverne, Minnesota, was the organization of religion classes for children who were developmentally disabled. Some of these children were in the school system, but Pat was sure that there were many more unidentified who were being kept hidden away by their families. To reach these children, Pat began organizing parties in the big gymnasium of the parish high school. She convinced the high school students, most of whom had never worked with developmentally disabled children before, to come to the party and act as hosts and hostesses. The events were highly successful and led to the establishment of a day activity center for the developmentally disabled in Luverne.

One of Pat's problems during that time came about when she ran afoul of a local Irish priest. He had asked her to help clean up the parish church. Poking through the building she found a pile of coal that had been abandoned in the basement since 1941. Pat told a poor family that they were welcome to have the coal, but when the priest learned of it he was irate and accused her of giving away his coal. As she thought about the experience she realized her error. "I made the mistake of not suggesting that it was his idea to give the coal away."

When Piper moved to Slayton, Minnesota, she looked about her and found that this community, too, lacked a day activity center for the disabled. As she put it, "I was just a person in the community, but I have a big mouth, and it didn't hurt that I was wearing a habit." When she began to promote the idea of a center, she was told that there weren't any developmentally disabled children in the community. "I'll bet there are," she said to herself and began driving around the countryside in her car. "People would give me clues where to go. I would pretend I was lost and visit these families. I found many disabled children. Their families were so embarrassed about them that they had never brought them out. They did not even go to their church."

Pat convinced the pastor of the local Catholic Church to let her use the basement hall for a center. Some people wanted to delay the opening until they could conduct a census to see how many children would make use of a day center. Pat said, "No, if we just open the center, it will be full the second day." Pat discovered that she could motivate people to give her supplies for the center. She could not get them to give her large sums of money but they would donate equipment such as chairs and tables. They understood that she was not asking for anything for herself, she did not have children and she was not going to be the teacher. "It was marvelous how the whole community got involved and created the Slayton Day Activity Center," she remembers.

Her work founding the center in Slayton brought Pat into her first contact with governmental bodies. The state law at that time said that a teacher could not be the director of a day activity center. The director had to be a nurse. Pat believed "that law was the dumbest thing," so she began writing letters to the State Department of Health and to legislators and was so thrilled to receive a reply from a legislator to whom she had written that she saved the letter in a scrapbook. Many years later, when she was a legislator herself, the writer of the letter was still a member, and she was able to show him the letter he had sent her.

Pat's next project in Slayton was to begin doing ecumenical work with the Protestant churches in the community "something that was unheard of at the time." Pat convinced another old Irish priest to share the classrooms in his church with the nearby Presbyterians and Lutherans. The church was close to the public school and all three denominations could use the classrooms in the Catholic facility to teach release-time religion classes to their own students. The arrangement was not without its difficulties though Pat was usually able to resolve the problems.

"The Lutheran minister from across the street would come over to see me on Saturday night after dark to borrow my Concordia Press filmstrips. His congregation was very conservative Lutheran and if they had known the filmstrips came from me, a Catholic nun, even though they had been produced by a Lutheran publisher, they would have been sure I had done something to them. And this old Irish priest never knew that the kindergarten curriculum I used was produced by the Methodists."

When Pat left Slayton to move to Austin, she told her superiors that she would only work in an ecumenical setting. "I won't work just for the Catholic Church because the Catholic Churches fight with each other all the time," she explained. "And the Lutherans do too. I had learned that it is when you get the Catholics and Methodists and

Lutherans all together that they will work together. Get three Catholics together and they fight."

When Pat Piper moved to Austin, she set as her goal the establishment of an ecumenical resource center in that community. It was during this period that she made her decision to leave the convent. "This was not a dramatic or unique decision," she explained. "A lot of women were leaving the convents. It was no major deal for the religious order—more a natural transition. I'm very close to them and people in town still call me 'sister.' Why not accept women in the church without their being nuns? By then we weren't wearing habits but kind of tacky clothes. I kept my same job and continued to work for the nun's salary."

Her first year in Austin was very hard going for Pat. She received little cooperation or assistance from members of the community and at one point became so discouraged that she visited a priest friend and began to cry. "Where are we going to create this ecumenical center?" she said. "I want to do this work but there's nobody here to help me." The priest was sympathetic and encouraged her. "You just do your thing," he told her. "Forget about the people who are discouraging you." Six months went by without Pat's receiving any salary. The Mother Superior of the convent allowed Pat to live there without paying rent. "I was supposed to be paying but it wasn't that I'd get kicked out if I didn't. They had plenty of space and they always had food. I found my clothes mostly in rag-bags."

Though Pat and her small group of supporters had no money they persisted and eventually were able to obtain the use of an old bar on the east end of Austin that belonged to the Knights of Columbus. With the assistance of the Knights, who helped her clean and paint the space, Pat was able to turn the old bar into an ecumenical center. Once she began walking around Austin describing her idea for the center, people began to help her. She received help from groups as diverse as the Chamber of Commerce and the local Presbyterian congregation. Eventually twenty-eight churches joined the center.

"I think I got so much support because I put all my energy into it and fixed everything up. I hung sheets on the walls and found chairs and with a little artistic talent fixed them up so we didn't have to use very much money." Two years later, Pat moved the center to larger quarters in an old Gold Bond Stamp store. "We did everything on a shoestring," she remembers. An attempt by an older priest to be help-ful her first year caused her some initial embarrassment. Pat had not yet left the convent and was still wearing a short habit and veil. Realizing she needed transportation, the priest leased a car for her. When she went to pick it up, she was embarrassed to find the priest had leased a bright yellow sports car with spoke wheels for her. "I sure as heck did not need a sporty car," she remembers.

Pat ran the ecumenical center for eighteen years, speaking at local churches and attending DFL meetings. Her commitment to the com-munity was unquestioned. When a legislative seat became open, she was asked to run for it. "I was intrigued, flattered and scared to death. I went to the library and got a book out to find out how much a legis-lator made. I didn't know if it was less than the nun's salary that I was still living on and I was too chicken to ask."

While Pat was trying to make up her mind about running for state representative she got what she called "the best sermon I ever heard in my life," from a state senator. Piper and the senator were attending a peace meeting in the basement of the Congregational Church in Austin. After Pat got the movie projector running, the senator beckoned for her to come back to the church kitchen where he could talk to her. "We won't have a democracy," he pointed out to her, "if our people aren't willing to run. There is no reason why you shouldn't run for the legis-lature." His lecture deeply impressed Pat and helped her make up her mind. "I was so duty oriented that I just said 'Okay,'" she explained.

Pat's opponent was a judge who had retired from the bench to run for the seat. To most observers, it was a miss-match, a powerful judge running against a former nun who had never before held political office. The judge was well-financed and had hired two full-time cam-paign workers. Since this was a strong DFL district, the presumption was that whoever won the primary would go on to prevail in the elec-tion. The endorsing convention was held in Albert Lea, and balloting went on until two-thirty in the morning. When it was over, Pat had lost the endorsement by three votes. She drove alone back to Austin in the early hours of the morning, shedding tears, certain that, though she had given it her best shot, her political career was over before it had even begun.

Her supporters thought differently. The next morning they brought flowers to her office and assured her of their support even though she had not received the party endorsement. DFL officials from St. Paul called and urged her to continue in the race. Reluctant to abandon her supporters, Pat left her name in the race and continued doing what she had been doing, running her center and speaking at the churches. Under-funded and outmaneuvered, she had little hope of success. Then the judge made a foolish mistake. He wrote an article and circulated it among all the media stating, "Once a judge, always a judge, and once a nun, always a nun." The implication was that the judge's allegiance was to the law, while Pat's was ultimately to the Roman Catholic Church. Her many years of working ecumenically with all of the churches in the community refuted that suggestion and, despite the apparent odds against her, Pat Piper defeated her opponent and, in 1982, was elected to represent the 27th district in the Minnesota House of Representatives. After serving two terms in the House, in 1986, she ran for and was elected to the Minnesota Senate where she worked on two landmark initiatives in Minnesota, the CARE Health Insurance Program and the creation of the Department of Children, Families, and Learning.

MinnesotaCARE is a program to provide health insurance on a sliding fee scale for working people who are not covered by their employers. Senator Linda Berglin was the major architect of the bill and Pat credits Linda's brilliance and dogged determination with its eventual passage. Pat was a member of the "Gang of Seven" legislators from both parties who worked with Linda for the two years it took to get majority approval of the bill. Upon its passage, in 1992, Senate Majority Leader Roger Moe made an unprecedented speech on the floor of the Senate praising Berglin. "The speech was powerful, extraordinary — an historic moment. You don't get that kind of acclaim even when you are dead," Pat commented.

The Department of Children, Families, and Learning began with Pat and Senators Jane Ranum and Jerry Janezich who wanted to reorganize the Department of Education to provide services to children and families from a different, more holistic perspective. During the first year the three worked on the reorganization, they called it the Department of Good Things. Then Roger Moe told them they had to get a better name for their bill so they called it the Department of Children, Families, and Learning. The reorganization became law in 1995 and Pat suspects that "when the three of us are gone, they will probably go back to the old name of 'Department of Education.'"

State Senator Patricia Piper

Pat believes women approach legislation with a more emotional "from the heart" perspective than do men. This, she says, has been a benefit to the legislature, allowing men to act with greater sensitivity and, paradoxically, helping women to be "tougher." In her opinion, men and women have moved closer to the emotional center through their interaction in the legislature. Pat envisions the state of Minnesota as a large family with all of the tensions and conflicts inherent in families. "Our work as lawmakers is to deal with the needs of this larger family," she says.

As a child, city council member Joanne Cushman lived on Hoyt Avenue in the Como Park neighborhood of St. Paul, and attended Chelsea Heights Grade School. An only child, she played baseball and kickball with the neighborhood children and became a figure skater. She was an expert skater and, for a time, her parents considered enrolling her in the St. Paul Figure Skating Club before they realized they could not afford the expense.

The influential figure in Joanne's life was her father. He had been teased as a young boy, had had a difficult childhood, and, as a result, was continually on the lookout for others who might be in trouble. "My father always felt sorry for kids that were having a tough time in the neighborhood," she remembers. "He'd go to bat for them." An elderly couple lived in their neighborhood, across an empty lot from Joanne's home. When her mother had cooked dinner, Joanne's father would call the couple to ask if they had started their supper yet. If they had not, which was generally the case, he would send a tray across the empty lot with food for them. The next day, the couple would send back the tray with the dishes washed. "There was a path worn across that empty lot," Joanne remembers. When he learned that the elderly couple's funds had been cut back, he went to the welfare office in St. Paul on their behalf to make certain their money was reinstated. On another occasion, he appeared in court for one of the neighbor boys who had gotten into trouble.

Joanne's father had been a medic in the first World War and was always interested in drugs. He worked at a wholesale drug house but wanted to become a pharmacist. "Back then you could take the state board test to become a pharmacist," Joanne explained. "I can remember him, with his three-by-five cards, studying the generic names." Though he learned a great deal, he could not master the chemistry involved and so never achieved his dream. "My dad was very disappointed," Joanne remembers.

In contrast to how she felt about her father, Joanne was not close to her mother. When she would go home at noon from elementary school, she made her own lunch because both of her parents were working. Though her mother had not graduated from high school, she became a registered nurse. "She didn't pass her state boards the first time around—she had to work at it," Joanne remembers. "She liked private duty nursing and taking care of people rather than doing the paperwork."

Joanne has many memories of what life was like at home during World War II. "I remember the washing and flattening of cans. My dad was an air raid warden and he had his air raid warden hat. He would go out and stand on the corners when we had practice air raids. Because she was a nurse, my mother had a car and a C gas-rationing sticker which gave her a lot more gasoline than people who had the A sticker. My father did not have a car. My dad's family was greatly impacted by the war; his cousin, Wendell, was killed in the invasion of Guadacanal. My aunt Grace, who lived on a farm, had a picture on her wall of Franklin Roosevelt. My dad thought an awful lot of Eleanor Roosevelt."

The summers between Joanne's seventh and ninth grades were spent on her grandmother's and aunt's farms. She helped with the farm chores and drove the team of horses when the hay was brought into the barn. Nevertheless, much of her time was spent alone. "Being an only child, maybe I've learned more about having to cope," she says.

When Joanne was in high school, she told her father about a boy with the same last name as their family who was living in a foster home and getting into trouble. Joanne's father got to know the boy and eventually brought him home to live with them. Joanne and the young man graduated from high school together. Though the youth continued to get into trouble, spending some time in Totem Town, Joanne's father arranged for him to have his class picture taken with the rest of the high school students. When the boy did not have the proper attire, Joanne's father bought him a necktie and lent him a sport coat so he could look like the other students. After graduation from high school, Joanne went on to the University of Minnesota and the young man joined the Marines and served in the Korean War.

Joanne had a lot to cope with as a child. She came home from school one day to find one of the neighbors loading up her mother's possessions because her mother was moving out of the house. "That was an awful experience," she remembers. The neighbors took Joanne in and fed her supper. "There have always been good people around to kind of help pick me up." Joanne's mother permanently left her father when Joanne was a senior in high school and moved to California. Her parents were divorced while she was in college. During her parent's divorce, a neighbor took the witness stand to tell about helping Joanne with her formal for homecoming because her mother wasn't there.

Joanne says that her father encouraged her to go on to school. "He always told me to speak up and to not be afraid to ask questions. I will never forget that I didn't complete school in June the year I graduated from the University of Minnesota, which almost all of my classmates did. That wouldn't be any kind of a big deal these days, but back then it was. I had to go that extra fall quarter." Joanne remembers that her father "was pretty down when I was in college and not around much. He even encouraged me to stay on campus as he felt it would be good for me."

Joanne's father's encouragement may have been critical in keeping her in school as there were other influences encouraging her to drop out. An aunt asked her why she wanted to complete her education since she was "just going to get married anyway." This was the prevailing attitude among many of her parents' friends and relatives. As a result Joanne became an early supporter of the women's movement and of increased opportunities for women in athletics. In later years, when she served on the Roseville School Board, Joanne witnessed with disgust the board's grumbling when equal funding for women's sports was mandated. "If we are going to give them all these programs, where are we going to put them?" board members asked. "We don't have any space, we don't have the coaches." Joanne's response was, "It's about time, we find the coaches and space and fund them."

Though her father also eventually moved away from the Twin Cities, he was present for her graduation from the university. When the president recognized the parents in the audience at the graduation ceremony, Joanne's father wept. "My graduation meant so much to him," she explained, "because there were times he was afraid I would quit. He wanted me to have the confidence that he felt he lacked." Joanne did not disappoint her father and, while in college, she won a leadership award. The family of Joanne's husband-to-be was also in the audience at her graduation and they gave her a graduation party.

In contrast to many of the other women in politics, Joanne found college work difficult. "I was intimidated by the academic achievements of some of those around me. The U was not easy for me. I really struggled." She admits that she had an active social life during that time and also worked part time from the time she was sixteen years old until she graduated from college. Her first job was at Schuneman's Department Store in St. Paul. From there, she went to the St. Paul Companies and worked there all through college. She has a great deal of sympathy for people who have to struggle in school. "I tried to get across to those who had an easier time with school and got the good grades that they should not be dismissing those of us who were having a tougher time and were struggling. I felt that we had a lot to offer too. School was just harder for us."

Joanne believes that idea has been validated in her own children. Her son graduated Phi Beta Kappa and magna cum laude from the university and her daughters did not achieve that. "But when it comes to other common sense things, they do a better job than he does," she says. "He's not really the absent-minded professor, but different traits do come out."

It was the PTA that opened the door to the political world for Joanne. An area near her home, on Lexington Avenue and County Road B, would flood when there was a heavy rain. The school buses would be halfway up to their hubcaps in water while bringing the children home from school. Joanne hosted meetings for neighbors in her home to explain the sewer problem. As a result of her and other people's efforts, their district was the first one in the St. Paul area to get new storm sewers. With her husband's encouragement, Joanne next took over the presidency of her local PTA and went from there to the Roseville Area Board of Education, serving from 1976 through June of 1985. She was elected to the Roseville City Council in 1985 and served there until December of 1993.

Joanne learned the value of persistence while working to get the John Rose Ice Skating Rink for the community. "People get themselves locked in a corner instead of being willing to sit down and negotiate. We spent thirteen years working on that. And then we would be defeated. We'd go to the House and Senate committees and we'd get shot down. We couldn't get it through the bonding bill in the legislature. We would just have to regroup and get other people involved. We worked for years bringing various groups of support together." In the end, the ice rink was built.

"I'm not one who throws the towel in easily," Joanne says of herself. "I always think if it is something you really want done and it is worth-

Roseville City Council Member
Joanne Cushman

while for the community, then you work at it." She has little patience with people who condemn government. "Government is where you get a lot of things done," she says. "I get really tired of the anti-government themes that are running rampant these days." She was shocked when close friends with whom she was having dinner on Election Day remarked that they were not voting. "What do you mean you are not voting?" Joanne asked. The friends replied that voting did not make any difference. Such attitudes are very discouraging to Joanne who believes that "being a participant does made a difference."

The battles have taken their toll on Joanne. Even though she admits that "I have been most frustrated with myself when I have not spoken out," she says that she has lost some of her willingness to fight political battles. "I don't like having to carry one if I'm attacked in a letter to the paper. I am not good at sitting down and writing a reply. I think I just really got worn down in regard to the bumps and bruises. Now I'm much more apt to pick my fights. I still have one or two left."

Another woman who became a leader in her community in the 1980s was Marge Anderson. Marge, whose Ojbiwe name, Bedaba-nooquay, means "Dawn of the Morning Sun," grew up with her family in a one-room tar-paper shack on the Mille Lacs Indian Reservation in central Minnesota. Marge was the second of eight children. Their home had no conveniences, electricity or running water, but Marge says "we did not miss any of that because we did not know what it was."

Her father was a seasonal worker whose own father had died when Marge's father was fifteen years old. While only a youth, Marge's father took on the responsibility for supporting his mother and brothers and sisters working for the railroad from the spring through fall until he was laid off during the winter. About her father, Marge says, "I always admired him. He was a really proud man and would not ask for help or welfare. He wanted to do it all on his own. There weren't any unemployment benefits for seasonal workers. My father taught himself and us how to fish, get deer. We ate squirrel and porcupine just to survive. In the spring we tapped the maple trees and boiled the sap to get sugar and syrup." The subsistence life Marge lived in her childhood was little different from that of pioneers who lived a century before her.

"My mom was a real inspiration for me. She made do with what she had. I remember one day when my Dad was out working somewhere with the Sioux Line and we did not have anything to eat. Mother took us children out in the woods and we gathered bitter-sweet berries. We tied them up in bunches and stood on the side of highway 169 and tourists stopped and bought them from us." Marge estimates that she was seven or eight years old when she and all of her brothers and sisters ("Mom did not leave anybody behind") sold bittersweet on the roadside. When the berries were sold, Marge's mother went to the store and bought groceries to feed the children. "She did not go back out to make more money," Marge remembers. "She just took enough so we could have something to eat."

To survive through the winter, the family harvested wild rice. If there were elders who did not have anyone to pole their boats, Marge's father would assign some of his children to pole their boats for them. The boats were heavy, wooden boats with flat bottoms. One person would pole while another, the "knocker," bent the stalks of rice over the boat and hit them with a stick to knock off the grains. Marge's father had a campsite where the rice was spread out on a tarp to dry. Then it was bagged, some of it sold and the rest kept to feed the family through the winter. "That's how we got our school clothes," Marge remembers. Her mother had a garden and canned produce, the family stored potatoes, and in November they netted fish. "We would sit there and gut them, clean the insides out, pour salt on them and put them outside in a barrel to freeze." Eventually the Bureau of Indian Affairs built some two-room houses for Indians and Marge's parents were given one of the houses, located across the street from where she now lives. The house had no plumbing or electricity but it had a kitchen and a cellar that made food storage easier.

While the family was still living in the one-room shack, Marge's father became a member of the Tribal Council of the Mille Lacs Band. Because they did not have a place to meet, the council met in the members' homes. When the council members came to her home, Marge would listen to the council members talk. Much of the discussion centered on conflict with the Bureau of Indian Affairs (BIA) and this impressed the young girl. "The Bureau used to tell the Indians what they had to do. If the Indians told the Bureau what they wanted to do, what their visions were, they were always dashed. The Bureau would tell them, 'You can't do that.' Things like that. This formulated in my mind the idea that we needed to tell them, instead of letting them tell us, what to do. Because they don't live on a reservation. They live far away. They don't know what life here is like."

Other discussions centered on the Bureau of Indian Affairs' policy of taking Indian children away from their families and putting them in boarding schools. Marge's mother's sister had been taken from her family against her will, placed in a boarding school, and Marge's mother never saw her sister again. The parents lived in fear that the children might be taken. "Some of the children, during that time, were sent to boarding schools," Marge said. "So I think my parents did a great job of shielding us. Sometimes the BIA would pick kids up and kidnap them so my parents always made sure they knew where we were. They were worried about that."

During much of her childhood Marge's best friend was a girl who lived across the street from her home. (The woman still lives in the same place.) Marge says that her mother made her clean the house first and then she was allowed to go play with her friend. The two girls spoke Ojibwe with each other as that was the language of their families and the community. The girl lived with her grandmother and because the girl did not have parents, the BIA sent her to a boarding school. Marge did not see her friend for a year or two and when she finally came back to her grandmother's home, Marge ran over to see her, speaking Ojibwe. "She just looked at me like she did not understand me. I asked her what was wrong. She was just blocked. It was such a traumatic thing they did to her in the boarding school that she did not want to be associated with the language. She and I kept on seeing each other and she finally came out of it and started speaking Ojibwe again. She speaks fluently now. That was the kind of thing that was going on." From an early age Marge learned that her Indian culture was important and that she should work to preserve it.

Despite their concerns about the boarding schools, the Tribal Council members were in favor of education. Marge remembers their conversation. "What can we do so our kids can have what everyone else's have?" they asked. The elders decided, "They need to go to school and get an education. That is the key."

Marge and all of her brothers and sisters attended the local Bureau of Indian Affairs School that offered grades one through nine. Schooling was not a pleasant experience for the Indian children. The teachers scolded them and said, "Shame on you!" if they were overheard speaking Ojibwe, the only language most of them knew. All winter the children walked over a mile to the highway where they were picked up by a school bus. After graduation from the ninth grade at the BIA school, many of the Ojibwe children transferred to the public high school in Onamia. Here they were subjected to more abuse. The girls were called "squaws" and the newcomers were spit on by other students. When the Indian youth fought back, they were punished. "The teachers blamed us for everything," Marge remembers. One day she hit back at a boy who had been taunting her and she was taken to the principal's office and threatened with expulsion. When she got home that night she told her parents she was not returning to school. While her parents sympathized with her problems, and understood the abuse she was receiving, they would not allow her to drop out of high school. "They knew education was the key to getting some of the things everyone else just took for granted," she said. In Marge's high school graduation class, only three of the graduates were Native Americans.

After graduation from high school, Marge married and because there were no jobs at that time for young people on the reservation, the young couple moved to Minneapolis. There she made a decision that she regrets today. Remembering the way she had been made to suffer from racism, she and her husband decided not to speak Ojibwe to their three children. "I did not want them to go through what I went through, getting slapped because you were speaking your language, being told 'shame on you.' So I did not teach them any of the Ojibwe language. I regret it. At that time I thought that was the right decision. I was trying to protect them." The children learned some of the language from their grandparents, but they did not become fluent. Though she did not teach her children Ojibwe, Marge maintained close contacts on the reservation. "We did not break our connection there," she explained.

During the eighteen years her family lived in Minneapolis, Marge did not work outside of her home but did volunteer work at her children's schools and at a hospital. In 1975 she received a call from the tribe asking her to come back to the reservation to work as an accountant at a resort the tribe had built. "I knew some bookkeeping and I was good with numbers. The kids were grown. I told my husband and he did not mind so I said I would go and try it." Marge moved back to her parent's home and commuted back and forth to Minneapolis. She found she liked keeping books and after a year, when there was a vacancy on the Tribal Council, several friends urged her to apply for the position.

"No, I don't think so," she said. "I like what I am doing." Marge's friends kept after her so finally, to end the discussion, she told them, " Okay, I will file. But I am not going to go out and campaign." She filed for a district council seat on the Tribal Council only to satisfy her friends. "I did not do anything—just put my name on a piece of paper that said I was a candidate." No one was more surprised than Marge Anderson when election day came and she discovered she had been elected.

After she was elected representative from District 1, she learned that there was a nutrition program in place to feed elderly members of the District. But the program only had enough money to feed twenty people and there were many more in need. Marge began investigating and learned of a federal program from Washington, D.C., that would allot $70,000 to programs that qualified. Marge sent for the guidelines and suggested writing a proposal for the money. The tribal leadership discouraged her. "They told me it was impossible, that it would not happen. I said, 'Don't tell me what I can't get done. I am going to try.'" The first objection offered was that there were not enough elders to qualify. Marge was sure there were and began going door to door, house to house, getting names and dates of birth. When she wrote her proposal she had well over a hundred elderly people who qualified. Up to the day she mailed in the proposal, her fellow Tribal Council members were telling her she was not going to get anything. Marge admits to feeling discouraged but told herself she would never know until she tried. Then, one day, she received a telephone call from Washington. She had been awarded the grant of $70,000, enough to feed all the elders in all three districts of the Mille Lacs Band of Ojibwe. "That was really a wonderful day," she remembers. "We had to hire cooks for those districts. A lot of people were fed after that."

In July of 1986, Marge's brother, Henry Davis, was elected Secretary-Treasurer of the Tribal Council. They were the first brother-sister team to serve on the Tribal Council and it was a source of pride to both of them. Then, in November, Henry was killed in an automobile accident that triggered a special election. Again Marge's friends urged her to file for her brother's seat as Secretary-Treasurer. She did and ran unopposed that year and again in 1990. She was one year into her second term as Secretary-Treasurer when the Tribal Chairman, Art Gahbaco, died suddenly. After the funeral her fellow council members approached her and said she had to accept the position as chairperson of the council. In a special meeting called for that purpose, Marge's fellow Tribal Council members unanimously appointed her to serve out Art Gahbaco's term. She was the first woman to serve as a Tribal Chair and Chief Executive Officer of an Indian tribe in the state of Minnesota.

"When I first walked into that office after I was appointed, I thought to myself, 'What am I doing here?' I didn't have a clue what to do. I didn't know where to start." That question was soon answered when she received a call from the State Gaming Commission to come to St. Paul to negotiate contracts for blackjack at the Mille Lacs casino. She had barely gotten blackjack approved for the casino when she was called to Washington to testify before Congress in regard to a self-governance demonstration project for Indian tribes. "I was nervous," she remembered, "but there were not too many questions I could not answer. I guess I got my message across because self-governance is now permanent legislation. I think I had an effect on that."

In the late 1980s, Marge was looking at the money appropriated for Indians by Congress and the amount that eventually ended up with the tribes. The differences seemed to her to be enormous. She did a study and learned that only fourteen cents of every dollar appropriated made its way to the people it was supposed to be benefiting. The other eighty-six cents were going to the central office, the regional office, and the district office of the BIA for administration. The tribal leaders' outrage at the misspending of funds eventually reached Congress, which funded another demonstration project to look at the situation and make recommendations. Mille Lacs was the first tribe to sign a contract with the Federal Government that allocated funds more or less directly to the tribe.

Marge's greatest achievement while in office was winning the Supreme Court decision regarding Indian treaty rights dating back to the treaty of 1837. Problems began for the Ojibwe when they began to be arrested for hunting and fishing without licenses—something they had done for centuries and believed they were still allowed to do under their treaty. While he was still alive, Art had investigated and found that the Indians did, indeed, have a good case. When he died, Marge picked up the banner and carried the case through the District Court, the Court of Appeals, and, when the State of Minnesota appealed, to the United States Supreme Court.

When the problems first began, officials from the Tribe and the State worked to negotiate a settlement. Marge explained, "We worked long and hard to come up with one. We had everyone involved and we had a referendum vote on it here. Everything was arranged. We just wanted to be able to fish out from our land here—about a mile into the lake."

The negotiators for both sides thought they had a good agreement but when it went to the Minnesota legislature, the legislature turned it down. After that happened, the only recourse was the courts.

Marge is proud of the way the Tribe behaved. "We took the high road. We did not do anything to hurt our neighbors; we tried to educate them to Indian culture which says to take only what you need. We weren't going to take all of the fish out of the lake. We understood that we needed to live together and did not want the violence that happened over in Wisconsin to happen here. And it didn't. We did not have any violence here."

When the case was due to come before the Supreme Court in Washington, D.C., emotions were running high. On a wintry November day in 1998, three Indian boys bearing a staff with eagle feathers began running from Lac du Flambeau, Wisconsin, all the way to the steps of the Supreme Court. As the runners left Lac de Flambeau, an eagle suddenly descended from the sky and flew along with the racing youth. "It was an awesome sight," Marge recalled. "We were very confident it was a good sign."

On the morning of March 24, 1999, Marge was going to work slowly, dragging up the stairs, feeling tired and a little dispirited. She was met by the tribe's Commissioner of Finance coming down the hall toward her calling out, "We won!" Marge stopped. "Won what?" she asked. "The treaty rights case," was the reply. "Oh my God!" Marge exclaimed. At that point everyone began crying. The receptionist was crying and Marge went over and put her arms around her. "I still couldn't believe it," she recalled. "I turned the radio on and there it was. Our victory."

Marge Anderson's philosophy was formed when she was a small child and witnessed the Indian peoples' struggles to survive. Her father instilled in her the value of work, that people need to work to get what they want. When money from the casino began coming to the tribe, Anderson insisted that the money be invested in the community. "We had protests and all that and I just said, 'If you want a check, get a job. I cannot in good conscience promise people money they have not earned.' That has been my philosophy. There is so much need here and we need to invest in the long-term future of our children and in taking care of our elders."

Marge never forgot the privation of the generation before her. Remembering a younger brother who died at age five because there was no medical care available and another brother who died at age twenty-nine of heart failure as a result of undiagnosed rheumatic fever, she made certain the tribe built a modern health clinic on the reservation. The clinic is the tribe's—not the Bureau of Indian Affairs'—clinic. She is proud of the fact that members of the Mille Lac Band have health benefits no matter where they live in the United States.

Marge has found that women political office holders, in general, do not seek a political office for the glory but to get things done. She believes women like to complete tasks

Chief Executive of Mille Lacs Band of Ojibwe Marge Anderson

and then move on whereas "men kind of procrastinate. They put things aside and let them build up. I like to be proactive, get ahead of the game and deal with things that way."

Marge Anderson has taken up golf. She finds it is a way to relieve stress and to get off by herself. She says that when she was Tribal Chair her daughter and granddaughter found that if they wanted to spend any time with her they had to take up golf. Marge is almost as busy now as when she was Chief Executive of the Tribe. She is a director of the Federal Home Loan Bank, serves on a state housing agency and is beginning work with Harvard University on an Indian study. Her concern is taking care of people. "Welfare of the people is most important to me." Marge Anderson still lives on the reservation across the street from where she grew up. The street, however, has a new name. While Chief Executive Officer of the Tribe she saw to it that the street was renamed Harry Davis Drive. Harry Davis was the name of her father and also her brother who served so briefly with Marge as half of the only brother-sister team ever to serve on the Tribal Council of the Mille Lacs Band of Ojibwe.

◅ ◆ ▻

"I think being a woman is like being Irish. Everyone says you're important and nice but you take second place all the same." —Iris Murdock

Lieutenant governors, like most constitutional officers in Minnesota, have, until the 1980s, all been male. It was Governor Rudy Perpich who broke ranks with his brethren and named a woman to be the successor to forty-two male lieutenant governors stretching back 124 years to William Holcombe, a Stillwater lumberman. Since Perpich's groundbreaking selection of Marlene Johnson to be his running mate in 1982, all succeeding lieutenant governors have been women.

Marlene Johnson grew up in the small town of Braham in Isanti County, Minnesota, where her father was the founder and CEO of the electric cooperative as well as the mayor of the town. He had been a pioneer in the cooperative movement, founding the first electric coop in Minnesota, and was nationally known for his work. In many respects, he brought the principles he used in managing the cooperative to his role as leader of his family.

Marlene grew up believing that, through her words and actions, she could influence others. "We had family discussions about everything from politics to where we were going to go on our family vacations and what we were going to eat for dinner," she says. As a child, Marlene discovered she could have an impact on her world when she convinced her family to stop planting lima beans in the family garden. Knowing that she was expected to eat everything on her plate and hating lima beans, she convinced her family to stop planting them. After Marlene presented her arguments against lima beans, her mother said, "Well, we're not going to plant them anymore because there's no reason to

186

plant vegetables you're not going to eat." That was an important concession because the family lived frugally and the garden was a principal source of food. "I never ate a store-bought vegetable until I was in college," Marlene remembers, "and I don't think I had one store-bought coat until I went to college. We never got extravagant gifts."

Despite her parent's frugality, the life the Johnsons lived was a rich one. Because of their father's leadership role in the community he was both a well-known and respected individual and a target for controversy. "I grew up having my father called a Communist and having people demonstrate against him at the annual meeting of the co-op. It was understood in our family that you had to cope and deal with that kind of controversy if you were doing something you believed in."

The annual meeting of the cooperative was a major event in the community. "Everyone who lived in the region was a member—it was the most inclusive event in the area," Marlene recalled. Hundreds came to enjoy the free meal that was served and listen to the presentations. "It was like a big reunion on one level. There was always entertainment so it was fun and then there was an important speech. It was a big event. We dressed up and went and supported our dad and cheered on the company."

Besides conducting the business of the co-op, Marlene's father used the occasion of the annual meeting to bring nationally-known speakers to the community to expand the thinking of the local residents and expose them to outside ideas. As a result, the meeting became a community event that was social, political and, at times, intellectual. One year, he brought Carl Rowen, a black columnist for the *Minneapolis Tribune*, who went on to national prominence. "Carl was probably the first black person who ever came to Braham. It was very bold of my father to bring him."

Other speakers caused wild controversy. Johnson remembers the year her father brought Governor Orville Freeman to the annual meeting. Because demonstrators were picketing Johnson's home and outside the front of the building where Freeman was to speak, Marlene and her brothers and sister were slipped in by the back door to avoid the risk of their being hurt. "We always went to the annual meeting," she remembered. "We didn't consider not going. After the governor's speech, people started yelling at him, booing and throwing things." Later in the day, when Marlene had returned to her home, Freeman called her house to inquire how the rest of the day had gone after he had gotten out of the hall and to make sure the members of the Johnson family were safe.

Though they had little money and her father had not gotten past the eighth grade in school, Marlene's parents believed in education for their children. "Going to college was never an option; it was just what you did after high school." Her parents paid for their children's education themselves, not allowing them to apply for scholarships because Marlene's father feared that the money might be taken from people who needed it more.

Another value Marlene's parents instilled in their children was that of travel. They believed it was important for their children to understand the richness and differences within the United States. Travel was considered a basic part of their education. Camping all the way, Marlene and her family had visited thirty-six states by the time she graduated from high school. (Her younger brothers and sister made it to forty-eight.) The travel gave Marlene "a deep understanding of the big picture. I saw the country and thought about it in a more complex way than I would have if I had stayed at home."

An added benefit was that through her family camping experiences, Marlene gained a strong love for the out-of-doors. "We were kind of pre-hippie-era environmentalists," she said. Her father's "second bible" was Rachel Carson's book *Silent Spring*. His devotion to Carson's principles of conservation was the reason people in Braham believed he was a Communist. Marlene's father would not use chemicals in their garden, nor would he spray for mosquitoes. Instead he put up birdhouses for martins because martins eat mosquitoes. "To this day," Marlene says, "you can drive around Braham and you can see where the executives of the electric co-op lived at that time because they all have martin houses in their yards."

At a young age Marlene demonstrated an ability to organize by holding buggy parades in her neighborhood. Children four and five years old decorated their tricycles and baby buggies, set up lemonade stands, and held a parade. "We did that knowing that everybody in the neighborhood would stand out there and watch us go by and buy lemonade from us and cheer us on." (The people who showed up to watch the parade were the same adults who, if they saw a child misbehaving, would come out of their houses to correct the behavior or call the child's parents.) From buggy parades, Marlene moved on to organizing six friends into the Helping Hand Club. The girls met every week in one of their homes and thought up projects to do for their community. The group made decorations for the local nursing home and the hospital at Christmas.

By the age of eleven, Marlene was babysitting, performing in piano recitals (she loved her piano lessons), singing in a trio, and participating in the activities of the 4-H Club. Looking back on herself as a child, Marlene says, "I think I am still much like her. I have very strong leadership skills. I end up being in charge even when I don't start out being in charge. I am often the person who is articulating the vision, who is helping clarify issues for people or helping them see things in different ways. I am more analytical than I was then and I am still quite disciplined."

The community's support of its young people, which began with attendance at the buggy parades, continued through high school. The entire town turned out for athletic events, high school band concerts, and plays. Marlene remembers, "There was never any question that the whole town would show up if there was a school play. I never went to a school play that didn't have a full house when I was growing up."

Marlene credits the influence of her family, especially her father, for the fact that she has never been intimidated by position or authority. "I have a lot of respect for authority, but I'm not afraid of it," she says. "Because I grew up knowing people of influence and leadership, I have never been uncomfortable around them or particularly impressed by them either. In my family, I never knew we were poor, even though when I subsequently learned how little my father had saved, I was shocked. We always lived as middle-class people."

Marlene's first experience taking a cause that was important to her into the political arena was when she was a sophomore in high school. She had started investigating colleges and learned that many schools required their students to have had two years of a foreign language before applying. The Braham High School did not offer any foreign language instruction, nor was the school administration interested in adding language courses. With their parents' support, Marlene and her friends began circulating petitions requesting foreign language instruction in their school. The issue was highly controversial. It was the first time that students had ever petitioned the school board and, initially, their petition was rejected. Marlene remembers that "we just kept repeating ourselves. That was when I first understood what became the marketing message of the nineties which is you have to say something at least fifteen times before anybody starts catching on. Although in Braham I think it sometimes took longer than fifteen times." After saying 'no' for a year, the school board finally said 'yes.'" Spanish was introduced at the beginning of Marlene's junior year so she was able to take two years of a foreign language before she entered Macalester College in St. Paul in 1963.

Marlene says her own persistence and determination came from observing her father with the co-op. "He was active with political people of both parties to accomplish things for farmers and the communities he served. That's how we thought about things — that the co-op mission was service. We thought about things in terms of what was required to serve the community."

The most memorable controversy of Marlene's youth was her father's attempt to get Section 8 housing for the elderly. The concept behind Section 8 housing was to provide affordable housing for the elderly so they could leave their big houses, yet stay in the community within walking distance of services such as the post office, churches, and stores. With Section 8 housing, the elderly would not lose contact with their neighborhoods and their former homes would be available for younger families. As mayor, Marlene's father applied for one of the federal grants to build this housing for the elderly in the town of Braham.

His efforts turned into what Marlene called "the controversy of the century. It was one of those 'not-in-my-back-yard' scenes. It was unbelievable. Parents of some of my best friends quit speaking to my parents for a year or two." The project was so controversial that it was put on hold for several years and was not built until the year Marlene's father died. When ground was finally broken, the waiting list for the housing had almost as many names on it as the total population of Braham. Marlene remembers that there were many such situations in her home as she was growing up. "That's just the way it was. Life was like that."

Like many of the other women in politics, Johnson did well in high school. However, when she went to college, she ran into difficulties. "I went into a real funk in college, lost a lot of my self-confidence. I think I was actually clinically depressed for a good chunk of college." In her sophomore year at Macalester, Marlene got an F in French and was placed on academic probation with the suggestion that she should not return. She went to the school counselor who told her that the reason she was having trouble with French was because she was a slow reader. This made no sense to Marlene because she was a voracious reader. The message she came away with from her visit with the counselor was that she was a terrible person.

Since she did not want to drop out, Marlene went to the one professor she trusted, Chuck Green. They talked for two hours and worked out a strategy. Marlene was president of the Young Democrats Organization, and the rules of the college were that students who were on academic probation could not participate in extracurricular activities. To have to give up her office would have been deeply painful for Marlene, in part because she would have to publicly acknowledge that she was on probation, and also because she got so much pleasure from working in the organization. The professor agreed that she was right in wanting to keep her position with the Young Democrats. He helped Marlene come up with a rationale for continuing her extracurricular activities along with staying in college and helped her prepare and rehearse her argument for the dean. She went straight to the dean's office and sat in the anteroom until he let her in. There she made the speech of her young life, and when she walked out, she was still in college, still on academic probation, and also still president of Macalester's Young Democrats. "I stayed on academic probation for the rest of my college career. It was good for me because it forced me to come out of my shame and start healing. I didn't tell the world that I was on academic probation for two years, but I did tell the world that I wouldn't have finished college without the advice of Chuck Green."

Marlene's leadership of the Young Democrats at Macalester College had far-reaching consequences. Though she herself was not old enough to vote, she helped organize her fellow students to attend the precinct caucus in 1966 supporting Sandy Keith who was running for governor. At that time, students could not vote where they were attending school but only in their home communities. The act of packing the Macalester College precinct with student supporters of Sandy Keith led to the court case which eventually changed the law—allowing students to vote where they attend college.

The change did not come easily. Marlene did not realize until later the naivete of their actions. The precinct they had packed with students was Doug Kelm's, who was the most powerful Democrat in the fourth district. His father was Elmer F. Kelm, head of the state Democratic Party in the 1940s who led the historic merger with the Farmer-Labor Party, and his younger brother was Tom Kelm, Wendell Anderson's chief of staff. "Doug Kelm did not suffer fools lightly and he was mad," Marlene remembers. "They took us to court and we spent final exam week in court." Marlene was not the one who was on trial, as she had not been old enough to participate in the caucus, but she was the leader of the student group and the one who had organized it. Marlene was in court every day, and the students lost their case.

From that experience, Marlene learned that she would not run away from controversy and that political actions have consequences that can seldom be anticipated. Though she had realized that their packing of the caucus would be controversial, it never occurred to her that the students would be hauled into court and would then have to raise money to pay for their defense. Though their lawyers worked on the case without charge, the students had to find $600 to pay for a transcript of the proceedings. That challenge was Johnson's first experience in political fund-raising. The students raised the money by selling 600 buttons at one dollar each.

In the mid-1970s, Marlene Johnson became deeply interested in becoming a politician. By this time, she was the owner of a public relations business, had founded the Minnesota chapter of the National Association of Women Business Owners, and helped found the Ramsey County Women's Political Caucus. However, as she thought about what she wanted to do with her life, she found herself shying away from the idea of politics because, in many ways, it conflicted with how she had been reared in northern Minnesota. She had observed that while men were respected by their peers for running for political office, women often suffered the opposite reaction from their associates. "I was raised to be understated and never to brag and never to be arrogant or push myself in any way. We lived in a very poor community and you just never let people feel that you were better than they were. I had a lot of ambiguity about what it meant to seriously put myself forward for politics."

While she was wrestling with her personal inhibitions about politics, a close friend, another business owner, advised her not to deny her talents and to recognize how good she was in the political arena. Her friend told her that it was Okay to love politics. With her friend's encouragement, Johnson began talking with others about her ambitions and finally told them that she wanted to run for governor. She chose the position of governor because she did not feel she had the skills to be a legislator or a county commissioner. Not having any idea how to accomplish her goal of running for governor, she nevertheless prepared herself for it, believing that it was just a matter of waiting until her political break would come. It did, in 1981, when Rudy Perpich called and asked her to be his running mate for governor. "A lot of people didn't understand how I could say 'yes' on twenty-four hours notice," she remembered. "For me, it wasn't overnight because I had been thinking about it for a long time."

In reflecting on her eight years as Lieutenant Governor of Minnesota, Johnson believes one of the reasons there are not more women holding political office is that they lack the mentoring that many men receive from other men. Men mentor other men, help them get back in the running when they lose elections and work to position them for the next run. Men are mentored, she says, from early in their political careers. "People mentor people who they see as being able to continue their power. It's like I mentor you to take over for me. That's the traditional model of mentorship in corporations and in politics too. Whether it's Mayor Daly mentoring his son or the Kennedy boys mentoring each other. Look at who is running for office in Minnesota now [1998]. It's all those boys who have got dads who spent their lives getting them ready to run for governor. That's not true for any woman I know."

However, men do not act as political mentors for women, Johnson says, in part because they are not sure how to do it for women, and in part simply because men are more comfortable with other men than they are with women. Unfortunately, she laments, women do not know how to mentor each other. "Women don't have a concept of power and the connectedness of power that is required if you're going to be a successful mentor." Another problem is that young women who could go into politics often are busy rearing children and caring for their homes, while young men traditionally have someone doing those things for them. Johnson admits this is a difficult topic to discuss. "It's a hard thing to even talk about because women are so much better off than they were twenty years ago. You can't spend your life complaining about what you don't have. But it's still an issue."

The difficult aspect of politics for Marlene was the sense of always being a target of controversy because of social changes she was trying

Lieutenant Governor Marlene Johnson

to bring about. She felt the burden of responsibility to stay true to what she believed and not let herself get sidetracked by the negative things that came her way. At the same time, she enjoyed the energy that came from political involvement, the genuine good times and the friends she made. "Those are very bonding experiences," she says, "and you get to know people under adversity. If someone does well in a crisis, can stay calm and centered in a difficult situation, they're a pretty good person."

The second woman to hold the office of lieutenant governor and the first and only woman to serve as mayor of Red Wing is Joanell M. Dyrstad. Joanell credits a second grade teacher and her family, including her extended family of grandparents, aunts, and uncles, with giving her a strong sense of connectedness to others. That teacher in the community of St. James was so significant in Dyrstad's life that she still remembers her maiden name (Miss Law) and her name after the teacher married (Mrs. Sorenson). Sorenson must have also felt a special connection to Dyrstad's class of students because, even though she had moved away from St. James, she returned for the class's graduation from high school.

Like many other female officeholders, Joanell found her childhood playmates among the boys in her neighborhood. "I was always participating in their games and playing ball with them. The boy next door and I made a horse out of a saw horse. We put a head on it and made a saddle and might even have taken roller skates apart and put them on it so we could push it down the sidewalk," she remembers. When the boy became an all state football player she would hold the ball for him so he could practice kicking it through the branches of the trees. (During baseball season he was the shortstop on the high school team and she would throw grounders to him to help him improve his game.)

Though Joanell had a strong interest in athletics, her participation was limited to the few opportunities offered girls by the Girls Athletic Association (GAA). She compensated by playing an alto saxophone in the high school band and by working as secretary to the high school band director, helping organize band events.

When Joanell was nine, in 1951, her mother developed polio and was hospitalized at the Sister Kenney Institute in Minneapolis. Though the children's grandmother came to help care for her and her two-year-old brother, Joanell took responsibility for her younger brother and became a kind of surrogate mother to him. Her paternal grandparents lived in the town of La Salle, Minnesota, where her grandfather owned a country store (Sletta's Store). The store was a typical small town enterprise of the time, housing the post office and selling everything from clothing to groceries. From the time she was eight years old, on Saturdays and during the summer, Joanell went to La Salle and worked in the store, stocking shelves, waiting on customers, and helping clean up.

Despite her young age, Joanell was trusted by her grandparents and given responsibility. When she was ten or eleven, she carefully drove her grandfather's car the few blocks from his home to the store, ground the meat for hamburger and ran the cash register. In return, Joanell's grandfather worked with her on her arithmetic. He would give her columns of numbers to add up. She would stand on one side of the counter, adding the numbers right side up while her grandfather stood opposite her, on the other side of the counter, adding the numbers upside down. She often stayed at her grandparents' home in LaSalle, along with two unmarried uncles and a maiden aunt who also lived there and provided a nurturing extended family for her.

The town of St. James provided opportunities for its young people. Joanell was active in Brownies and Girl Scouts through high school, attending the International Girl Scout Roundup in Colorado Springs, Colorado, where she was the patrol leader of her delegation of scouts. The St. James Rotary Club sponsored Joanell to attend the Model United Nations program in Canada where she represented the country of Ghana and had to speak on two issues of significance to that country in a United Nations-type setting. While in high school, Joanell taught Sunday School classes and, one summer, ran the entire summer school program at the church by herself. At the time, it seemed the expected thing to do. She had seen her mother accept the responsibility to head the Lutheran Women's Society and her aunt serve for twenty-five years as the Sunday School Superintendent in another church.

In looking back on her early years, Joanell suspects that her neighborhood may have provided some incentive for her to prove herself. As she explains, "My dad was a carpenter and we lived on the north side of town that, in those days in St. James, was the wrong side. We lived in a very nice home, but the south side was where the doctors and the lawyers and the dentists and their families lived." Joanell believes she may have been trying to demonstrate that she was "certainly as good as those people on the south side of town who sometimes might have looked down a little at those of us who lived on the north side of town."

That same desire to prove herself influenced Joanell's decision to attend Gustavus Adolphus as the first member of her family to attend college and earn a degree. On a high school visit to Gustavus with her St. James Luther League, another student expressed skepticism that Joanell would be able to attend the college. "What right do you have to say to me that I can't go?" Joanell said. The doubt expressed by her fellow Luther Leaguer only strengthened her determination to find a way to attend and encouraged by her high school band director and school superintendent, and with loans and a scholarship, she was able to enroll in college. Joanell attributes her "feistiness" to her mother and her internal strength to her father whom she characterizes as being "a very positive, easy-going kind of person, always very loving." She also credits the support of her extended family, grandparents, aunts, and uncles who gave her confidence in herself. At graduation, instead of calling on the valedictorian and salutatorian to address the audience, the superintendent selected two other outstanding students to give commencement speeches. Joanell was one of those chosen.

Alhough her parents always voted, Joanell does not remember politics being a topic of discussion in her home as a child. She was largely unaware of what was going on in her community of St. James. Now she sees politics evident in many more areas than just the activities of elected officials—such as in churches or in business. However, growing up as a young woman in St. James, she was conscious of the fact that women were never elected to the presidency of their school classes and other institutions. "Young men were always elected to those positions. I felt I was capable of being president of an organization but I was not ever given the opportunity to do it."

The closest Joanell came to politics in college was when her friendship with Jean LeVander led her to helping out in Harold LeVander's campaign for governor of Minnesota. She was not involved in the issues of the campaign, however, and her principal memory of the election was of Iontha and Harold LeVander walking across the stage of the Civic Center at their inaugural ball. At the time, she was overawed that she, Joanell Sletta, could be attending such an occasion. "Little did I know that many years later I would be walking across the stage as Lieutenant Governor," she said. "I certainly never dreamed of running for political office myself. That thought had not entered my mind."

Between her junior and senior years in college, Joanell spent the summer traveling in Europe. "I didn't have the money to do that but my grandfather went to a bank up in Minneapolis and withdrew $1000 and gave it to me so I could take that trip. Together with three girls from Gustavus, we spent thirteen weeks driving around Europe." Joanell had relatives in Sweden and Norway, so she had people to visit. Looking back she says, "I don't know how it all happened. It just did."

The first office that Joanell ran for was Mayor of Red Wing, Minnesota. She had been appointed to a citizen task force to study the need for a new police facility for the community. The Red Wing Police Department, at that time, was operating out of the basement of the sheriff's building. There was poor air circulation in the basement and the occupants of the offices were breathing the exhaust of cars. There was no area where the police could speak privately to a family. The office of the chief of police was situated in the front so that visitors who walked in found themselves in the chief's office instead of facing a receptionist.

After some delays, while the city council attended to other needs in the community, the task force finally got going and Joanell was made the chair. She worked with the architect to help design the new police department building and to determine what it would cost. She then took the project to the city council and the community to convince the voters to pass the referendum required to raise the funds for the building. "That was the first time that I went out and promoted something that I felt was necessary for the good of the community," she said. She and her committee made slide presentations to civic clubs and held an open house in the old building to show citizens the poor conditions in the police department. When the votes were counted, the referendum had passed by sixty-five percent.

Joanell's experience with the police department task force showed her that she enjoyed speaking at the public meetings and explaining the need for the new facility to the community. Her children were growing up, and though she did the books for their family-owned drugstore in Red Wing, she felt she now had the time to become more involved in their community. While she was assessing her options, she received a letter from the mayor asking her to consider running for his office when his term ended in eighteen months. Unfortunately, the mayor died in office. The city council asked for candidates to apply to fill out the mayor's term. Joanell was one of five to apply.

"I decided at that time that I really wanted to be mayor." Despite her desire, it was difficult for her to call the nine members of the city council and tell them she was interested in the mayor's position. "I can remember saying to myself, 'Joanell, if you want to do this you have to call these people, even if there are some you don't know or have any kind of relationship with [sic].'" The city council, which had the task of electing the new mayor, took five ballots to decide. After the first ballots, three candidates were eliminated, leaving Joanell and a man who had been on the city council for seventeen years and had also run unsuccessfully for mayor. On the fourth ballot, the council was tied four to four. On the fifth ballot, a chamber member changed his vote and the man was elected five to three. When the new mayor's term ended one year later, Joanell ran in the primary in March, 1985. She received the largest number of votes and went on to win the general election in April, taking office in May, 1985. She had garnered sixty-four percent of the vote.

Joanell Dyrstad served three terms as mayor of Red Wing, winning reelection with as much as ninety percent of the vote. She looks with pride on her accomplishments as mayor. "We redid the downtown streets and restored Riverfront Center and the new park and the parking ramp behind it. The train depot was renovated and we purchased a business park and development area and brought a couple of businesses in."

The Sheldon Theater, built in 1904, was dilapidated and the community had to decide what to do with it. While she was mayor, Joanell led a private fund drive that raised $1.5 million and passed a public referendum that raised an additional $1.5 million to pay for the theater's restoration. Red Wing now has the first municipally owned theater in the country. She recognizes that while some of this would have happened regardless of who had been mayor, she takes credit for two achievements that would not have taken place without her leadership.

One was a downtown memorial to war veterans. The First Minnesota Regiment had distinguished itself at the battle of Gettysburg during the Civil War, with over seventy percent killed or wounded, and many of the soldiers who fought had been from Goodhue County. Joanell worked with the historic preservation group in Red Wing and local veterans to design and build a memorial that lists the names of all county residents killed in service to their country.

The second accomplishment, of great significance to her, was the building of sidewalks along some streets in the newer areas of town that were used by children walking to school. "Fortunately, that was not triggered by a child being killed walking to school," she says. "But we just couldn't let this go on any longer. A tragedy was going to occur."

To gain support for sidewalks, Joanell organized a group of citizens who counted children walking in the street and illustrated the problem with videos. As a stop-gap measure, Joanell ordered white lines painted on the thoroughfare and the children were told to stay within the three-foot space. "In the wintertime, when there was snow on the road, it was so dangerous it was unbelievable," she said. Some property owners complained that they did not want sidewalks put in because it would destroy their shrubs—plantings that they had actually planted on the city right of way. Other property owners objected because they would have to change the angle of their driveways or move retaining walls. By getting the citizens together, Joanell worked out a compromise. The property owners paid just for the sidewalk in front of their property and the city picked up any additional expenses. Joanell's husband lost business at the drugstore because some of the people who lived on the affected streets and objected to the sidewalks would no longer patronize the mayor's store. Joanell had no problem with that. "It was the right thing to do," she says. "Those sidewalks would not have been put in if I had not been mayor," she says. "To this day I see them and feel good."

Joanell resigned her position as mayor of Red Wing at the end of 1990 to become Lieutenant Governor of Minnesota in the administration of Arne Carlson. She was the twenty-fifth woman in the United

States to be elected a Lieutenant Governor. Four women, all Republicans, were elected to that office in the same year she was. Joanell credits Marlene Johnson with setting the stage for another woman in that position. During Marlene's tenure, her office had been in a suite of rooms on the far east side of the capitol where she seldom saw or had contact with Governor Perpich.

Joanell and Governor Carlson decided to change that arrangement. Joanell and her staff of three moved into offices directly off the Governor's reception room. Her office was on the east side of the public reception area and the governor's was on the west side. "That made a big difference," she said. "I was right in the middle of everything and was there for policy discussions with the governor." Among the areas Joanell participated in was the selection of judges. "The governor, the chair of the Judicial Selection Committee and I would interview three people and then would discuss among ourselves who we felt would be the best appointment."

One of the tasks Governor Carlson assigned to Joanell was to look into the abortion issue. She formed a committee composed of both pro and anti-choice representatives, medical personnel, and state legislators that met to seek common areas of agreement on the divisive issue. "We did not focus on whether abortion was a good or bad thing, but on what could be done to prevent unintended pregnancies." Our final report was a major achievement but, perhaps because it wasn't controversial, the press ignored it. Our recommendations were never implemented."

An initiative that Joanell undertook herself was to get anti-stalking legislation passed. A St. Paul judge had had an enormous problem with a stalker who left dead animals in her mailbox, slashed her tires and called her at all hours of the night. Because the judge had not been physically harmed, there was little the police could do about it. Legislation to deal with such a situation did not exist. Although Joanell, in the executive branch, could not author legislation herself, she consulted with attorneys and legislators and organized a press conference in the offices of the Women's Consortium in St. Paul. Women who had been victims of stalkers came forward to testify about their experiences, the press gave the meeting major coverage, and anti-stalking legislation was passed. "There are a number of legislators who now get the credit for the legislation, but I got the ball rolling," she said.

Joanell found that, even though she was Lieutenant Governor, other people tended to overlook her. She especially remembers a meeting in the governor's office with representatives of MPR (Minnesota Public Radio) and other staff members. The BBC was planning a program with MPR and wanted the governor to fly to England to participate in events from that side. Arne Carlson felt this was not something he wanted to put his time into. "Though I was sitting right there it never occurred to the people around the table that I would be a good representative from the governor's office." Joanell did end up going but she had to make the suggestion herself (and not openly at the meeting) that she was the appropriate spokesperson. "To this day I remember how frustrated I was." She flew to London with Bill Kling and hosted a reception at the American Embassy in London with British author P.D. James.

Joanell feels there are many times when people take women officials more lightly than they would a man or they do not recognize women who hold public positions. Often when she and her husband were together and would be introduced as the Lieutenant Governor of Minnesota, the person being introduced would hold out his hand to Joanell's husband. "My husband would get this big grin on his face and say, 'It's my wife.'" To save money (the state had a big deficit at the time), Arne and Joanell shared some staff members. She found that the staffs' first allegiance was to the governor and it was sometimes a challenge to get them to do things for her. Joanell believes that was due more to the fact they were dedicated to promoting the governor and his program than because she was a woman.

As part of her duties, Joanell participated in the National Association of Lieutenant Governors and in 1994 was the first woman to be named chairperson of the organization. When the association met in Washington, D.C., it was customary for the Vice-President of the United States to address the group and be introduced by the chair. However, when Joanell was chair, Vice-President Al Gore's staff would not permit her to introduce Gore because she was a Republican! Following her term as Lieutenant Governor, Joanell ran in the IR primary in 1994 for the United States Senate seat won by Rod Grams.

Being a mayor was great preparation to serve as lieutenant governor, Joanell discovered. "Because of the variety of services Red Wing provides I was familiar with things ranging from the cemetery to the fact that the city owns an airport over in Wisconsin, to issues regarding the nuclear power plant (Prairie Island) and the Indian reservation within the city

Lieutenant Governor Joanell Dyrstad

limits. I had had experience with water and sewer treatment plants plus an understanding of the political process." She found it was much easier to get things done as a mayor than as a state official. "You can see the results of what you have done. Overall it takes much more to accomplish something on the state level than it does on the local level provided you have a positive, forward-looking community."

Joanell has found women approach policy decisions in a manner different from men. "I think women are much more willing to listen to other people," she said. "They don't have to be the only power figure, the only one in charge. Women like to take in all of the information before making a decision. Sometimes people think because you are listening and not making snap judgments, that you are incapable of making decisions. Women have to show by their manner and body language that they are able to make timely decisions."

Joanell loved being Lieutenant Governor. She finds it interesting that every Lieutenant Governor since Marlene Johnson has been a woman and that when Skip Humphrey and Allan Quist ran for governor with male running mates they lost. She wonders if the public views the position as one for which a woman is qualified "but they don't want a woman governor."

The third woman to hold the office of Lieutenant Governor was Joanne Benson. Joanne had spent her early childhood on a farm outside of LeSueur, Minnesota, where she and her cousins played freely in the open fields. "We had to devise our own entertainment because we didn't have a lot of things. We were poor, but I didn't know it because everyone else was living the same way. Our entertainment was in the outdoors and in lots of creative play—make-believe and hide-and-seek in the alfalfa field. I would say I was a very happy child."

Joanne's relatives lived near her immediate family on the big hillsides of the Minnesota River Valley. The families would often get together in each other's homes. No one had money for recreation so they would push back the rugs and dance and play cards. At the end of the evening, the women would go into the kitchen and make sandwiches, slice pickles and cut the cake for the group. The children would play around the adults until they dropped off to sleep on the coats on the beds. Joanne remembers an event like that as being "a very warm and wonderful community gathering because it was simple and pleasant. It was just people happy to be together."

Joanne grew up in a strong supportive environment with parents who gave her the belief she could do anything she wanted to do. In addition, Joanne had a brother who was five years older who also encouraged her. She literally cannot recall a single occasion when her brother was ever mean to her, or hit or teased her. As a result she adored him. Looking back on her childhood, Joanne remembers that she and her brother had "a very respectful upbringing. My parents trusted us a lot and gave us a lot of credit for having good instincts and values. They never had to use anything other than very gentle persuasion."

Joanne remembers with great affection the one-room country school where she began her education. The children were a closely-knit group whose parents were supportive of the school. When she entered first grade, Joanne was already reading. As a result, the teacher soon had Joanne giving the reading lesson to the class while she worked with other children. Joanne was not so skilled in arithmetic. She recalls that the teacher and all of the other students would stop their work to celebrate the fact she had mastered something simple, like learning to count by twos. "It was a great experience of loving to learn." The sense of being supported both by parents and a community was a strong influence early in Benson's life. Even as a young child in school, she found that she was valued and had a meaningful role to play. By the time she was in junior high, she was president of many of her school organizations such as Student Council, Spanish Club, Honor Society, and the Future Homemakers of America.

When she was in the third or fourth grade, Joanne decided that she wanted to attend church. Though her parents belonged to a church, they seldom attended. One Sunday, Joanne went with her cousins to a Christmas program the Sunday School was presenting and as she sat there watching the participants, she decided she wanted to be a part of that group of people. On her own, she made arrangements to attend church on a regular basis. "When I was older, I realized it was very strange for a child to lead a family into that. My parents were believers but they just weren't regular church goers."

When Joanne was a junior in high school, her family moved to Glencoe, Minnesota, where they owned a small family business. When they first bought the drive-in restaurant, Joanne, her mother, and brother moved into a small trailer parked in back so they could run the business during the week while her father kept his job as a machinist at Northern Ordinance Company. He came to Glencoe on weekends to help with the restaurant. Joanne's family built up the drive-in business and when it had become successful they purchased a new restaurant in Glencoe. At this point, her father left his machinist job, and together the family ran the new restaurant, which, because it was part of a service station, had to be open, with a family member present, twenty-four hours a day. Joanne remembers that they had only one day off a year, from 4:00 P.M. on Christmas Eve until 4:00 P.M. on Christmas Day.

Joanne worked daily at the restaurant "from the time my nose cleared the counter" until she graduated from high school. She believes that she missed the last five minutes of every school activity, unless she was a participant, because she had to dash back to the restaurant ahead of the school crowd. "Lindy's [the restaurant] was the hang out for the whole town. When school events were over, everyone came to Lindy's." Joanne waited tables, cleared off the dirty dishes, ran the cash register. "In a small restaurant in a small town, you do whatever needs to be done."

Though she began her college career at the University of Minnesota, she soon transferred to St. Cloud State. Because she was married and had children while she was going to college, it took Joanne ten years to complete her degree in elementary education with a minor in special education. Unlike many other professional training programs, one of the required courses for prospective teachers was in human relations. "Only teachers need to be human," she says with some irony. During one of the first days in the class, the instructor asked the students to tell the rest of the students something that they did not like about themselves. Almost every hand in the class went up. Joanne was amazed at how eager the students were to reveal something bad about themselves. When the teacher asked for volunteers to say something they liked about themselves, something they were proud of, no one, except Joanne, raised a hand.

In the discussion that followed, Joanne said that, contrary to most people in our culture who do not accept compliments well, she was eager to accept any good comment that came her way. "I figure it this way. If someone wants to say something nice to me, I will accept it and take it all in. If someone says something bad about me, I may not accept it, but I will take it under advisement."

For another class exercise, the professor asked Joanne to lie down on the floor. Six fellow class members were instructed to hold her down. Joanne was told her task was to try to persuade them to let her up within the three minute period of the experiment. When the three minutes had passed, Joanne had convinced her captors to let her go and she was sitting up. "I just appealed to their better sense, to that better nature in people, and talked them into it," she explained. Another student, a burly young man, was not successful. "He couldn't get up because he kept fighting."

Joanne credits her parents with teaching her the power of empathy. For example, before going to school dances and sock hops, her parents would remind her to look out for a shy cousin and make sure she, too, had invitations to dance. "That was very much a message in our family, that you were responsible not only for yourself but for others." It was this attitude that eventually propelled her into the public arena. "I did not grow up thinking I wanted to be in politics. Rather it was the sense of responsibility that had been instilled in me that, as a citizen, you have to do more than vote."

When Joanne and her husband moved to St. Cloud, they soon became involved in local affairs. Joanne became active in Republican politics, serving as precinct chairperson and chair for her senate district. Though she helped many candidates by working in their campaigns, she had no thought of running for political office herself.

The legislature's closing of the St. Cloud State University's Thomas Gray Campus Lab School in 1983, where Joanne Benson was a teacher, was the event that led her into thinking more seriously about taking an active role in politics. The university Laboratory School was an outstanding institution, more than one hundred years old, with a waiting list in the hundreds. Parents enrolled their children at birth. Shortly before it was forced to close, the school had been visited by experts from Colorado and Michigan who had declared it a national model of stellar elementary education.

"There was an economic downturn in 1982," Joanne explained. "The university was expanding its mission, becoming more comprehensive, and the administration put less value on the lab school. If every department on campus would have taken a little less money, we could have absorbed the costs and kept it going. But we had an interim president at the university, not a permanent president, so there was no one from the higher levels of administration to help us."

In desperation, the parents, faculty, and members of the university's Education Department turned to their state senator, James Pehler, chairman of the Education Committee, for help. Through him they requested funds from the legislature to save the school. Up until the last minute, the parents and staff believed they would receive state assistance, but Pehler was unable to use his influence to get the measure through his own committee, and the school was closed.

"It was very difficult for me because I loved that job at the lab school so much," Joanne said. "My husband asked me if I would teach there even if they did not pay me and I said, 'Yes, I would.' We did workshops for teachers in the field, trained the young students who were becoming teachers. We had a wonderful faculty, with great students and parents. And it was just chopped off. It was bad timing and a bad decision." When funding for the school was turned down, Joanne took a closer look at the legislature. "Boy, you sure need the very best people down there because look what happened to us."

After the lab school closed, the parents came to Joanne and asked her to take it over and move it to a nearby empty school building. They would pay tuition for their children to attend. Benson was surprised that the parents had come to her rather than to the school's principal or other administrators. "They came to me because I was the most passionate and most willing person to take their children and keep the school open." The offer was tempting and she often wonders now what would have happened if she had said, "Yes." Influencing her decision to turn the parents down was the fact that her own children were young and it would have been a huge undertaking, one for which she may not have been professionally and emotionally prepared at that moment. "I didn't have the finances or the guts to do it at the time," she remembers, "and I've often regretted it."

Joanne's experience as a teacher in the lab school did have long range effects. In the mid 1970s, Joanne had started a program with her kindergarten students that has influenced her career ever since. The older students and their teachers became involved in recycling and Earth Day projects and the kindergartners asked their teacher how they could get involved. "What can we do?" they asked. "We are just little kids." Benson asked the children to look around and tell her what they saw that they did not like in their environment. The children pointed out the litter on the playground and in the streets surrounding the school. When Benson asked what they could do about it, the children replied that they could pick it up.

That began Benson's program of every child picking up three pieces of litter a day. With forty kindergarten students at work picking up litter, trash soon became hard to find around the school. Then the children began picking up litter around their homes and neighborhoods, with the result that the entire community became noticeably cleaner. For Joanne, it was a powerful lesson.

"I call it my 'three pieces of litter a day' philosophy. If you see a problem, you figure out what you can do about it. You don't have to solve the whole problem. Just do something that will move toward the solution." Using her class of kindergartners as the example, Benson says, "Start with something you can do. Don't look at the big problems; look at what you can affect right here, in your work, in your family, in your community. If enough people join you, you can make great strides." Benson never abandoned her anti-litter campaign. When she was lieutenant governor of Minnesota, each member of her staff picked up three pieces of litter a day.

For several years, Joanne worked as chairwoman of her senate district essentially by herself. One former chairman had been elected to the state senate and another had moved out of the district. When, after several years, she decided that she had had enough of doing most of the work, she resigned and gave a stirring farewell address. Called her "Just say yes" speech, Joanne told her listeners that if they expected to have good government, they would have to be a part of it. "When you find a candidate you believe in and trust and he comes to you for assistance, just say yes," she told her audience. She ran through a variety of ways to 'just say yes' — to respond to candidates' requests for money, for help with door knocking, to stuff envelopes. By the end of the speech her audience was repeating her "just say yes" litany.

A few months later the Republicans were looking for a candidate to run against Jim Pehler, the long term, entrenched DFL senator who had failed to get the funding to save the lab school. No one would run against him because he had been an incumbent for many years and was thought to be unbeatable. People asked Joanne to run but she turned them down until Bernie Gruenes, a well-respected bank official in St. Cloud, told her if she would run, he would be her campaign manager and she would not have to worry about money. All she would have to do was go out and meet people and sell herself. At 11:00 P.M. on the night before the nominating convention was to begin, Joanne agreed. She was the only candidate and was endorsed at the convention with only one dissenting vote.

No woman had ever before run for a senate seat from that district and while she was well-known in certain circles, in the larger district, Joanne's name recognition was very low. Nevertheless she took a leave from her job as alumni director at St. Cloud State University to mount a vigorous campaign. Midpoint in her efforts she received a call asking her to be part of the National Plowing Contest being held on a farm just outside St. Cloud. Joanne was wary. "Is my opponent doing it?" she asked. When she was told that he was, she agreed to participate.

When Joanne arrived at the field, she discovered there was a celebrity contest before the main plowing event. She was the only woman. The celebrities (politicians and some sports figures) were lined up on one side of the field, and the real plowing contestants were lined up facing them. Each celebrity was to partner with the individual facing him. "An eighteen-year-old young man from Iowa got me. When he realized I was to be his partner, I could see his face fall. He was thinking, 'of all the people I could have been teamed up with, I got this little woman.' He was so competitive. I thought it was funny. I could just read his feelings from his face."

Before the competition began, the partners were allowed to practice on a test plot. Joanne and her partner rode their tractor to their test plot. The young man was permitted to coach Joanne, but he could not do anything to help her except raise and lower the plow share to place it at the right depth for the soil. They started out and the young man began to brighten up. "You're not bad at this," he said. "We could win."

When they went to the field where the real plowing was to be done, they found the soil was sandy and quite different from the test plot. The young man kept having Joanne stop the tractor while he adjusted the plow-share. Every time he made her stop, the tractor zigged and zagged from one side to another. When she came back for her second pass on the field she noticed two farmers standing at the side looking at her field. One said to the other, "She plows the way my son does after he comes home from a Saturday night bender." Joanne and her partner came in next to last in the plowing contest. But she was jubilant because last place went to Pehler. "He had been so cocky he had not come in for the practice, so I won."

A few weeks later, she used the incident when she introduced Vice President George Bush who had come to Minnesota for a fund-raiser for Arlen Stangland. When Bush stood up to speak, he looked at Joanne and remarked, "I don't know about you, but I think she is going to give him fits." Election night came, and Joanne lost to James Pehler by 300 votes. Though she felt sorry for the people who had worked hard on her campaign, she felt as if she had had a victory. "I was a candidate who came out of nowhere," she said. "And I went from there to almost winning."

When the next election cycle came around she ran again but Pehler did not and Joanne won election to the Senate by a large margin. She knew her second campaign was going well when, at a St. Cloud community celebration surrounded by friends, she felt a tap on her shoulder and a woman said, "When you turn around, don't faint." Joanne turned around and did almost faint because the person who had tapped on her shoulder was one of the leaders of the DFL party in St. Cloud. The woman said, "I just wanted you to know that I am going to vote for you. I can't think of a thing you've done that I would change."

One of Joanne's most difficult experiences in her political life took place while serving in the Senate. The Women's Right to Know Bill had been passed by the House and was coming to the Senate. The bill would have required women seeking an abortion to have a waiting period between seeing her doctor for information and making her decision. Joanne has been pro-life all of her life and she voted for the bill, which passed the Senate. Right after the vote was taken, the Republican senators met with Governor Arne Carlson's chief of staff who told them the governor would veto the bill if it stayed the way it was. No one had any doubt that Governor Carlson would do what he said he would.

The Women's Right to Know legislation was attached to a larger welfare reform bill, one that Joanne had worked on for hundreds of hours. A veto of the Women's Right to Know Bill would mean a veto of the entire welfare reform bill. Joanne wanted both sections of the bill to survive. Dean Johnson, the Senate Republican leader, went to Joanne and asked her to meet with three Republican women senators, two of whom were pro-choice and one of whom was pro-life, to see if they could not work out a compromise that would be acceptable to the governor. For an intense few days, Senators Linda Runbeck and Joanne Benson, who were pro-life, met with Senators Martha Robertson and Sheila Kiscaden, who were pro-choice, to work on the parts of the bill the governor found problematic. The four women worked diligently and eventually came up with language that was acceptable to all of them. "We were quite proud of ourselves that we could get together and close this huge gap between us. We thought, symbolically, if we could do it, if we could get beyond this division over abortion, the larger group could as well."

Joanne was the one chosen to give the speech about the bill on the floor of the Senate. Arne Carlson later told Joanne it was the best speech he had ever heard. "It came from the heart," she says, "and it was very emotional for me. You can't get into this subject without it getting really rough. I knew I would probably be criticized by people whose support I wanted, but it was worthwhile to see if we could get somewhere on this issue. And then Senator Don Samuelson tabled the bill. He took it out of consideration. I tried and tried but he would never take it off the table. Samuelson was being pressured by the pro-life organizations who did not want our modified bill to go through."

Joanne paid a huge price for her actions. "The pro-life organizations were upset with me for working to modify the bill. They characterized me as trying to kill it because they said I was trying to help the governor—which I wasn't trying to do at all. I was trying to help us get something passed and signed. It was very hard. I am pro-life. They should have been my friends." Joanne learned that the issue would not go away and she would not be forgiven for her efforts at compromise. She found that the incident pursued her when she ran for her party's endorsement for governor. "They were still saying the same thing, which was untrue. Some of it was malicious. I thought I was purer than pure because I had tried to make it happen." Friends asked her, "Why did you even try to do anything with abortion? It is like touching an electric wire."

A happier result of the experience was the close bond that developed among the four women senators who had worked together to modify the bill. They had adopted the philosophy that they really shouldn't be arguing about it. If the governor was a stumbling block because of a few words here and there, they believed they could change the wording and still have a good bill. Others also rallied to Joanne's defense. Duane Benson, a Republican leader, wrote that she had done a very courageous thing and was right to have done it. Tim Penny called and said, "I know what you are going through. I've been there. You did the right thing."

Joanne has wondered, since that experience, if she would do what she did again, knowing that her actions may have been a factor in her being rejected by her party for governor. She thinks that she would. "If you get into a position where you have an opportunity to make things happen and you don't take it, you regret that, too. I'd rather do it and fail and suffer for it, than always wonder if I'd tried, could I have made a difference. You can't second-guess it later. I thought it was the right thing to do then. I still think it was right now."

Joanne discovered, when she became lieutenant governor, that there was no little handbook that told her how to be a lieutenant governor. While she could look at what other holders of the office had done in the past, the job was essentially hers to shape. Requests came in to her office by the hundreds, and she needed a framework with which to evaluate them. She decided that her work would be guided by three Cs: citizenship, communication ("because that is what government is all about, listening and responding and sharing ideas"), and celebration. "The governor and lieutenant governor have to be the celebrators of all that is good that is going on in the state," she said.

Benson characterizes herself as being an optimistic person who believes that most people want the same kinds of things. The politician's role is to marshal that concern so that people understand they have a common self-interest. She is a strong believer in the power of small individual acts. Benson advises anyone in politics to keep perse-

Lieutenant Governor Joanne Benson

vering. "You can't overestimate perseverance. There is a little trail in St. Cloud that exists today because I would not let it drop. It was vetoed and I just kept coming back and coming back. Politics is really the art of persuading and accommodating other people's issues and needs as much as you can and just pushing on. Some people go at their work with a very cerebral bent and some go at it very emotionally driven. I think the combination of the head and the heart together makes a person really effective. You can't be driven too hard by either one — you have to have both."

The fourth woman to hold the office of lieutenant governor is Mae A. Schunk, an elementary school teacher and administrator from St. Paul. She was elected with Governor Jesse Ventura, whose first term expires in 2003.

$\text{C}\text{R}9\text{ED}$

"Now we are expected to be as wise as men who have had generations of all the help there is, and we scarcely anything." —Louisa May Alcott

As the women's movement slowed in the 1980s and some feminists experienced self-doubts, others called for a renewed traditionalism celebrating homemaking and child-rearing and urging a renewed focus on family life. They argued that the women's movement had confused and misled women by urging them to deny their natural functions. They held feminists responsible, in part, for the disruptions in American society—everything from the divorce rate to troubles affecting the nation's young. The theme of a return to more traditional sex roles became prominent in political speeches, sermons, television programs, and, most especially, women's magazines, where articles abounded pointing out that working women were reportedly yearning for more time at home with their children and spouses.

Despite these calls for women to return to traditional roles, by the end of the decade, some facts were apparent. Polls showed that large majorities of Americans supported the principles of equal rights for women and a woman's right to choose abortion. Indeed, most women believed that the women's movement had significantly improved their lives. In 1982, over 900 women in the United States held positions as state legislators, compared with 344 a decade earlier. EMILY's list, an organization to raise funds for female candidates nation-wide, was founded in 1984.

The number of working women rose in the 1980s. Nearly two million women with infants, or over half of all new mothers, were in the labor force in 1988 compared with less than one-third in 1976. The increase in working mothers put a strain on already inadequate child-care facilities. Cuts in federal funding for child-care, passed in the early 1980s, profoundly affected its availability, especially for lower-income mothers. As baby-boomers began to have children of their own, the demand for adequate child-care increased still further. By 1988, politicians took note of this new concern as polls showed that most Americans favored the use of their tax money to create child-care options for working parents.

Entering political life at the end of the 1980s and the beginning of the 1990s was a group of educated, socially savvy women. They had grown up with the women's movement, watched women being awarded equal status in sports under Title IX, had a realistic understanding of their talents and potential, and came onto the scene prepared to be heard. Not for them was a secondary, helpful-woman-in-the-background place in politics. They would confront head-on the stereotype of "naïve women" and challenge anyone who tried to assign them a lesser role.

Karen Anderson, the future mayor of Minnetonka, remembers an early childhood in which she was able to roam freely over a countryside that was largely open space. Though Anderson's home was in a suburb of Chicago, the area was rural at the time. "We had chickens and rabbits and ducks right there on our property. At the age of eight, I had a lot of freedom to explore the natural environment" she remembers. "I would go alone into the woods and creeks and fields, and that was fine with my family. They must have had some faith in my being able to take care of myself. I ice skated on the river that was near our house. That was a dangerous activity and kids aren't allowed to do that nowadays. I took baths in the creek and found a pasture with horses in it. I knew I wasn't supposed to go in that horse pasture but I did and I made friends with the horses. I treasure that physical freedom I had. Kids can't have that today because the world is not a safe place. I was a good girl, obeyed and respected the rules. So while I was adventurous and a tomboy, I toed the line. I was fearful of my father and my father's punishment. I don't recall him being physically abusive but he could be verbally abusive."

The sense of physical freedom, of being able to roam over a countryside and take small risks, even those of parental displeasure, helped Karen become self-reliant, courageous and not afraid of a challenge. Growing up, Karen, the third of four children, was also an avid reader.

Her parents provided a variety of books for their children who were encouraged to read. Karen could read anything she wanted with one exception, comic books. "My father and mother encouraged me to read and would find books for me. So I had intellectual freedom and physical freedom."

Karen's father was on the city council of the Chicago suburb where she grew up so being a part of local government seemed like a normal part of life to her. Previously her father had served as police magistrate and his best friend, through the early years of her childhood, was the town mayor. This did not mean, however, that she grasped the finer points of political competition. While Chicago politics under Mayor Richard Daley were dominated by the Democratic Party, residents of the suburbs, including Anderson's parents, were Republican. As a young child, Karen heard her parents make disparaging remarks about President Franklin D. Roosevelt. When his death was announced on the radio, Karen went jumping through the house shouting with glee, "The president's dead! The president's dead!" Having heard nothing but terrible comments about President Roosevelt, she thought this was a wonderful event and everyone would be happy now. Very quickly, she learned that it was one thing to criticize a politician's policies and quite another thing to rejoice over his death. "I think I was spanked for that," Karen said.

That incident, and her parent's attitude, gave her a strong respect for authority. "If you don't like the rules," she says, "work within the system to change them. Until you can work within the system to change it, don't complain about it."

She also learned respect for other people from observing her parents in their small community. Supermarkets had not yet come to her town, and she went with her mother on her weekly rounds to the meat market, the grocery store, the hardware store and saw how respectfully her mother treated everyone, and how they, in turn, responded to her mother. "That's how you operated in a community. There was a man who pushed his cart down our street twice a year to sharpen scissors and knives and my mother treated him with total respect. He was doing a valuable job in the community and that was how you treated everyone."

Because of this attitude of respect, Karen believes that as a young girl she had concerns about issues of fairness and equity. Her teachers in elementary school did not treat the boys and girls differently from each other in terms of learning and performing. Until she reached the junior high level, she remembers being treated on a par with boys. "My class and my classmates were very gender neutral as I remember. I value that." Karen remembers getting into an argument with her second grade teacher over the pronunciation of some words. "I made sure I showed her I was right. I still feel guilty about that."

The sense of equality, though, was tempered by her shyness. From an early age, she wore glasses for near-sightedness and someone started calling her the "intellectual." Though she was not sure what it meant, she knew she did not like the sound of the word. Nor did she like it when her father teasingly called her a "scientific goon." Because she believed herself to be shy, Karen seldom voluntarily participated in class while she was in elementary school. Though she remembers that she usually knew the answers to the teacher's questions, only if she was called on would she give a response.

However, Karen remembers that the women teachers she had in grade school accommodated her shyness and called on her often, enabling her to participate in her classes through elementary school. Male teachers at the elementary level were rare. Karen's fifth grade teacher was a man, but he taught for only two years before being made principal of the school. "I see now, in retrospect, that some of the women teachers in that school certainly should have been promoted before he was."

It was when Karen entered junior and senior high school and had more male teachers that she experienced her first gender differences. Most of the male teachers, for some reason, failed to call on her. "I wasn't assertive enough to say, 'I know those answers, too,'" she recalls. "I always knew them. I was proud of being smart, but I felt that I had to be careful about where I showed how smart I was. So I began to be lost in the shuffle."

Intimidated, afraid of being teased, Anderson found it easier to sit silently in her classes that were taught by male teachers than it was to participate. Fortunately, she was able to develop a close relationship with a few male teachers who went out of their way to engage her. Still, it was always easier for her to participate in classes taught by women teachers. "I think I kind of closed off from the men in those years, starting in junior high."

Despite her reluctance to participate in the classes taught by men, Karen became a leader among her peers. She dates her emergence to a schoolyard fight and her interest in athletics. Karen was playing coed softball in junior high when something she did suddenly triggered the wrath of another player. Karen suspects she got a base hit when the boy wasn't expecting it. In a rage, the boy jumped on top of Karen and started pounding on her.

"I remember turning my head so I'd get his blows on the side of my head and not the front and I saw this friend of mine coming from the opposite side of the school ground as fast as she could and she just beat the devil out of that kid." The two girls eventually got the better of the boy and were continuing to pummel him when teachers pulled them apart. The fight marked a change in Karen's relationships with the other students. They saw that this shy girl had stood up for herself. And Karen felt vindicated when the other student had come to her defense. After the experience of the schoolyard incident, Karen and her friend gained status with their group.

When her teachers assigned group projects, Karen now found herself taking charge. She would make sure all the students had the directions and that everyone followed them. Other students began looking to her as a leader, a role she continued to assume through high school. In Karen's mind, leadership was simply a matter of applying common sense and a system to the problem, "You get the project, you define it and then you go ahead and do it."

Karen perceived, early on, that her approach to work was different from that of most of her friends. "I was a hard worker to the point of being compulsive. As a young girl, I had trouble playing, and I would have to schedule time for play. When I was asked to clean up under our apple trees, I would pick up every last one of those damn rotten apples. I wouldn't quit until they were all picked up. And I would stay outside playing in the snow far beyond getting cold. That's where I didn't have common sense. I would get so intent on doing something that I wanted to finish that I would do it beyond the point of reason."

When she entered junior high, Karen discovered that girls were excluded from organized athletics. In elementary school, she had competed in sports with the boys. But when she entered junior high, she found that there was an absolute separation of the sexes. While the boys were encouraged to continue competing in sports, the girls no longer had an opportunity to participate.

A major effort was required of both the girl athletes and their coaches if they were to engage in competition. To enable the girls to compete

in sports at even a minimal level, the women coaches had to locate a station wagon and, on their own, set up events with coaches they knew in
other schools. Girls' sports were not allotted school time so their athletic events had to be conducted on Saturdays. The girls had to contribute
money to pay for their transportation and other expenses. For Karen,
who had grown up playing sports with the boys, had been accepted as
part of the team and had had positive experiences with athletics, it was
profoundly disappointing to find that, in junior and senior high school,
her achievements in this area no longer meant anything. "I questioned
why the boys could do things the girls couldn't do but I never acted on
my concerns. No one acted on them. I guess the way we acted on them
was to find a way to compete among ourselves."

The girls who were willing to be identified as athletes also took
some social risks. "Because the women high school teacher-coaches
were looked on as being lesbians, it was somewhat risky to put yourself
in their camp. But we just did, that's all. We didn't take our cause into
the public arena but we took a risk by identifying ourselves with the
athletic group. We were not the cheerleader group, we were the jocks."

The question of religion was a complicated one for Karen Anderson.
Her parents had been reared in different churches, but when their children were small, they attended the same church as a family. When a
major political upheaval took place in the church, Karen's father left, to
return only for ceremonial occasions as weddings and funerals. Karen
and her mother continued to attend and participate in the life of the
congregation until two events occurred that caused Karen to put some
distance between herself and organized religion.

When she was in the eight-to-ten-year-old age group, she participated in a modern dance program at her church. "It must have been
someone new in the community who got a group of young girls together and taught us this wonderful modern dance that was very free spir-
ited and moving. We had these flowing white dressy costumes that
were modern and free form." When the group performed their dance
for the congregation, instead of giving its approval, the audience members were appalled. "They obviously saw something sexual in it. Young
girls, they believed, should not be encouraged to move freely and wear
loose garments that you could almost see through. We had had such a
wonderful time doing the dance, and I was shocked by this reaction
from the church. It made no sense to me."

The second incident occurred when it appeared to Karen that the pastor of the congregation was not living up to the precepts he was expounding from his pulpit. The congregation was an all-white one, and the pastor repeatedly urged the members to welcome people from different racial backgrounds to the church. The pastor's attitude visibly changed, however, when his daughter came home from college with an African-American friend and brought him to church with her. "I saw the hypocrisy there. So at an early age, while I loved my friends at the church and the social part of the experience, I identified the hypocrisy. The church wasn't that important to me. I was able to deal with my issues and satisfy my community needs in other ways."

Karen's mother had gone to work full time when Karen was ten-years old and she was looked after by her paternal grandmother. This woman was a strong figure, independent and active in the community. She told Karen that she could do anything in life that she wanted to do. "I got that message more from her than from my own parents," Karen remembered. "She lived longer than my mother, and I received a great deal of unconditional love and support from her."

When she entered college, Karen lost some of her reticence and became more outspoken. Though she was initially unsuccessful, Anderson worked with her college sorority to admit Jewish women. "Some of my good friends whom I had met in the dormitory setting were Jewish and I really valued them, and I was shocked and alarmed that they weren't allowed to join the sorority. Several of us spoke out to the leadership of the sorority and appeared before the board and encouraged it to be open. I also invited my Jewish friends to come with me to the house and participate in things. It was several years later that the organization opened up."

Growing up in the Chicago area, Karen Anderson early in life observed that the city was run by a very closed and possibly corrupt Democratic system based on money and underhanded, dishonest deal-ings. Few women were involved in politics. Karen and her husband moved to Minnesota in 1964 when she was twenty-four years old and soon realized that while ethical government may not have been valued in the Chicago area where she grew up, it was in Minnesota. The con-trast between Minnesota and Chicago was immediately apparent. "It was a wide-open political system in Minnesota in those days and you could get involved in your community," she remembers. "Women were still not accepted into public office but I worked for the first woman who ran for the city council in Minnetonka and joined the League of Women Voters as soon as we moved here." Karen and her husband joined a church the day after they moved to Minnesota. "It was a Unitarian Church and the members were very progressive, with forward thinking women who were into issues and causes and that just hooked me."

Karen credits both the League of Women Voters and Alanon with helping her understand and validate her feelings as a woman. Because she had been a tomboy in her youth, she felt that she had devalued many of the feminine aspects of her nature. Showing emotion, such as crying, or relying on feelings for making decisions had not been looked on favorably. By working through the Alanon program, she was able to appreciate the feminine side of her nature and look more favorably on the early women in her life. "I was able to recognize the competitive part of my nature and value it rather than putting it down as something that women shouldn't be. It's all right for women to be competitive and powerful and take the credit. That was something I had to work on and learn."

When Karen is considering an issue, she now takes into consideration her feelings about the problem first. From there she gathers the facts and the data. It was not easy for her to learn to trust her emotions. "I had to learn by experience to trust my gut. I know successful elected men who are able to do that too, and I've learned from them. That's helped me reinforce valuing those traits that are sometimes seen as more female. When I have seen male role models calling on their own intuition and feelings and making decisions based on them, that has helped me."

Drawing on her feelings of being kept out of sports as a girl, Karen has fought for equal athletic opportunities for women. When her own daughter was on the first girls' soccer team in Minnetonka, she discovered that the girl's team did not have its own first aid kit, but had to share one with the junior varsity boy's soccer team. If one of the girls got hurt, the coach would have to get the first aid kit from the boy's team to treat an injured player. Karen was outraged and began making phone calls to the high school when her daughter took her aside. "Mom," she said. "You've really done a good job fighting your own battles. This one is mine. And I need you to stay out of it." Karen backed off, and soon the girls' soccer team got its own first aid kit.

Karen Anderson was elected to the Minnetonka City Council in 1986 and served through 1994 when she became the first woman to be elected mayor of the city. Her initial network was the PTA and the League of Women Voters. "The League really trained me for my elected positions, taught me how to research issues, to always have a factual base, and to call upon networks of support when I wanted to move something ahead." In the beginning, her resources were predominantly female but over time they broadened to include most of the community.

Karen says it took eight years of service on the council to become part of the "male hierarchy and male processing system" before she could run for mayor. Then when she ran for mayor she had the support of the two previous mayors of Minnetonka and the male and female members of the city council. As a result of her council experience, she felt at home with the position of mayor and found that she knew how to work within the system and its processes. "I don't have to force the issue as a woman any more," she says. "I know how to open doors, how to call on all the resources in the community and within my network. I do not have to rely so much on women to get things done as I had to early on. I don't feel like a woman alone any more."

Karen did feel like a woman alone when she ran for Second Vice President of the National League of Cities, an organization in which she is active. Three candidates, two women and one man, were running for the position. To Karen's shock, a prominent women's organization endorsed the male candidate because he appeared to be the strongest voice for women's issues. "They never asked us the questions about women's issues and I never thought to raise them," she lamented. "I thought all these women were my buddies. I had worked with them on women's issues for years." The man was able to co-op the women's vote for the endorsement but he lost the election. Karen won and learned from that experience that each new generation of women needs to be educated about women's issues and the problems faced by women. At the time of the endorsement vote, there had been many younger women in the room. Enough of her old friends had failed to show up that the endorsement had slipped away from them.

Women bring a different style to leadership and government, according to Karen. They look for partnerships, cooperation and ways to work with other people to get the job done. "In the past five years, all of a sudden, it has become popular in cities to have collaborative efforts of all kinds. I give women a great deal of credit for this. Women have introduced this partnership style and brought a willingness to do the job without needing to take the credit. Women can organize a partnership and it won't matter if there are seven people in it, so long as the job gets done and it serves the citizens. Women see the right thing to do and do it. It has to do with sharing power. Women are willing to share power rather than hoard it or use it in a political way." Karen says she sees changes in the direction of cooperative power-sharing taking place in city governments all over the country and believes the shift began about ten years ago when more women were elected to office.

Despite the changes they have been able to bring about, women mayors are still only about ten to fifteen percent of the total number, both in Minnesota and around the country. Women chief executives govern slightly more than half of the population of the Twin Cities Metropolitan area, holding the mayor's office in Minneapolis, Bloomington, Eden Prairie, Plymouth, Minnetonka, Burnsville, Eagan, and Coon Rapids.

When she took office as mayor, Karen set about revamping the citizen participation on boards and commissions and opening up the process by which people were recruited and appointed. Then she began to forge partnerships. Though there is now a long list of them, the first partnership was with the Hopkins School District to build the Lindberg Center, a community athletic facility. When she came into office, people told her that there was intense rivalry among the three school districts within the City of Minnetonka. She was warned not to work with any of the districts because of the impossibility of giving each district equal attention, with the result that the other two would be jealous.

Karen was not deterred. She determined that there had never, within anyone's memory, been a meeting between the Minnetonka City Council and the Hopkins School Board. Karen called a joint meeting of the two institutions to talk about things they could do together. Two years later the Lindberg Center was inaugurated. Since then she has had a partnership with the City of Hopkins to rebuild the Shady Oak Beach Facility and similar relationships with other surrounding communities. Every two or three months, she meets with the mayors of the fourteen towns that surround Lake Minnetonka. While it has been the women who have taken the lead in collaborating with other organizations, Karen says "once they get going, the men foster them just as much. It is wonderful."

The provision of affordable housing is another area in which Karen takes pride. (This was an issue that Joan Growe championed for Minnetonka in the late 1960s as a member of the League of Women Voters.) The city has received national awards for a model mixed-use housing complex. In the past four years, under Karen's administration, the city has approved over 500 units of new or renovated affordable housing within the city. This was not accomplished without opposition and "the city council had to make some very courageous decisions." She credits members of the faith community with helping educate their congregations. Working with MICAH (Metropolitan Interfaith Council on Affordable Housing) she called together a dozen priests, rabbis, and ministers and explained the problem. "Will you help us?" she asked. "Without exception, they jumped right on board and began preaching about housing from the pulpit and assisting us in community education efforts. That has paid off."

The most volatile and hostile issue she has had to deal with as mayor is the deer management program. There were more white-tailed deer in the city than it could deal with and the deer were involved in over 150 car-deer accidents a year, causing considerable damage. "It became a public safety issue." Working with the DNR (Department of Natural Resources) she started a program at first called a "deer removal" program. In actual fact, it was a "trap-and-kill program." As Karen explained, you cannot tranquilize deer and move them a distance away from the city because they die. Less than ten percent of deer survive being removed. The only solution was to slaughter the excess deer and give the meat to a food shelf. "Our goal was to keep a viable, healthy deer herd in the city. And we are successful in doing that. The numbers are manageable and people can see deer in their back yards but not with the terrible public safety problem." There was much opposition to the program at first and Karen received a serious threat at her home. The city maintains ongoing education about the animal control program, especially with children and new residents. She still gets calls from homeowners saying either, "Get those deer out of my yard!" or "Why are you killing Bambi?"

Women will occasionally ask Karen why she works full time as mayor for such a low salary ($9,600 a year). She replies that she does it for the power. "I appreciate being in a position where I can make positive changes in my community. That is the kind of power I am talking

Minnetonka Mayor Karen Anderson

about. I acknowledge that power and believe it is important for women to talk about it. It takes power to bring about good things in our communities. Give me power and that's fine."

Karen has also observed, to her sorrow, that the initial opposition, and even roadblocks, for women running for office often comes from other women. "That jealousy is still there, less than it was in the beginning, but it is still there." Both men and women still expect a female official to be better prepared than a man. More is expected of women in leadership roles than is of men. "I just kind of accept that and keep going. None of us can meet everyone's expectations."

Karen seldom sees herself as a woman elected official any more except when she is meeting with the Girl Scouts, the Brownies, and the kids in the schools. "Then I am a role model and I connect with the girls and young women," she says. "That's fun."

As a young girl Rep. Mindy Greiling saw women being teachers, secretaries, or nurses, and thought that those were the only career options open to her. She had an aunt who was a nurse and her mother worked in a clerical position at the Mayo Clinic in Rochester. Members of her mother's family farmed near Rochester while her father's family was from West Virginia. "We were very much the you-don't-fight-city-hall type of people, or at least the women didn't. I had a lot of women relatives who would not ever have challenged anything. Children, too, were to be seen and not heard. We were taught to respect our elders. I don't remember ever being encouraged to do anything but what we were told."

The big annual event in Mindy's life as a child was her family's Fourth of July picnic. The picnics were held on a farm outside of Rochester and relatives came from as far away as Indiana to attend the family affair which was a big reunion of aunts, uncles, and cousins who lived on neighboring farms. "They took the day off, which for farmers who had cows (which most of them did) was quite an occasion," she remembers. "They had to milk the cows in the morning and then get back home in time to milk them again in the evening."

During the picnic, to Mindy's bemusement, the men would usually engage in heated discussions of politics. "They looked like they were having a lot of fun, but it was also kind of funny that they got so riled up about it. We'd all been well fed, it was a hot afternoon, and yet there they would be going on about things they didn't have to get quite so emotional about." Mindy observed that the women, who were either in the kitchen or cleaning up after the meal, did not participate in the discussions. Politics, Mindy decided early in her life, was a man's domain.

In the evening, everyone would go into town for the Fourth of July fireworks sponsored by the city of Rochester. It looked to Mindy as if the whole city parked by her house. Mindy lived a block from the lake, so the children could sit on their front steps to see the people go by and then watch the fireworks. Half of Rochester, it seemed, would be there. "It felt like a real small-town civic activity. We had the family portion in the morning on the farm and then the whole city and our neighborhood kids in the evening. Best of all, we . . . got to stay up late."

It was when she was in the third grade in the Rochester Public Schools that Mindy made the career decision that she wanted to be a teacher. Every year, when school was out in the spring, Mindy and her sister, who was a year older, would collect the school papers the teachers were throwing out and use them to play school during the summer. Because she was older, Mindy's sister played the role of the teacher while Mindy was required to be the student who took orders and did all of the work. Despite that disadvantage, Mindy continued to play the game with her sister because of her tremendous enjoyment of school. She remembers that she excelled in everything except athletics and music. "I took piano for five years, struggled along, and still could hardly play anything."

In third grade, Mindy formed a friendship with a boy named Dennis, who was also a good student. The two competed with each other to see who could get the best spelling papers or the highest grades on their assignments and in the process became good friends. Dennis was a fat little boy who, though he was good at school, was picked on by his classmates. Mindy observed that Dennis, when he was teased, "would crumble into this kind of whiny kid because he wasn't sure of himself." Once safe in his own yard, however, Dennis would regain his self-confidence and he and Mindy would skate together on the rink in his back yard.

Observing his son's problems, Dennis' father ordered the boy to fight back at his tormentors. "You shouldn't take that from them," he said. "You have to fight. When they do that to you, go ahead and sock them in the nose." One day the father came upon his son and Mindy with a kid who was tormenting Dennis and he insisted that Dennis fight. "I don't want to," wailed Dennis, as he swung. Dennis was crying harder than the boy he hit. Mindy, who was observing the whole exchange ("typical girl thing, just watching"), thought that Dennis' dad was making a mistake. She realized that the aggressor boy was afraid, not of Dennis, but of Dennis' father, who was a large man. "I think they were both afraid of the Dad, kind of playing out this little drama." Dennis was in Mindy's school for only a year when his family moved to Iowa. For a time they corresponded, her first pen pal, until the letters from Dennis finally stopped coming. Though she never heard from Dennis again, Mindy remembers the incident as the time she first became aware of the sometimes hidden motivations and pressures that affect the way people behave.

Mindy's discovery that she could influence other children came about when she had two playmates, a boy and a girl, who were always bickering. When she played with them individually, they got along, but when both were together with Mindy there would be a battle. One day she announced to the two children that if they were going to argue and fight she would go home. In the future, if they wanted to play with her, they would have to do it one at a time and take turns. To her surprise, they agreed. The two children actually kept track of whose day it was to play with Mindy. One would come one day and the next day the other child would come. This continued for an entire summer with Mindy continually amazed at the effect her determined stand had had on the other two children. "That gave me a sense of power at that young age," she remembers.

In school, Mindy was not a leader who would challenge authority but a follower who did whatever the teacher said. She was never a troublemaker and she idolized her teacher. Though she was not good at athletics, Mindy excelled at everything else at school and was competitive in her academic subjects. She believes that she tended to be competitive in the areas where she was competent. "If I'm not so good at something, then I hang back and I'm not competitive at all. Whatever the teacher wanted to have done, I would do as well as I could. I never tried to do anything there in terms of leadership. Outside of school, among my circle of friends, I was the leader. If I didn't want to play something, all I had to do was withhold myself and they would usually change the game because they didn't want to play without me. They usually had more fun with me than they did without me. I was kind of manipulative, I think, in that regard."

In elementary school, when children nominated their peers for class offices, Mindy would always be nominated and elected. In high school, however, the candidates nominated themselves. Mindy never nominated herself for an office because there wasn't any office she was particularly interested in. "Besides, I don't think it would have occurred to me to nominate myself." Nevertheless, Mindy often found herself president of organizations. "I saw it as doing a service. I was more interested in having things working properly or serving the organization than I was in a title."

In high school she was named the class representative to the student council, a position she did not appreciate. "Actually I thought it was kind of a waste of time. We all left the classroom and went down to the library to discuss things. One of the things I have always hated is a lot of people sitting around talking just to hear themselves talk with nothing coming of it. I didn't see that we were making any real decisions. It seemed like a make-work thing. All we did was take down notes of what the principal said and report back to the class. I think the principal had the idea that it looked good to have a student council in the school. But if we actually had had ideas and wanted to do something, he wouldn't have been open to that. When I went to the meetings I would be sorry that I had missed what was happening in the classroom. That was always more interesting to me than the student council."

Mindy's first political debate took place at one of the family Fourth of July picnics. She got into an argument with her cousin whose father was supporting John Kennedy for president. Mindy was arguing for Richard Nixon because her family was Republican. "We discussed the

Catholic dimension because we were all Protestants. That was the hey-day of the Catholic jokes and folks told nasty Catholic jokes about priests. There was a lot of prejudice against Catholics among my rela-tives, so religion was something they held against Kennedy. Even my relatives who supported Kennedy took great pains to say 'It's not like he's going to be one heartbeat from the Pope.'" Mindy's social studies class held a mock election that year and John Kennedy won over-whelmingly "because everybody thought he was cuter." In the general election, however, to Mindy's gratification, Richard Nixon carried the Minnesota city of Rochester.

When she was in the fourth grade, Mindy's class took a field trip from Rochester to the state capitol where Governor Rolvaag spoke to her class. She was surprised to find him to be a short man, not much taller than she was. Governors, she had supposed, would be tall men. Later, the class visited some committee hearings and saw the rooms filled with men. "There were no women anywhere. It was all men dis-cussing politics at the Capitol. If there were any women there at the time, which I don't think there were, I didn't see any of them." The field trip to the Capitol reinforced Mindy's belief that politics was an activi-ty reserved only for men.

Not until she was in college at Gustavus Adolphus did Mindy find a cause to which she could devote herself. Though it was the height of the Vietnam War protest movement, only a few students at Gustavus (those Mindy thought of as a fringe element) were involved. What engaged her attention was the system of registration for dormitory rooms for the next year. The system being used by the college for room selection was for stu-dents to show up on a first come, first serve basis. Because a new dormi-tory had been built, there was large demand for the new rooms. Mindy had been through "room rush" in the past and had been dismayed by the mob of students who pushed and shoved to get to the front of the line and secure their choice of rooms. Those who were not so aggressive were left out. That struck her as being essentially unfair.

Mindy and a friend organized a number system for room assign-ments. They printed off the numbers, got student approval of the new system, passed the numbers out in a manner that seemed reasonable to the students and expected the college administration to go along with the plan. However, when the time came to assign rooms Mindy and her friend suddenly discovered that the administration was not planning to follow the number system they had devised "because it wasn't their idea, I think" and were intending to keep the old method in place.

Though Mindy's friend crumpled at the administration's resistance, Mindy went in alone to argue for their system. "I was really mad about it, so I decided I might as well go and vent about it. Usually my periods of bravery are tied in with my being mad. If I'm not mad, then I'm not nearly as brave. We had invested all that time and they were just kicking us aside because we were young students — maybe even because we were young female students."

Mindy's advocacy was successful. The number system she and her friend had devised was used to assign rooms that year and the year after, which was Mindy's last year at Gustavus Adolphus College. As to the room she was assigned, it was in the new building where she had wanted to be but the building itself "turned out to be a dog of a dorm. All the older dorms were much nicer." According to Mindy, the new building, the first co-ed dorm built at Gustavus, turned out to be noisy with small rooms built of cheap cinder block construction. "All these years later it's probably the last dorm anyone would pick," she remembers ruefully.

The Fourth of July picnics and community celebrations of her childhood in Rochester gave Mindy an appreciation for neighborhood cohesiveness that has never left her. She finds that sense of community lacking in the suburbs, which she represents. "I'm always kind of envious of the legislators who have a community," she comments. "I can go to Roseville and be as apt to see someone from another state as from Roseville, and there is no gathering place." Taking the place of community for Mindy and also making up her political base are three organizations: the PTA, the League of Women Voters, for which she served on the state board, and church friends from the Hamline United Methodist Church in Roseville.

Mindy's role models for political action came from her mother's side of the family where many of the men served on school and county boards. "There was a kind of community service bred within the male part of my relatives." The men were at the level of government where they provided the services needed, sometimes housing the rural school teacher or helping pick out the books for the school. (She also has a cousin who serves on a township board.)

Mindy's first experience with elective office came when she was recruited to run for the Roseville Area School Board. She was PTA president at the time and the only woman member of the board urged her to run. "She had certain issues she was strong on and she knew I agreed with her on those," Mindy recalls. While she was serving on the school board Senator John Marty asked her to run for the legislature. "I never would have gone into politics if I hadn't been recruited," she said. "I think that's probably true of a lot of women." John Marty, she said, was looking for someone who had been active in the community, had name recognition and agreed with him on issues. "He was having to run in a new territory and he knew I would work hard so I kind of fit into his agenda." Mindy was elected to the Minnesota House of Representatives in 1992.

Following that election old-timers, Joan Growe, Phyllis Kahn, Linda Berglin, and other female veterans of the legislature, invited the new women to lunch at the Minnesota Club (a bastion of male power) in downtown St. Paul. There the experienced legislators explained to the newcomers the good work that already had been done and welcomed them into the fray. The message Mindy got was that women had come a long way in the legislature. "But when I got into the thick of things, I realized we had not come all that far," she lamented.

Mindy came to the legislature as a former elementary school teacher with a female principal where staff members worked together as a team. She either worked in her own room where she had total authority or she worked together with the other school staff. Her ten years of involvement with the League of Women Voters, the PTA, and the Girl Scouts all involved consensus type organizations where no one individual claimed credit and everyone worked together. "No one put their names on League stuff in those days," she said. "Everything was a cooperative effort and no one was so ego-bound that they would want to take credit for the group's work. When she went on the Roseville Area School Board, though it involved both men and women, it was still collaborative because no one was introducing bills and claiming chief author status. "If someone had an idea, that idea did not happen until it became everyone's idea — and there were six of us. Though we argued and fought, by the time we faced the community, we were in agreement. We were not interested in who had the bright idea, or who was wrong — that sort of thing."

The legislature was different from anything Mindy had previously experienced. "I was completely depressed when I was first here," she said. "I was in culture shock." Mindy was appalled at how big many of the members' egos were and, being a first termer, at how powerless she was. She found it hard to distinguish between what was harassment and what was just the nature of the legislature's power and the seniority structure. Mindy believes women get a "double-whammy" because they are not used to fighting for themselves. Most women are used to working for consensus.

Mindy found that the culture of the legislature was geared to fit the male paradigm of hierarchical thinking better than it did the female. As Mindy explained, "In the legislature, there has to be a chief author. That individual gets his name in the papers, receives editorial notice. He does it and it's his thing. He has to be always promoting himself. The idea that you would actually work on something together and everyone would share the credit or blame doesn't work out. An unintended consequence of allowing only one chief author's name on a bill is that lawmakers are motivated to create many small programs, even if they are redundant, so they will have something to show their constituents. To me that is the biggest difference between men and women. Because women are more into achieving consensus, it is harder for them when they come here and try to stick it out."

The class of freshmen legislators who came in with Mindy had two major goals, campaign finance reform and ethics reform. In campaign finance reform, the newcomers succeeded in putting spending caps on how much a large contributor could give to a campaign, spend on lobbyists, contribute to PACS, and on how much a candidate could accept in an election year. Candidates running for the first time were allowed to receive more money than the incumbents. "The idea was to try to level the playing field." They were not totally successful. As Mindy commented, "We did a poor job of plugging up the soft money holes. Now the money goes to the caucuses and it effects the agenda. In some ways it is worse today than it was. But we tried to do it right."

The attempt to bring about ethics reform ran into a bizarre complication. The bill, sponsored by John Marty and Mindy, placed a cap of five dollars on what a lobbyist could spend entertaining a representative he was trying to influence. The idea was to curb the excessive big parties and extravagant dinners the lobbyists were continually throwing for members of the legislature. (Women seldom were a part of the going-fishing- or out-to-dinner-with-the-lobbyists culture at the legislature. When sessions ended, most women went home to their children). Under the proposal, with the five dollar limit, lobbyists and legislators would be able to have a cup of coffee and a doughnut together. When the bill reached the Senate, opponents (mostly out-of-town legislators who enjoyed the big parties that had helped pass the time in the evenings when they were away from home) lowered the amount that could be spent to zero, thinking that that sum would be so ridiculous that the bill would not pass. To their dismay, their strategy failed and the zero spending bill passed.

Everyone expected the bill to be overturned in the next session of the legislature and Marty was prepared to bring back his original five dollar spending limit. But with the passage of a year, the mood of the legislature had changed. Common Cause and the press had applauded the zero spending limit saying, in effect, "This is fine, leave it as it is." And so the zero spending limit, put in as a device to defeat the bill by its opponents, remained the law.

Mindy, however, paid a personal price for the passage of the two measures. "We will always be blamed for having gotten rid of the culture that was here," she said. "Some of us will never be able to live that down. That is how this place works. There will always be baggage that people like me will have to carry with them."

For example, Mindy has run up against the "male retaliation tactics" that women see at work in the legislative process. A Democrat, she once voted with Republicans when they appealed one of the House speaker's floor rulings. After that, she said, the vice chair of the K-12 Education Finance Division, Chuck Brown (DFL), refused to let any of her bills be heard. The way the legislature operates, by seniority, drives everything, keeping the existing leadership—almost entirely male—entrenched. Changing that system has become a galvanizing goal for newly-arrived women.

Every year Mindy and Betty McCollum have introduced a bill to get rid of per-diem legislation, believing that legislators should be on a straight salary. Their bill does not cut anyone out but makes clear that per-diem payments during the legislative session are salary and count toward legislators' pensions. The bill never gets serious attention but the two women continue to make their statement, hoping over time to gain supporters. (Mindy is also one who favors a unicameral legislature. "I see it as a good government issue, making government visible with accountability and less game playing.")

During Mindy's first terms in the legislature, Phyllis Kahn was routinely adding to every bill that came forward that contained a board of any sort, the requirement that the board be gender balanced. Phyllis was on the Government Operations Committee and put this stock amendment onto every bill that came through her committee. Mindy supported Phyllis's amendments, but to little avail. As Mindy noted, "Arne Carlson routinely vetoed them all so they didn't go anywhere."

One day a bill came onto the floor of the house authored by Peggy Leppik, a moderate Republican, that stated the IRRRB (an institution on the Iron Range) should be gender balanced. Mindy said to herself that "what is good for the goose is good for the gander" and crossed party lines to vote for Peggy's bill. No sooner had she voted than the male DFL legislator seated in front of her turned on her and spitting his words out demanded that she change her vote. "You don't know what you're doing," he shouted. "You don't know who your friends are and they aren't the Republicans. There aren't any good women to put on that IRRRB board anyway!"

The legislator was so angry that he left the floor and would not sit in his seat in front of Mindy for the remainder of the day. This incident occurred near the end of the week and the first thing the next Monday morning the man was in Mindy's office. "I have been thinking about you all weekend," he said, "and I feel badly that I yelled at you so much. I can't get it out of my mind, and I have been feeling really bad about it all weekend." He paused and his voice rose. "*But you were wrong*," he shouted. Before Mindy could respond he had worked himself into being angry all over again.

Mindy believes that many men in the legislature are still struggling with themselves over their tactics, the relationships of power, and the limits and appropriateness of threats and coercion. "Some of the men yell at everybody," she said. "They can be both curmudgeons and loveable guys too."

Mindy has observed that the women who have been in the legislature the longest tend to take on the characteristics of the men. Research indicates that if women are forty percent of an organization, they change the organization. If they are less than that, the organization changes them. "I clearly saw that women who had been here for a long time and had to operate with men became like them. There was an occasion when a group of us, Pam Neary, Becky Kelso, and others talked publicly to the *Pioneer Press* about Tom Osthoff's overstepping his bounds and harassing us. When the story came out, Phyllis Kahn ran to Tom's rescue and sent a letter to the editor about what a dear, sweet, well-meaning soul he was—one of the best legislators."

After the letter appeared, the women took Phyllis to dinner and reminded her that they, too, were feminists like her and they did not appreciate her lack of support. They explained that they were trying to change the atmosphere of the legislature. Mindy admires Phyllis for being a great feminist. She also understands something of the bind Phyllis was in. Osthoff was a good friend of Phyllis' who had helped her in many tough battles, including feminist fights, and she wanted to pay that back and protect him from the other outraged women. The situation was a complicated one. Women had to walk a narrow line—especially in the early days when there were only a few women in the legislature—because male allies were essential to getting anything accomplished. "Women are very loyal, just like men, and when they are here in small numbers and need allies they get co-opted."

Mindy recalled the famous caucus "where Becky Lourey made her motion for Irv not to be in charge of elections. One of the women representatives came storming in saying that we should not be challenging Irv." Mindy received an award for being the only person to vote against Irv Anderson on the House floor. "I felt that I had nothing to lose. I had been completely cut adrift. It wasn't like my voting for him was going to change anything."

Many women had run afoul of Anderson who, though personally likeable, represented, along with other older legislators, an outworn style of power politics. According to Mindy, Anderson's problem as House Speaker was his controlling tactics. "He took no prisoners. You were either with him or you were not. If you had ever crossed him in any way, then you were permanently off his list. You could never recoup yourself. He went as far as he needed to with his circle and no further. That is how he held his power, by punishing others. Anyone who was considering crossing him or reaching out a hand to those who were permanently in the abyss, were too frightened to do that. It was Irv's ruling by fear that eventually did him in because he made the circle of those he trusted too small."

Mindy has found that the legislature itself, when members are in agreement, forms a kind of community. One of those times it felt like a community was when members came back for a day to vote flood relief for northwestern Minnesota. She remembers that all the members were happy to be called back, the issue was not a controversial one so they were in a good mood—and they were glad to see each other. All the members felt as if they were doing a good thing and it was "apple pie and motherhood. Nobody had to hang around long enough to get tired of each other or argue about anything. We just came back for one day and left before any damage could be done. The legislature is a very good community. Some of the neatest people in the world are in the legislature—when we're not fighting—because we're all basically social people."

State Representative Mindy Greiling

State Representative Alice Hausman grew up on a farm in Kansas where she and her four sisters and one brother, from the time they were small children, were obliged to do hard labor. Her rural experience proved to be an isolating one. "We had such a narrow childhood when I compare myself to others," she remembers. "Our life revolved around church, school, and home—the triangle that was reflected in very early America. There was nothing else. I think where we lived in Kansas was a very backward place. When I compare it to people who lived on farms in Iowa and Minnesota, they had a totally different kind of existence than I did. We had such a simple life."

Because their community was so isolated, Alice engaged in a world of imaginative play. "The whole farm was our playground. In the corn-crib, we would set up a grocery store complete with shelves and all of the old cans and things. We would stock the shelves with grocery items.

Then in the junkyard (which was where we dumped all the household trash) we would set up whole houses." The houses were peopled with paper dolls Hausman and her sisters cut out of catalogues. She would lay out the rooms of houses, using pencils for the walls, and would then walk her catalogue-dolls through the rooms.

Though Hausman lived in an isolated setting, she had seen enough of her surroundings to know that her home was primitive compared to the homes others lived in. When she was not doing chores for her parents, she would sit on a particular fence in the barnyard where the wood was weathered and soft. With a sharp stick or a nail she would sketch into the wood the rooms of her parents' house and then draw in improvements she wanted to make to them. Even with no point of reference, she was drawing floor plans and designing improvements. She also escaped into books. "I read and read and read. I would find private places, like a tree with a branch in the pasture—we called it the swing. Often I would be there alone, reading and thinking."

One of Alice's aunts was married to a man who drank and may also have abused his wife and children. From time to time, Alice's parents, because they were the stable members of the family, were called on to rescue the children. Alice remembers a little cousin who, when he came into their house, appeared fearful and sat on a chair in the kitchen with his head down. Alice's mother prepared scrambled eggs for the meal. "When my mother made scrambled eggs, she made a certain amount and we all had just one helping. We all knew there was just one helping. Either my little cousin had never had scrambled eggs before or he was starving, because when she put the eggs in front of him he just gobbled them up and when they were gone he looked up and said 'More.' My mother said, 'There isn't anymore.' I can still feel today the overwhelming sympathy I felt for this little kid who loved those scrambled eggs and how sad I was that there wasn't more to give him."

Though Alice's mother and father had had only an eighth grade education, there was no question that education and doing well in school was a value they cherished in their family. Her father read books and was a good story teller—sometimes to the annoyance of Alice's mother when he would tell the same stories over and over again. From her father, Alice learned that one need not have a formal education to be wise. For Hausman's father, fence building was a metaphor for character. He believed a person should do everything well and not be careless in his work. "He did not like people who did things in a sloppy way and the thing he used as a symbol of that was the kind of fences they put around their farms. Did they build neat fences or sloppy, messy fences?"

Hausman's father could frighten his children with his anger. "We would be petrified if the pigs would get out and we had to go help him chase them back in. He would be furious if we'd miss some. Pigs are hard to chase and he would really yell at us. It was a scary thing to talk with my dad, so much so that when I was in high school and wanted to tell my parents that I had a date, I would wait until my father was in the bedroom, changing clothes with the door closed, before I would say whatever I had to say through the door. My mother showed her anger in a different way. She did not smile much and she had a tense look. She did not have a happy look on her face at all." Hausman attributes the emotional reserve and gravity of her parents, in part, to the life of unremitting labor that Kansas farmers of the period had to endure.

Even though Alice and her brother and sisters did not receive many expressions of affection and approval from their parents, they figured out ways to be close to them. When Alice's father would be sitting in his chair at night reading, she would get a comb and, standing behind his chair, comb his hair. "I must have been about the height of the recliner," she remembers. "He combed his hair straight back so it was easy for me to do." Alice had many earaches as a child. When her ear was hurting, her father would take her on his lap and blow smoke into her ear. It was a folk remedy called "campbelling," but to Alice it was a demonstration of her father's affection for her.

Alice Hausman attended a rural one-room Lutheran parochial school in Kansas. Every school day would begin with opening devotions—the children singing a hymn accompanied by the teacher on an old-fashioned pump organ. Each morning the teacher would ask his students, "What is our hymn for the day?" Invariably the hymnal on the organ would be open to the hymn they were to sing that morning. Whoever had thought to look at the hymnal on the organ before class began would be able to wave his hand and call out, "I know, I know."

Before her first day in first grade, Alice's older sister and her friends, who were eighth graders, had primed Alice to respond to the teacher's opening question about the morning hymn. "I can still picture my sister's and her friend's faces, how excited they were that I, on my first day in school, would be able to answer the question about the hymn. They drilled it into me. 'This is the hymn. This is the hymn. When he says, 'What is the hymn?' you answer with the name of the hymn.'"

On the first day of school, the moment arrived when the teacher asked his question. "What is our hymn for today?" The smiling faces of the conspirators turned and looked at Alice. And she froze. Despite all her sister's prompting, the shy first grader, on her first day of school, was not able to open her mouth in front of all those big eighth graders. Despite the inauspicious beginning, Alice excelled in school. Reading became her escape and when she was not working she was reading, to the annoyance of her mother. "She always has her nose in a book," her mother would complain. It was not said kindly because Alice's mother needed her children's help and, in Alice's case, she had to take the extra step of getting her attention before she could send her on an errand.

In religion class the children had to memorize long passages from the Bible. Hausman was always given the longest passages because she could memorize easily while some others, for whom memorization was more difficult, would be given "God is love."

Though Alice thought of herself as a shy, quiet, invisible country girl that was not how others saw her, as she discovered when she left her small rural Lutheran school to enter the high school in town. There were 100 students in her freshman class, most of whom knew each other because they had been attending the town public and parochial schools. The few students who came from the rural school were total strangers to them. At the beginning of the year, the entire class would meet in the school auditorium to elect class officers. At the end of the day on which her class had elected officers, Alice was milking the cows in the barn with her older sister. ("All our really good conversations happened in the cow barn," she remembers.) "We had the election of class officers today," Alice remarked to her sister. Her sister smiled back and asked, "What office were you elected to?" Alice was amazed that her sister had assumed, correctly as it turned out, that she had been elected to a class office. "It is strange that I didn't have any concept of myself at all. I only saw myself through a few reflections of others."

Despite her acceptance by her peers in high school, as she grew older Hausman became more and more resentful of living on a farm. "All of my friends in high school lived in town and could go to slumber parties. I really couldn't because we lived fifteen miles out of town and that was too far to be taken back in at night. I felt terribly sorry for myself being kept out of the social mainstream because I lived on the farm."

Another problem for the growing adolescent was the evidence that farm work left on her hands. The children in the Hausman family were responsible for the preparation of the fruits and vegetables grown on the farm. They shelled the peas and pitted the cherries, an activity that stained their hands. The brown color from the cherries would not easily wash off and when she began dating this caused Alice humiliation and resentment. "I hated the farm and what it meant to me. There is no question that growing up on the farm left me with a feeling of being disadvantaged, of being a misfit, of not fitting into groups in quite the same way as others."

The Lutheran school Hausman attended presented two programs each year for the community — one in the church on Christmas Eve and the other in the Spring. Everyone in the community, not just the parents, attended these events. In this one-hundred percent German-Lutheran region, the church and the school were essentially the same institution. On Christmas Eve the children would tell the Christmas story, presenting the entire service. There would be a procession and music and every child would participate. "I got the long Bible passages. I don't think I was ever scared or thought I couldn't do it." Though her parents were sparing with their praise, Alice says she "knew deep down that my whole family was aware I got the big part."

The Spring program was conducted in a grove of trees in a pasture. Every Spring the men in the community, investing considerable effort that could have been expended on their farms, would put up a stage of planks with board seats for the audience. Then, on the appointed day, everyone in the area would come to the pasture and find their seats in the outdoor auditorium. Throughout a long, sunny Kansas afternoon the hard working farmers and their wives would put aside their labors for a few hours to sit in the shade of a grove of trees and watch their children as they sang songs, recited poems, put on plays. For Hausman these were "defining moments when the children stood up in front and the whole community came. Clearly, the children were the deliverers of the message."

Looking back on those experiences, Hausman is impressed that every child, no matter how slow, was given a part in the program. She remembers holding her breath as some of the students struggled with their parts. "Nobody laughed. Nobody thought it would be funny if they couldn't do it or made a mistake. The sensitivity that had to have been there in the teachers and the pastor who analyzed the gifts of all the kids and gave each of them a part that they could handle was wonderful. None of us thought about it very much. But I know now what a sensitive, caring, affirming practice that was." In the German Hausman family, though there were few expressions of affection or praise, Alice knew she was supported. Riding home from one of the Spring performances where Alice had sung a solo on the stage by herself, her father remarked to the occupants of the car in general, (but not to Alice herself), "Well, she certainly did a good job, didn't she."

Alice Hausman's first memory of politics is of her father talking in their farm kitchen with the men who came to pick up the eggs and milk. It was the morning after a national election and the men were good-naturedly arguing about it. Her parents, who were Republicans, deplored Harry Truman's use of the words "hell" and "damn" and supported Dwight Eisenhower. From her parents' attitudes, she learned that politics was an important arena of life and something she would have to take seriously in the future.

In college, Alice was active in student government, running the campaigns of others and holding some offices herself. The first national political campaign she worked on was Barry Goldwater's when he ran against Lyndon Johnson for president. Still a Republican like her parents, she passed out literature and rang doorbells for the Goldwater campaign. The reading of the Christian Science Monitor newspaper during the Vietnam War changed her politics. "I was reading and thinking to myself, 'This is horrible and I should not be just sitting here in this living room reading about this. I should do something about it. I have to get involved.'"

In protest against the Vietnam War, Hausman and her future husband, who had also been a Republican, joined the Democratic campaign of Eugene McCarthy. They became active campaigners against the war and were photographed during a demonstration reading the names of soldiers who had been killed. Alice soon discovered that she would not be in a group for very long before she would be promoted to a leadership position. In a group, Hausman became the planner and organizer, the one others saw as being steady and having common sense. "You can get an awful lot done if you don't care who gets the credit," she observed. "Being concerned about who gets the credit has always seemed a little unseemly to me. For heaven's sake, just do it and don't expect credit."

When she moved to Minnesota, Hausman volunteered to work in Ann Wynia's 1978 campaign for State Representative. She went to Wynia's house as a volunteer and Ann soon discovered that Hausman was someone who was willing to work. She asked her to find the best price for envelopes. Hausman did, and eventually ended up managing a Wynia campaign. In 1989, when Ann Wynia became the Commissioner of Human Services, Alice was elected to her seat.

The St. Anthony Park neighborhood in St. Paul, which was in the district represented first by Ann Wynia and then, in 1989, by Alice Hausman, has a history of electing strong women to public office and is accepting of women candidates. Voters in other districts have not been so welcoming. The area directly to the north of St. Anthony Park, for example, did not send a woman to the legislature until 1992 when Mary Jo McGuire and Mindy Greiling were elected to represent it in the year known, among the women, as the Year of the Woman. With fifty-five women serving in the legislature in 1992, it appeared that women were indeed entering the mainstream of political life. Unfortunately, after the 1992 term, some women were not reelected, and the number of women serving in the legislature dropped to forty-four.

Alice notes that when she was first elected to the Minnesota House there were two other women House members from St. Paul, Sandy Pappas and Kathleen Vallenga. Both have since been replaced by men (Sandy Pappas went to the Senate) leaving Alice the only woman in the House of Representatives who is living in the city of St. Paul. Despite the difficulty in getting elected to office, once women take their seats, they often find a receptive place among their colleagues. The individual who accepted Alice the most readily in the House of Representatives was Willard Munger, the longest-serving member of the Minnesota House. Every time Alice made a speech on the floor about issues that were important to him, Munger would get out of his chair, walk over to her and say, "That was the best speech I ever heard given on the floor." Whether that was true or not, Alice found his comments very affirming.

At the end of the 1993 session, a group of women lawmakers, including Alice, met throughout the interim before the 1994 session to work on a bill to establish a state energy policy. The bill was modeled after a 1970s bill that established the context for developing state environmental policy. That bill had proven to be extremely helpful in judging future environmental proposals and the women felt the same kind of analytical tool was needed for energy policy. Rather than just react when a utility brought a bill to them, they wanted to have a context, something to measure it against. They were also aware that NSP (Northern States Power) would be bringing issues on nuclear energy to the legislature and they wanted to have a broad energy policy in place to help guide their decision-making.

The bill they produced, after months of work, pointed out that the state's high dependence on coal was damaging the lakes, killing loons, and possibly contributing to global warming. Billions of dollars were being sent out of state to purchase fuel. Nuclear energy, clean in itself, left a waste product that was radio-active for centuries and presented a massive disposal problem, the costs of which no one could quantify. Alternatives were wind and solar power and the generation of electricity from biomass, all of which Minnesota had in abundance. The bill laid out an energy policy for the state, outlining a direction for the future and established a hierarchy of energy sources with the renewable resources at the top, and coal and nuclear at the bottom.

The final bill was presented with a great deal of fanfare—and then it never got a hearing. Joel Jacobs was the chair of the Regulated Industries and Energy Committee and he told Alice, when she pushed him, that he "wasn't hearing any controversial bills this year." Though he and Alice were both members of the party in power, she was unable to move him. However, a controversial bill was heard that year because, a short time later, NSP requested permission from the legislature to store nuclear waste above ground in containers called "dry casks." The dry cask controversy became what Roger Moe called the most contentious and controversial issue ever to come before the legislature.

The issue was a complicated one. NSP had run out of inside space to store nuclear waste. The federal government, despite decades of effort, had been unable to cajole a single state into putting this radioactive material underground on its land. NSP wanted to put the waste above ground in casks, licensed for 80 to 100 years, until the federal government could tell them where to permanently dispose of it. The cask site was near a neighborhood of poor, mostly minority citizens and next to an Indian reservation. Hausman, Munger, and others objected, saying the above

ground storage was dangerous, the state should not put its most dangerous waste next to its most vulnerable citizens and that while present residents of Minnesota were getting cheap energy, they would be saddling
future generations with bills of unknown and possibly gargantuan
dimensions. Hausman's group wanted NSP to explore the development
of energy from renewable resources which Minnesota has in abundance.

When Alice suggested that, instead of storing nuclear waste next to
a poor minority community, it be placed near wealthy, white residential
neighborhoods, the topic of dry cask storage suddenly became everyone's concern. The House passed a bill stating it opposed dry cask storage, but if NSP felt compelled to store the waste above ground, they
would have to put it some place other than Prairie Island. (The bill was
disingenuous. The legislators had been told by federal government
experts that the casks could never be moved. It is simply too risky to
transport nuclear waste materials.) The Senate passed its bill, authored
by Steve Novak, which said nothing about renewable energy and
allowed NSP to store waste in casks above ground at Prairie Island.

The House and Senate bills were sent to a ten-person conference
committee to iron out the differences. Novak represented the Senate
version and Loren Jenning the House version. Alice was the only
woman member of the committee as well as the voice of the minority
opinion which called for the development of energy from renewable
resources. Because of the enormous interest in the issue, the hearings
were televised and the hearing room was packed.

As the debate went on, spectators began to notice that Alice was not
being allowed to speak. The House conference chair, Loren Jennings,
twice refused to acknowledge her. Neither the House nor the Senate
chairs, who alternated presiding over the meetings, would recognize
her nor would they let her ask questions. If she did begin to speak, they
would cut her off saying she was not addressing the point at hand.
Members of the audience took note of this before Alice herself had
become aware of it.

One afternoon Mel Duncan, a progressive community activist, sat
next to a reporter in the hearing room and began pointing out incidents.
"There it is," he said. "See, they interrupted her again." The following
day the spectators, including most of the women serving in the legislature, came to the hearing room wearing round, yellow stickers printed
with the slogan, "Let Alice Talk." Soon almost everyone in the audience

was wearing them. Female lawmakers attended every session of the Conference Committee to show their support for Hausman.

Among the many telephone calls Alice received during the Conference Committee hearings was one from a Catholic nun in Wisconsin. She wanted Alice to know that "hundreds of nuns are praying for you." The other call was from a businessman in Minneapolis. He and his colleagues were watching the televised hearings at night and discussing them in the office during the day. His friends had asked him to call and tell Alice that "not all men are like that."

To a remarkable extent the dry cask storage issue divided along gender lines. Polls taken before NSP launched a print, radio, and television advertising campaign showed that more than half of all Minnesotans opposed NSP's plan while about twenty percent supported it. After the ad campaign, more than half approved. Men, but not women, had been convinced by NSP's advertising. Both before and after the ad campaign, more women opposed the plan than supported it. It was Alice Hausman who spoke for Minnesotans of both genders who opposed NSP's plan to store nuclear waste above ground, but they could only watch from the sidelines as the process played out before them.

In the end, NSP was allowed to store its nuclear waste above ground in a limited number of dry casks on Prairie Island. In the House twenty-two women voted against the bill and eleven voted for it. Rep. Sidney Pauly, a female six-term IR representative, voted against the bill despite strong pressure to conform from her IR caucus. Of the male members of the House, seventy-five voted for the bill and twenty-four voted against it. Only twenty-eight percent of male legislators voted against the NSP nuclear storage proposal, while fifty-eight percent of female lawmakers opposed the measure.

Phyllis Kahn did an analysis of the vote and hypothesized that if there had been an equal number of men and women members of the House (sixty-seven women), based on the way the two sexes voted on the bill, the bill would have received sixty-eight negative votes, killing the above-ground dry cask storage. The Senate was another matter; the same calculation would have just missed stopping the bill in the Senate.

Though NSP received permission to store nuclear waste above ground at Prairie Island, Alice did have a small victory. In exchange for the permission, NSP was mandated to research wind, solar, and biomass energy. The renewable energy mandates are in the bill only because Alice was on the Conference Committee. Her tenacity eventually convinced the two chairmen that they had to do something to satisfy the group she was representing.

State Representative Alice Hausman

In many ways, the modest view that Hausman had of herself as a child continues with her as an adult. She has lost her shyness and now feels that she knows herself well. "I would never now, I think, be elected as a majority leader or speaker of the House, just because I am too non-traditional. But I am often the natural leader in a group." Hausman no longer resents the isolation and limitations of her rural Kansas childhood. "I absolutely know that I'm a product of my past. There have been times when I thought I had been limited; I was sort of resentful about where I grew up and thought that if I had started earlier, maybe I'd be at a further point. Now I am glad it has made me the kind of person I am."

Alice's idea of a good time is still to sit and plan for something—a future vacation, a party, what she is going to do to her house in the long term. "I think that is what I am always doing," she says. "Sometimes I wish I could just turn that off and be content in the present moment and forget about the future. But that's a part of me that is still there."

‹♦›

∝10∽

"The one thing that doesn't abide by majority rule is a person's conscience." —Harper Lee.

By the 1990s, women had made economic gains, earning seventy-one cents for every dollar paid to a man. The range ran from sixty-four cents for working-class women to seventy-seven cents for professional women with doctorates. Black women earned sixty-five cents while Latinas were on the bottom with fifty-four cents. Nevertheless women-owned businesses employed more workers in the United States than did the Fortune 500 countries worldwide.

Issues concerning women continued to move forward. Title IX had a dramatic affect on women in sports. Women athletes won all five of the gold medals won by Americans during the Winter Olympics of 1992 and, at the 1996 Summer Olympics, women went on to win nineteen gold, ten silver, and nine bronze medals. The Family Medical Leave Act went into effect in 1993. The bill had been vetoed by President Bush but was the first bill to be signed into law by President Clinton. Beginning in 1994, every couple applying for a marriage license in California has been given information about domestic violence.

Congress passed the Gender Equity in Education Act in 1994 which promoted math and science learning by girls, and included resources to provide counseling to pregnant teens and information to prevent sexual harassment. The state of Virginia recognized that the male-only admissions policy of the state-supported Virginia Military Institute violated the Fourteenth Amendment of the Constitution.

Many churches also changed their policies. By the second half of the decade, there were 2,313 ordained women ministers in the Baptist church, 1,452 women Episcopal priests, 1,838 women Evangelical Lutheran pastors, 259 Reform women rabbis, 4,995 women Methodist ministers, 3,026 Presbyterian women ministers, 2,080 women serving United Church of Christ congregations and 4,443 women ministers serving Unitarian Universalist churches.

The decade saw the first Mexican-American woman and the first Puerto Rican woman elected to the United States House of Representatives and the first Black woman elected to the Senate. Both Senators from California were women. Legislative bodies no longer went into a startled silence when a woman's voice was heard on the floor. For Martha Robertson, Ellen Anderson, and Sheila Kiscaden, taking their seats in the Minnesota legislature in 1992 was far different from what it had been for their colleagues twenty years before. The world, and Minnesota, had changed in many ways—but in others it had remained the same.

Born and reared in Massachusetts, Martha Robertson was the eldest child in her family and, while still a youngster, took on major responsibility for her five brothers and sisters. Robertson's parents divorced when she was ten, the children lived with their father, and Martha became, in many respects, a mother to her younger siblings. Early in life she learned that she was the child who was expected to set the example for the others. A few years following his divorce, Martha's father remarried and the blended family contained eleven children. "We went cross-country with all of us in a car at one point," Martha remembers. "After we accidentally left one of my brothers behind we had to count off and I was always number one. There was always that kind of built-in reinforcement of being the oldest." Responsibility and commitment were lessons learned at an early age.

The evening meal at the Robertson household was a highly regimented affair. The family sat down around a large table at 6:00 P.M. The children had to eat everything on their plates, and the last one to be finished did not get dessert. As a result the children learned to eat very quickly. Seats at the table were assigned with the assignments changing every month. Chairs were placed at each end of the table for the adults and two children. There were high chairs for the two youngest and benches along the sides of the table for the rest of the children. Martha and her brothers and sisters carefully calibrated the advantages and disadvantages of each location around the table. Martha considered the chairs to be the best seats, except they had the disadvantage of being next to their parents. Her step-mother was very strict about table manners, so the child who had the bad luck to be seated next to her was nagged throughout the meal. Sitting beside the two youngest children was an advantage because if you were quick and dexterous, you could flip food you did not like off your plate and onto the floor under the high chairs.

Martha liked sitting next to her father, who served all the plates from his position at the head of the table. The disadvantage was that he started serving from the side away from Martha and the food was often cold before he had filled her plate. On the positive side, when he began serving he gave small portions, but by the time he reached the end, they had usually grown larger. (This was only an advantage if the menu contained something Martha enjoyed eating.)

Martha's step-mother served a wide variety of food and the children were required to eat every bit. As a result, there are some foods that, to this day, Robertson will not touch. And she seldom eats desserts. "I've tried an awful lot of food," she says. "Can you imagine a bunch of kids under fourteen all sitting around a table looking at calves' brains?" Each child was allowed only one glass of milk. Martha says that she never heard of having bread at the table until she came to the Midwest. "We never had bread on the table, just a vegetable, meat, and starch. If we had salad, that was the vegetable." All of the children had jobs at mealtime that were rotated monthly like the seating assignment. One was a server, one had to set the table, and one had to clear the table after the meal. During the meal, they often played a game called Bottacelli, which was a form of twenty questions. Other times they had to memorize poems and recite them at dinner. As Martha looks back on the experience, she believes the mealtime discipline "gave me boxes to work in. It gave me structure. I think there's some safety and comfort in structure. At the same time I learned at a very young age that it was okay to try different things." She now also appreciates what her step-mother was experiencing. "I can't imagine having eleven children. My step-mom was twenty-nine years old with eleven kids!"

Martha attended an all-girls school in downtown Boston where she excelled in sports as well as academics. "I really shone there and had leadership positions that I think in a co-ed environment I wouldn't have had. "She was captain of the swim team and also played field hockey,

Lacrosse, and softball and sang in the glee club. As a result of her experience (there were 400 girls from the fifth through twelfth grade) she is a supporter of single-sex schooling for girls. "I think there is a value in not worrying about what the guys think. So much of the confidence that I have in myself comes from that experience. There were forty-seven girls in my class. That's enough so that we all had something to excel in. I still remember when I wanted to be in the B math class because that's where all of my friends were, and my Dad said, 'It is better to sit on the bench in the major leagues, than be a player in the minors.'"

Following her senior year in high school, Martha went to Jamaica with a group of eight Americans in a program called Operation Crossroads Africa. They teamed up with some Girl Guides to build a school in Jamaica. Three years later, while in college, she participated in a similar program in Africa. With both groups, Martha ended up keeping the books. "I was the one who knew how much we were going to spend at the market." The experiences gave her an appreciation for what she had — running water, refrigeration, toilets. "I certainly got out of my system any sense of a two-year commitment to the Peace Corps," she said. "There was clearly a sense of trying to be in other people's shoes and have some understanding of what they were going through."

Martha attended college at Franklin and Marshall in Lancaster, Pennsylvania, going from an all-girl school to a college that had just turned co-educational from being all male. "The one criteria I looked for in a college was that it would be co-ed," she said. When she got to college, she found that she knew how to study and was not afraid to get good grades. She immediately became involved in establishing intramural sports at Franklin Marshall and by the time she graduated they had a full roster of sports. Martha started out as a mathematics major but switched to business administration, which was an unusual choice at that time. "Women just didn't do business then."

Both of Martha's parents were actively engaged in politics in Boston, Massachusetts. Her mother ran for the Boston School Board in 1957, and her father was involved in city politics. "My father was at Harvard between John and Robert Kennedy and was responsible for getting rid of Mayor Curley. Dad was always considered the thirteenth person on the Boston City Council." In 1990, Martha's brother ran on the Republican ticket, unsuccessfully, for the United States Senate seat from Massachusetts. Martha grew up stuffing envelopes for campaigns, handing out campaign literature at polls on Election Day (legal in Massachusetts) and attending political conventions, gavel to gavel.

Robertson became involved in Minnesota politics in 1988 when she went to her first district caucus. She had expected it to be a straw poll for the presidency and was surprised to find an intense discussion of issues. When the chairman asked for a volunteer to be the precinct chair and no one responded, Martha—reflecting her commitment to community service—put up her hand. Three years later, when her job at General Mills was eliminated, she received another call asking her to become the district chair. Four years later, in 1992, Martha was elected to the Minnesota Senate.

Because Martha came from a predominantly male corporate environment, prior to going to the legislature, she did not detect any significant difference in the way she was perceived or treated by her male colleagues in the legislature. She has found it more frustrating being in the minority party in the legislature than being a woman. The committee assignments she was given (K-12 education and health and human services) were those typically given to women although Martha had requested the K-12 assignment. She believed that her business background and experience would bring a different perspective to education than that brought to the committee by members who were teachers or parents.

She was also named to a Finance Committee but that proved highly unsatisfactory. Instead of there being a single Finance Committee, as had been the case under prior leadership, there were now three separate finance committees. "There was never anybody in charge and the Finance Committee I was assigned to had very limited power or even reason for being," she said. "Bills are assigned to one of the three finance committees, and then they go to the floor. It puts a lot more power, to be honest, in the majority leader's hands than in the Finance Committee's, and you don't have the ability to oversee the whole picture." Martha discovered, to her disappointment, that being assigned to the Finance Committee did not end up providing oversight on financial matters nor did it provide any sense of making a contribution.

Martha is convinced that there is a major difference in the way men and women in the legislature approach problems. Women are willing to accept the existence of a middle ground and will strive to find it much earlier in the negotiating process than will men. "This year [2000] was a classic example," she said. "You had Roger Moe and Steve Sviggum arguing most of the session and they could not even agree on what the size of the pie was, let alone on how to divide it up."

By contrast, Martha, an Independent Republican, and Mindy Greiling, a DFL member, worked together on several special education issues, including a divisive issue involving the hearing impaired community. They were able to lower the rhetoric, determine the issues, and redo many of the rules controlling special education that had gotten out of line. "At the same time, we looked at the whole child instead of just the special-education piece of it. None of this would have been accomplished if we had allowed politics to get into it." Martha believes that women legislators tend to work harder than men, and many want to "just get the work done, do what's right and find the solution rather than pushing to do it purely for the show or the game. I don't think we are there for our own glory as much as some men are."

All of Martha's negotiating skills were required to resolve the problems with the Profile of Learning. The Profile was an attempt to create state-wide standards for K-12 education. The concept had the backing of two governors, Arne Carlson and Jesse Ventura. However, hard-core conservatives lobbied to eliminate the Profile believing that it took away local and parental control. The legislature had been stymied for the entire previous year over how to implement the standards. The task before the legislature, as Martha saw it, was "we needed to have a reaffirmation that we needed state-wide standards but with added flexibility for the local districts to be able to implement them." The problem was easier to define than to accomplish.

Debate over the Profile of Learning and a variation, the Northstar Standard, went on for most of the session. The debate changed from day to day, the demands shifted and it became harder and harder to keep the goal in mind. Martha maintained the state needed some ability to compare an A from a Minnetonka school with an A from Hibbing and at the same time allow the local districts to have the flexibility they wanted. She found it comforting to watch the negotiations, to see the Speaker of the House "come to an understanding of what we had to do despite his own personal detestation of the Profile." The issue was eventually resolved in a Conference Committee with Martha's participation.

Women who want to serve in public office, according to Martha, should enjoy people and be willing to sell themselves as well as their

State Senator Martha Robertson

ideas. They should have a firm grasp on what they believe and who they are. They should also have a desire to give something back to the community—a strong belief in public service.

Martha describes herself as the classic oldest child, the leader of the clan, the one who makes the plans, takes charge of the funds, organizes the projects, and keeps the records. She likes having a good time but is not gregarious. "I'm kind of a perfectionist in some ways—into neatness. I like order and am not really comfortable with change." Like her mother before her, she enjoys doing crossword puzzles and, as a point of pride, does the Sunday New York Times Crossword in ink. She likes predictability. "I can't stand surprises. Surprise birthday parties are fine but I think I am going merrily along and then, boom, there's something out of the blue that I didn't know about. That makes me very frustrated. I don't mind that there are problems. I just want to know about them ahead of time. I don't want to be embarrassed by them."

Martha was elected to the Minnesota State Senate in 1992 and again in 1996. She credits living in Minnesota on her own, away from the influence of her family, for her present involvement in politics. "When you are living so close to a family and a dad who is as strong and influential in Massachusetts politics as they are, I don't think I could have done there what I've been able to do here," she said. At the same time, she believes she could not have been elected to the Minnesota Senate without her family's support, encouragement, and financial assistance.

Senator Ellen Anderson attended elementary school in a small town in Pennsylvania and remembers getting all A's in the third grade. It was the first time she had been given letter grades in school and that report card was her first intimation that she might be smart. "People saw my report card and said, 'Wow, you got straight A's,' and I thought, 'Oh, that's a big deal isn't it?' So I knew I was going to be a good student." Ellen's parents expected their six children to achieve academically — her two older siblings also got straight A's. Ellen's mother had her master's degree in chemical engineering and her father had his Ph.D in the same field.

The family was close and did many things as a group, going on vacations together every summer, driving from the East Coast to New Mexico to visit relatives. "It was three days in the car — a pretty intense traveling experience that has wonderful memories for me." They stayed at Ellen's grandparents home where they were surrounded by cousins and other relatives. "It was a big extended family and I just loved that," she remembers.

Despite her success at school, Ellen remembers herself as having been very shy as a child. "I never would have dreamed, at that time, of being someone who could speak in public," she says. Ellen overcame her shyness when she learned to defend her twin sister. The twin had been born a few minutes after Ellen and was small and sickly throughout her childhood. As a result, the little girl was picked on by the other children. When the attacks first started and boys followed the little girl trying to hit her, Ellen became frightened and ran home, abandoning her sister. She felt so horrible about having done that, that the next time this happened, she stayed and attacked her sister's tormentors. "I kicked them in the shins and yelled at them. I felt much, much better fighting back even though my sister was sort of upset because she didn't want me to fight them. But I felt so outraged that they were doing this."

Ellen's twin continued to be fearful of people and when she was fifteen years old began exhibiting signs of mental illness. She was eventually diagnosed with schizophrenia and was hospitalized. For Ellen, who was close to her twin sister, it was a special tragedy and she wonders now if, as a child, she did not have guilt feelings about the differences between them and may have felt that she had to make up for her sister. She says that growing up she "definitely had a feeling that it was very important to use the skills you had to try and make things better for people."

Ellen says that, as a child, she was a total bookworm. "The year I was in the third grade, I read every Nancy Drew book. I used to sneak the books into classes when I was bored." When she was nine years old, her favorite thing to do when she got home from school was to escape into a story.

Ellen credits her love of reading for a certain independence of mind that developed early in her life. "When people told me things, I didn't automatically believe them." She believes her childhood reading gave her good verbal skills and the ability to argue effectively and persuasively. Skepticism was a cherished trait in her family and the children were expected to be able to challenge ideas and defend them. Family meals were the occasions for long discussions and Ellen was expected to present rational arguments to support her statements. Ellen remembers her older siblings and her father being the most involved in these discussions. Of her mother she concedes, "You could change her mind if you had a real rational argument, as opposed to persuading her for any other reason. She just wasn't as vocal as the rest of us in the process."

The abortion issue came home to Ellen in a very personal way when an older sister had an abortion ("a back-alley deal") and almost died. Later, in discussing the issue in a high school American Studies class she was surprised that a boy she was talking to opposed legal abortion. "I just assumed that anyone who was politically sophisticated would be pro-choice, like I was." Ellen learned from that experience how to approach people of differing viewpoints. She realized that she had "turned the boy off because I was so critical of him and his point of view. I was incredulous that he believed what he did and I was condescending. It was a very ineffective way to convince him." The incident taught Ellen that abortion is a very sensitive topic and people will have diverse opinions on it regardless of how much they seem to have in common. Following that incident, she tried to be more tolerant. "I learned to at least sound more tolerant even if I didn't believe it."

Ellen cannot recall that any limitations regarding gender were ever put on her, and she grew up expressing a kind of healthy skepticism about issues. In school, she challenged authority figures, skipped classes and engaged in escapades more to see if she could get away with them than from a desire to be disruptive.

In high school, Ellen hated her chemistry class and the teacher who taught it and cut the class as often as she could. The teacher was convinced Ellen was a deadbeat, a deplorable student, until the day Ellen was named a National Merit Scholar and the school had a ceremony and presented her with an award. When Ellen walked into the chemistry classroom after the ceremony, the teacher "just looked at me. She could not believe that it was the same person." Fortunately, the teacher was gracious and was not as unpleasant to Ellen as Ellen had been to her. "I loved being able to be sort of independent and not have to play by her rules and also be very successful," Ellen remembers. "It was an obnoxious attitude that I hope I've outgrown for the most part."

Anderson first became aware of politics when she saw how affected her parents were by the deaths of the Kennedys and Martin Luther King. "I have a memory of them being upset and crying. I never saw them cry any other time that I can remember." She was impressed that they took something that had happened far away from them so very seriously. Those events and her family's reaction to them taught her that "there are certain heroes in our life who are worthy of our respect. It was like something sacred had been destroyed and that was a real shocking feeling. It gave me the idea that there are certain things that are sacred and important."

Ellen's father, who died when she was fifteen, had participated in King's March on Washington in 1963, and she was impressed that her parents were involved in the life-changing events of the nation. When Ellen was ten or eleven her mother was president of the local chapter of the League of Women Voters. The League was giving out bracelets with E.R.A. on them for the Equal Rights Amendment. Those happened to also be Ellen's initials and she wore her bracelet everywhere. "I was really into it," she remembers. "I thought E.R.A., of course, women should have equal rights. Who wouldn't be for that?" She thought of abortion the same way. "It was just ingrained in me that women should have the right to decide what to do with their own bodies." Ellen remembers that in her family "we all had a very strong belief that justice and equality were the most important values in the world and had to be protected. You would fight for those." When she was eight years old, she went with her older sisters when they campaigned for Senator Eugene McCarthy for president and by the time she was sixteen she was campaigning on her own for a local congressional candidate.

Ellen was dressed up ("not looking like my usual teenage self") door knocking for a candidate for the United States Congress when a householder came to the door and began asking her questions about the candidate's platform. "This nice guy was about twenty and very good looking and I was very excited that he was interested in talking to me." Though still a teenager, Ellen found that she could stand on the steps and explain the platform to the questioner's satisfaction. The incident was memorable because it taught her that if she could project self-confidence, even when she did not feel it, people would accept her and listen to what she had to say.

Like many high school students, Ellen felt vaguely misunderstood and under-appreciated. When the time came to go to college, she wanted to go someplace far away where no one knew her and she could develop a whole new personality that would just "break out and wow everybody." In high school, it had been hard for her to step out of the mold and not be part of a clique that centered life around the mall and the swimming pool. In college, Ellen felt that "I could be an individual and be respected for myself and for my talents in a way that was difficult to achieve in the social world I lived in as a teenager. That really drove me to be involved in something different and to be successful at it."

Ellen Anderson's skepticism of the status quo and her adolescent need to rebel that she felt in high school continued into adulthood and helped propel her, after law school, into her first career as a public defender and criminal defense lawyer. "It felt so natural for me because my job was to try and poke holes in the other guy's arguments and explain why they couldn't prove what they were trying to prove. That's always been easier for me than to try and make the case myself."

At times, she finds it ironic that she is now holding a senatorial office and is herself one of the institutional figures she used to challenge. She credits her background with her desire to take an active role in affairs and change things herself. "I am willing to challenge some of the assumptions and things that other people automatically think are the way we should do things. I personally believe that's an essential part of politics. It allowed me to have some political courage, to be able to not just go along with what the majority of the powerful institutional entities were saying I should. I think it is just essential to have independent thinkers."

Ellen believes women in the legislature have particular difficulty in being taken seriously by their male colleagues. If the legislator is young, as Ellen was when she was elected to the Senate (thirty-two), the problem is compounded. "I don't feel young—I'm forty—but people still think of me as being young because I am one of the younger people here and was the youngest senator. Being a young woman and looking youthful meant that I had to work doubly hard to be taken seriously." Women in the legislature, Ellen says, have to walk a fine line between attending to their work and being sociable.

According to Ellen, in order to be taken seriously by their male colleagues, women in the legislature must "act serious but not too serious. If a woman is serious and intent on getting her work done, believes that what she is doing is important, and is not friendly or pals with her colleagues, she will not be very well received. The first task for women is to establish their credibility and convince others they know what they are talking about on the issues. After that, Ellen says, because politics is such a relational business ("everything depends on relationships") women have to get along on a personal basis with other legislators. "If a woman is perceived as all work and no play, not a fun person, she will be frowned upon for that. Men are allowed to be totally serious but women are not, because men don't like us if we are 'not nice.' It is strange but that is the way it is."

Ellen has found women in the legislature, on the whole, to be very serious about what they are there to do. They believe deeply in their mission. "I can't say that is true of all men." She finds the contrast between men and women greatest in the fact that men are able to get more done because they are not so passionate about issues and are willing to "just get along" with their colleagues no matter how much they may disagree. Ellen believes women find it harder to be part of the good-old-boys' club and hang out and have a drink together and chat when they disagree so vehemently about things. "I think the networking and the clubbiness is very different for men than for women in this setting which makes it more difficult for women."

From Ellen's experience and observation, men in the legislature get what they want by having tantrums and being bullies. "It is so childish that it reminds me of my two-year-old son. Women do not do that. Occasionally one of us might cry, which could be considered the feminine equivalent of a tantrum. Most of us try not to do that or get emotional. We go in and ask for things, we ask leadership to help us get things done, we make the case for why something is important. But we don't do it by bluster or by pressure, or by twisting arms. That is not something the women here believe in nor like to do. Men are much more inclined to use those kinds of tactics." Ellen finds that women tend to take the time to discuss issues, come to compromises, find common ground, really listen to where people are coming from.

Ellen's most wrenching experience in her eight years in the Senate was her involvement in the debate over storing nuclear waste at the Prairie Island plant on the Mississippi River next to an Indian tribe. "I was in the middle of that debate, passionately involved, and it was hard for me to see what happened. I was frustrated, not just by the outcome, but by the whole process. There was such a gender gap on that issue. On the Senate side were a couple of us women leading the charge against above ground storage. The leadership supporting it were men. The style of those who were pushing for the bill was what really caused me to be so frustrated and angry with how things get done around here.

"It was an example of politics at its worst. There was manipulation of facts, manipulation of the rules, manipulation of the democratic process, in my opinion, to get things that a lot of powerful entities believed should get done." Ellen says that certain bills and individuals get special treatment. The Dry Cask Storage Bill, she says, was one of those. Though it had been defeated once in the Environment Committee, it was brought back for reconsideration. "In between the two considerations, there was a great deal of arm-twisting and, in the end, just about everyone on the committee flip-flopped when they didn't need to." The only members of the Environment Committee who did not change their votes were Ellen and Senator Janet Johnson. Ellen was so disillusioned by the process that, for a time, she questioned whether it was worth it to be a State Senator. "It was a momentous experience for me," she said. "I was so shocked people would sell out their principles over an issue that was critical for generations to come just because important people wanted them to change their vote." Ellen points out that she has been in the Senate for four years since the Dry Cask Storage Bill affair and has reached a compromise on the issue in her mind.

A piece of legislation that gave her a personal reward was passage of a bill that allows and provides support for nursing mothers in the workplace. "I love that because it meant so much to me personally," she said. "As a new mother who was trying to continue nursing her child — pumping in my office with my breast pump whenever I could sneak out of committees and the Senate—I knew what a difficult thing it was for women to maintain that relationship with their babies when they were in the workforce."

Ellen got a bill passed that required employers to provide a private place and break time for women to nurse their babies. Since passage of the bill, Ellen has heard from women from all over the United States, praising the legislation and asking for copies of the bill so they could work for passage of similar measures in their states. A woman in Minnesota wrote, telling Ellen that when she showed a copy of the bill to her employer, though he knew little about breast feeding, he immediately set up a room for her to use. Though there is not a penalty in the law, Ellen says it has raised awareness and educated the public. When one employer refused to comply, a suit was filed, and the case was settled out of court. "That was a good sign that the law had some teeth and was having an impact. Personally that meant a lot to me."

Ellen finds the legislature to be a unique situation where the dynamics, how one accomplishes things, are vastly different from any other institution. Part of the process, she says, is relational ("you have to get along with people"); part is information, being knowledgeable and doing your homework; part is getting support from outside; and part is being able to use leverage internally, either being nice or pushing. The greatest education for Ellen has been to find out what a diverse state Minnesota is and the huge differences of opinion that exist among legislators. "Trying to get all of us to agree on things is a difficult process," she remarked. Ellen's personal strategy for change is "to outlast them, damn it! I am going to stay here until I get some power, become chairperson of a committee myself. It is hard to change those who have been

State Senator Ellen Anderson

here for a long time and have become the committee chairs. We have tried reforming the process, and hopefully that will have an effect. But in the long run, I will just have to outlast them."

Ellen feels strongly that the status quo is not necessarily good and that one needs to challenge many of the assumptions that govern how things are done in politics. She is also an optimist. "To be involved in politics, you have to believe that you can change things. Having been in office for several years, it's easy to believe you can't change institutions because they are so controlled by forces that are outside your ability to affect. I do have an on-going sense of optimism and a drive to keep working for that change. Otherwise I wouldn't want to be doing this kind of work."

Sheila Kiscaden, a future Minnesota senator, grew up the oldest of four children living with their parents in a tiny, two-bedroom home in Maplewood, Minnesota. She shared a bedroom with her younger sister and brother, and, by the time she was eleven, she was sharing it with a sister and two little brothers. The young girl's escape from this crowded situation was reading. Sheila read all of the time. She read to vicariously experience other things in life, to forget the crowded conditions of her home and to escape the tensions that existed in her family between her parents and between her mother and her grandmother.

During the summers, Sheila would spend weeks at a time with her grandmother. By the age of nine, she was taking the bus from Maplewood to downtown St. Paul, then transferring to another bus for the ride to her grandmother's house on West Seventh Street. Since her grandmother worked, Sheila would be alone during the day. This was not a problem for Sheila who found the solitude to be a great opportunity. Taking the bus back downtown, she would go to the St. Paul Public Library and fill a shopping bag with books. The bag would be so heavy she would have difficulty carrying it. Dragging the bag along the sidewalk, she would get it to the bus stop and boost it up the steps onto the bus for the ride back to West Seventh Street. Once there she would stop for an ice cream cone at Bridgeman's before returning to her grandmother's house where she would read for the rest of the day. Sheila spent most of the summers of her childhood reading. "When I think of my girlhood, I think of reading and reading and reading and reading," she says.

Sheila did well in school. School was a place where, in contrast to the turbulence of her home, she was at peace and successful. The principal of her school was also her sixth grade teacher. Sheila had scored high on the Iowa Achievement Tests and when her mother visited the school, the principal came out of his office to congratulate Sheila's mother on how well Sheila had done. Though only in the sixth grade, she was reading at college level. Sheila remembers that she received a great deal of praise from adults before she was ten years old. "I knew that my family needed me and that I made a difference."

During the first ten years of her life, a time when she characterized her home as "a very loving household," Sheila felt that she had the confidence of her mother and her grandmother. "They were both strong women and they thought I was great. Even in the turbulent years, I knew that what I did was appreciated and needed." While the first ten years of Sheila's childhood were relatively tranquil, the following ten were full of domestic strife and conflict. Her parents struggled financially and the money problems led to disputes. Out of economic necessity, Sheila's mother went to work. Her mother resented the fact that she had to take a job as a nurse's aide that was below her ability. She was brighter and better educated than her husband and in the hospital environment she quickly picked up medical terminology. Unfortunately, she would use the new medical terms at home to remind her family of how much she knew. "There was an edge to this display of knowledge," Sheila remembers. "She liked to show up my dad."

For his part, Sheila's father was unhappy that he was not able to support his family without his wife working and, to ease his own feelings, tried to control her earnings. "He would make her account for all of the money that she had. I can remember her having to account for how she spent ten dollars. That was a frequent thing. 'What do you mean you need more money?' he would say. 'I just gave you ten dollars!' And she would have to explain exactly how she had spent that last ten dollars."

As life became increasingly difficult for Sheila, she found herself caught in the middle of quarrels between her parents and between her mother and her maternal grandmother. Her mother and her grandmother each competed for Sheila's affection with the result that they were very hostile toward each other. Though this rivalry disturbed Sheila, she listened to them both and tried not to take sides. "That created conflict for me because I loved them both, and I knew they both loved me. They each had strengths and faults and they were both to blame for the conflict between them." Sheila was bright enough to know that the battles between her mother and her grandmother predated her and, though she was a pawn in their conflict, she was not to blame. The two women had a love-hate relationship and the conflict was long-standing.

Because of her family's problems, Sheila had irregular attendance at school. "I missed forty-three days of school when I was in seventh grade because I had to stay home to take care of my younger brothers and sister," she remembers. The dysfunctional relationship between her parents left the responsibility for managing the household and the younger children on Sheila's shoulders. "I had to do an awful lot of maintaining the household," she says. Her assumption of responsibilities was gradual. "You take one little piece and do it and then you build on the next little piece and pretty soon you're doing all sorts of things that you hadn't set out to do in a conscious way. In my family, I moved into trying to keep things calmer. I could figure out the things that triggered tension and hostility and anger. And if I could take care of that so that it didn't happen, I did."

Sheila was also sensitive to what the family conflict was doing to her younger sister and brothers. While those years of family turbulence were hard on Sheila, she saw that her younger brothers and sister were having an even more difficult time. "They were little and vulnerable and needed help." Even though Sheila often felt like acting out her own frustration and feelings of rebellion, she resisted because of her younger siblings. "If I had acted out then, it would have made it even worse for them," she explained. "They needed some one who was calm and stable who they could count on. They talk about me now as if I were their mother. They resented it when I went away to school at nineteen and felt that I had abandoned them. I had learned that I got rewarded by being compliant. I didn't get rewarded for acting out. I just wanted the problems to go away. I wanted life to be nice again. The compliant person tries to be ever more compliant, to make life smoother and smoother."

Sheila believes that her difficult family life taught her how to pay attention to non-verbal communication. She knows how to watch for emotional triggers, to see beyond the things people say to grasp what is really concerning them. "You need to get at the core of what is important to you so that you can carry it forward," she said.

Sheila's father was a veteran of World War II and had an intense interest in current events. Though he had had only an eighth grade education, he read the newspaper every day and was conversant with political issues. Sheila remembers him spreading the paper out over the kitchen table (they did not have a dining room table) and giving a running commentary on what was happening in the world. Even when she was in college, Sheila found that her father was far better informed on current affairs than she was because of his careful reading of the press.

In his late thirties, Sheila's father went through a religious conversion and became a faithful communicant in the Catholic Church. Sheila's mother did not attend, but all of the children did, making their first communions and taking religious instruction. "When you grow up Catholic, it is part of your culture but not necessarily part of your practice," Sheila pointed out. "None of us are Catholic now but we went through a ten-year phase of Catholicism. We always said we were Catholic."

Early in her life, Sheila's mother gave her a strong message that came from her own economic dependence, that Sheila and her brothers and sister should go to college, earn a professional degree and be able to support themselves. "That all came from my mother," Sheila said. "There was never a question but whether we were going to college. It was one of those 'thou shalts' in our family."

Sheila's mother had a strong interest in people from different cultures and backgrounds. Not only did she work outside of the home, which was unusual in their family, but she brought people home from work who were from different neighborhoods of the city. Sheila's mother had Hispanic and Native American friends, and one day she invited a family from India to their home for dinner. "I don't think any embassy could have put more effort into the dinner than our family did to entertain that family," Sheila recalls. She also has an aunt, whom she does not know very well, who is Sioux and another aunt who is Native Hawaiian.

Sheila's grandmother would have none of it. "My grandmother was very biased against anyone who wasn't Lutheran and white," Sheila remembers, adding that her mother's conflict and rebellion against her grandmother was intensified by her mother's seeking out of people who, most definitely, were neither Lutheran nor white. Despite the grandmother's disapproval, Sheila believes their home was enriched by the presence of her mother's friends, and the experiences enabled her to be at ease with people of other ethnic and racial backgrounds. The visitors also stimulated Sheila's interest in world travel.

Sheila's extended family was a large one. Her father was the eldest of eight children and many of his siblings had families with five to nine children, giving Sheila a great many cousins. Her father and mother socialized within the family and, for years, held large family gatherings — picnics in the summer and reunions at Christmas at grandmother's house. Sheila describes the gatherings as a "huge crowd of very different kinds of people." Though she shared an emotional bond with her relatives, she also felt as if she were different. "It was an Irish Catholic family and it was the tradition that the girls got pregnant and were married quickly to their boyfriends. This continued through the generations. I was the odd one out that didn't get pregnant, didn't even have a boyfriend, was very studious, wasn't into dating in high school. I didn't marry until I was twenty-four and didn't have children until I was thirty-five. So I was kind of odd." Though Sheila was the first one of her many cousins to attend college, others have since followed her example and some hold advanced degrees.

A year spent in Latin America as an undergraduate had a profound affect on Sheila's career. She became interested in family planning when she saw children going through garbage looking for food and read regularly in the Chilean press about infanticide. "At one point, sixty percent of the hospital beds in Chile were occupied with women with complications from illegal abortions." Visits to the "mushroom villages" where 10,000 people would be living without running water or electricity convinced her that people should have only as many children as they really wanted and could afford.

One of her first jobs was as regional coordinator for Planned Parenthood of Minnesota, helping establish family planning services in eight counties in southeastern Minnesota. When she had seen the Planned Parenthood job advertised, Sheila had felt "absolutely called to take that job. It was something I knew was important and needed to be done. It was my chance to have a direct role. Here was something I really cared about and, by golly, I should be doing that for a living. Yes!"

Though she was young and had not had much experience, her zeal and enthusiasm were persuasive, and she was hired. Within a few months, however, Planned Parenthood was sued for providing service to minors and Sheila was not only in the middle of the conflict but, for much of it, served as the lead person on the issue for her organization.

Fortunately Sheila had worked with a group of advisors to formulate the policy regarding service to minors. The advisors had included not only family planning advocates but people who were opposed to reproductive health services. Because the policy had been worked out by people holding widely divergent views, she found it easier to defend. "Once we had the policy, I felt confident that we had considered all points of view. It wasn't just my own thinking or my own views; it was a reflection of critical thinking by a variety of people. That left me in a position of being very confident about the position that we had taken—that we had done it thoughtfully. I tried to be respectful of opponents. I met with them and listened to them and gave them time, but because of all the preliminary work we had done, I really wasn't very amenable to much change at that point. I wouldn't allow them to bully me or intimidate me. But I would listen. I wouldn't ignore them."

The Planned Parenthood experience set the tone for her later political style. "I try to keep my mind open to the other person's position but when I have finally formulated a position I'm less able or willing to change my position. I try to honor the values that underlie the other person's point of view. But I am not one who will flip-flop very easily. I don't do what's popular but try to base my decisions on what I think is right after listening to advice and conferring with others."

Following her five years with Planned Parenthood and after her marriage and move to Rochester, Minnesota, Sheila took a job with Olmsted County. "I felt driven to do something that I found meaningful and I wanted to have influence of some sort." She became the county Human Services Planner, working with the county board to help them make better policy decisions. A good deal of her work was in the field of corrections, an area she calls "one of the most hopeful places I have ever worked." From the experiences of some members of her own family, she learned that individuals can make profound changes in their lives if they have the desire to do so.

One of the biggest role models in Sheila's life was an uncle who served a term in St. Cloud State Prison. "When you have such a huge family as mine you have people who do well and people who don't," she said. As a young man in his late teens Sheila's uncle got involved with some of his cousins in theft and ended up serving about three years in prison. Sheila's aunt-to-be believed in the young man, despite his criminal record, and they were married after he was released. "He was ashamed of what he had done but he went on to become an exemplary person. He never blamed his cousins, he blamed himself for being stupid enough to go along with them. His message was, 'You have to choose, be responsible.'" Sheila describes this uncle as being a man with "a lot of tolerance for people. He communicated affection for people without being affectionate. Without touch, without saying a lot of praising words, he communicated that he genuinely liked people, that he accepted them for who they were." When her uncle's own son, Michael, got into trouble as a young man, her uncle refused to condemn him, saying that the young man would learn from his mistakes. "And he was right. Michael now holds a master's degree and is an effective counselor."

Sheila has some distant cousins who have been in trouble with the law much of the time throughout their lives. "Some of the stuff they did was really stupid," she said. "One guy would hot-wire a car, drive it within four blocks of his house and walk home. He did it over and over again. It didn't take the police long to figure out that they could just wait there and catch him." Sheila learned that not everyone who commits crimes is malicious or gets any personal benefit for himself. "He just wanted a ride," she explained. "This cousin," she says, "never learned any skills. He got stigmatized and labeled and then who wanted to associate with him? The only people who would associate with him were the people who continued to commit crimes and got him involved. He just spiraled downward."

This cousin's mother was also a good friend of Sheila's mother. Though the two women were close, Sheila's mother was upset because her friend was dishonest. She shoplifted and regularly stole from her employers. Sheila's mother would talk about her friend, saying, "She's dishonest. Of course her son is going to be in trouble. When you see your own mother stealing what else are you going to do? He thinks this is Okay when he sees his own mother stealing." Sheila found it to be a powerful lesson that her mother could be close friends with a woman yet not condone her behavior. "I do that all the time now," she says. "I am friends with people that others are shocked to find we are friends."

Sheila believes she is blessed to have had a variety of experiences in her life. She says she can draw on the experiences of her extended family, experiences with early death, accidents, crime, chemical dependency, and out-of-wedlock pregnancy to have compassion for people. "Compassion is an important part of policy making."

When the State of Minnesota closed the Rochester State Hospital in the early 1980s, Sheila became the county's liaison with the state legislature, lobbying for the needs of the county. She left her job with the county in 1985 to start her own consulting business and helping other women run for office. She was having lunch with a county commissioner friend when the friend turned to her and asked, "When are you going to run for office?" Sheila replied that she might be willing to run for the state legislature. The word got around.

In the summer of 1992, Nancy Brataas, who had been a state senator for seventeen years, decided not to run for reelection. Nancy called Sheila and asked her to be her successor. "She persuaded me that I should run. If it hadn't been for all those other people who had been asking me for years to run, I would not have been ready when she called. And if she hadn't called and offered to run the campaign for me and pushed me, I would not have done it."

Sheila also credits her husband's support for her decision to run for the Senate. "I wouldn't have run if, at the point I was being asked, he hadn't given me the final kick in the pants to do it—which he has done several times for me." Sheila's husband reminded her that she had been supportive of his career, that now it was time for him to support hers and he would do whatever it took to make it a success. And he has. "My husband was quite accustomed to having all sorts of support from me. He doesn't have that now. I'm the one who is gone most of the time; he's the one who is home with the kids. For months of the year, I live in St. Paul and go home on weekends. You can't ignore the benefit of having an intimate relationship that is sustaining through a job that is very challenging, that is full of conflict. This job is absolutely full of conflict, full of anger. If you can't deal with anger, if you can't deal with conflict, you will have a terrible time in this job."

In the Senate, Sheila became aware of the generational differences among men which appeared to be influenced by the women's movement, much of which had taken place during her lifetime. Men just ten years older than herself, she observed, had many adjustments to make to shift their view of politics as a male-dominated profession to one in which women were equal participants. Younger men, she has found, do not have these problems. "The men my age are more comfortable having women as peers. They do not crack the jokes. They might kid you a little bit but they don't use the "you girl" kind of thing. For professional men, sex-based talk is not acceptable at all."

What Sheila does find different between men and women are the social relationships that play an important role in resolving conflict in the legislative process. The difficulty is that men and women like to do different things. Sheila remembers when, twenty-five years ago, her husband tried to get her to take up golf. "I should have listened to him," she said. "So many relationship issues get resolved on the golf course. Today's modern women know that and take up golf for their career development." She believes activities such as golf provide a time for extended social interaction and an opportunity to deal, on a secondary basis, with business issues. There is a group of older men in the legislature who, after a session go to a bar, have a few drinks and do pull tabs. One of Sheila's women colleagues goes with them and enjoys it. "I don't do that," Sheila said, "but because she does, she has a different relationship with some of those men than I do."

Ever since she held her first job, Sheila has been told that she "thinks like a man." She never understood that, and thought for a long time she was being told she wasn't very feminine. "I don't think like a man," she explains, "but I do approach issues in a rational, business-like manner. I look men in the eye and always expect to be treated as a peer." She observes that while she can be assertive in standing up for what she believes to be right, she is not particularly aggressive and can work with people. She believes that in the early years when there were few women in the legislature, men were uncomfortable with women's presence. Sheila says that attitude has now changed. "Men are much more comfortable with me now than they were with the other women who were first in their positions. By the time I got here, the legislature was twenty-five percent female and my caucus was forty percent women."

Republican women have a different perspective on gender equity issues than do Democratic women, according to Sheila. "Republican women tend not to think in terms of gender the way Democratic women do," she said. "Democrats send proposals to the legislature based on a gender-equity philosophy and we aren't disposed to do that. It is part of the Democratic women's platform. We tend to think people are judged more by their performance, initiative, and actions rather than anything based on gender." Sheila says that the gender-equity position of early feminists is based on a political philosophy that is different from her experience. "There are people, like Phyllis Kahn, who have been big strong feminists over the years. They fit a certain mental frame. Phyllis was one of the first ones here and she still has that mental frame from having been one of the first women in the House." As is true for men, Sheila believes women have evolved their styles of leadership based on when they came to the legislature. Attitudes are modified, she believes, in approximately five-year increments.

Sheila reflected on an experience she had in graduate school twenty years before. She had been about ten years older than some of her fellow students and was astonished to find that the younger women could not perceive some of the behaviors of the men as constituting male bias against women—behaviors such as men interrupting women when they were speaking, talking when women were making presentations or assigning women to stereotypical tasks. "They didn't see it and, when it was pointed out to them, they didn't believe it as it had not been part of their experience."

Sheila's legislative experience has been positive and, thanks to the mentorship of Senator Duane Benson, she was able to be a player and actively engaged in a range of issues beginning with her first year. Sheila was looking for a mentor and Duane had decided to give the freshman senator a hand. Sheila and Duane sat together on the floor of the Senate and next to each other on committees where he could answer her questions. The legislature was in the middle of health reform and knowing that that was one of her interests, Benson made sure Sheila was invited to sit in on briefings. Sheila made a point to go to Benson's office once a week and talk with him about issues and get his advice.

Though she was from the other party, Sheila also spent time with Linda Berglin asking for her perspective on issues and talking with her about how to approach problems. "I am more focused on public policy than I am on partisan politics," she says. "It has to be that way because most of the issues we deal with do not have anything to do with party philosophy. Certainly, we have some issues on which we become very partisan, but of the several thousand bills introduced each year, only a handful become partisan. It is a broader philosophy that prevails and that you use in making decisions."

In the summer of 1996 when the legislature was about to take up the question of welfare reform Sheila suggested a different approach to fellow legislator Fran Bradley, who took her idea to Governor Arne Carlson for his approval. Sheila suggested forming a committee composed of members of both parties from both houses of the legislature to study welfare reform in depth — much like a university study-group. Her idea was approved and for six weeks, twelve to fourteen legislators met two to three nights a week with staff from the Department of Human Services, Economic Security, and Housing to study welfare reform. "The staff sort of walked us through the federal requirements and what the policy choices were going to be. We would have our daytime hearings and then we would go into study sessions where we asked lots of questions. It was exhausting."

Though the people who were fearful of welfare reform accused the participants of holding secret meetings (they weren't secret meetings, only intense study sessions), when the bills came before the House and Senate, the legislators were well prepared to deal with the issues. Where debate over welfare in previous years had been acrimonious and bitter, by using the bi-partisan, study-session approach, the Welfare Reform Bill of 1997 was passed unanimously by the Senate and almost unanimously by the House. Sheila has since organized other study sessions for legislators around issues such as higher education and long-term care for the ill and elderly.

While Sheila says holding legislative office is a good job for women, she cautions that it presents some barriers for women with children under the age of twelve. During the session, the days and nights are filled with meetings, and even weekends at home are occupied with constituents' concerns and reading bills. Sheila's husband describes her presence at home during legislative sessions as, "the body comes home but the person doesn't." She says that a woman with young children "must have a really supportive spouse or other assistance to make it work. The legislature is a very intense experience."

Sheila is grateful for the strong female role models in her life and for her uncles who took an interest in her. Since her mother and grandmother were powerful individuals in her own family, it helped her to see strong individuals of both sexes and to observe uncles who were the strong members of their own families. "Because my mother was so strong, to see how strong men behaved was very positive for me. We had families where the women had to be strong and we had families where the men had to be strong." Sheila was impressed that her mother and her uncles were good friends who supported each other through the challenges of life.

Though her nature is calm now, Sheila says she has not always been this way. "My twenties were very difficult, and my family relationships were difficult. I had made up my mind in my mid-twenties that I was not healthy and I needed to become healthy and it was going to take a lot of work." Sheila believes that her position in the Minnesota Senate has helped her. "At this juncture, I feel pretty calm and centered and tested. I have had to get to what my core values are and to stand up for what I believe. When you do that, you get stronger. I'm stronger than I've ever been in my life because of this job. I don't think I could have done the job as well as I'm doing it if I hadn't had all those years of experience beforehand. I sort of feel like I've been tempered, as if I had gone through a furnace where the blacksmith puts the iron in the fire and he beats it and then it is stronger. That's how I feel. I'm tempered now. I'm not steel but I'm tempered."

A feature story about Sheila in the *St. Paul Pioneer Press* pleased her because it reported that she was respected by politicians from both major parties, that she had earned bipartisan kudos. "The story reflected what I think is important in policy-making which is to be bipartisan. There is a strong need for more people in the legislature to provide a place of common ground for resolving conflict. I learned that in my family of origin and I apply it here. I'm proud of that."

State Senator Sheila Kiscaden

The newspaper story was read by members of Sheila's family, providing outside confirmation that "the odd one out, the ugly duckling, grew up Okay. My family is proud of me now. At the beginning they didn't know what to do with me, when they were having kids and doing drugs and earning money. I was kind of this odd person. Now they are proud of me and that really feels good."

$\alpha 11 \infty$

"We can't take any credit for our talents. It's how we use them that counts." —Madeleine L'Engle

There are few political woman in Minnesota on whom the turmoil since the 1960s has had a greater impact than the Hmong former member of the St. Paul School Board, Choua Lee. From 1962 through 1975, the United States Central Intelligence Agency had recruited Laotian highlanders, called Hmong, to fight a secret war for the Americans in Laos. The action was in direct violation of the 1962 Geneva Accords and was unreported in the American press until 1969. When American forces withdrew from Southeast Asia in 1975, thousands of Hmong were forced to abandon their homes. Fleeing to Thailand and Laos as refugees many eventually came to the United States, resettling in California, Wisconsin, and St. Paul, Minnesota, which now has an estimated 50,000 Hmong residents. Choua was among those refugees.

One of Choua's early memories is of fleeing the bombs falling on her Laotian home and being sequestered for weeks in a cave-like bunker. "My parents didn't want to take any chances so they put us (Choua and her older sister) in that bunker and we were there day in and day out with little lamps to accompany us. We played with mud — dirt that we dug up from the ground and made tiny pots and utensils. At the end of those two months, we had a whole shelf of plates and spoons." Choua liked to draw and by the time she was four she had collected hundreds of drawings of figures and flowers that she had made. "I rolled them into a big bundle and carried it everywhere with me. Unfortunately, there was a fire and I lost it. I was upset for two months. It was like losing a treasure."

273

Choua arrived with her family in the United States from a refugee camp in Laos in 1976, when she was six years old. Choua quickly learned English and because many of the members of her Hmong community did not speak the language, from an early age she took on the responsibility of translating for them and filling out applications for permits and government assistance. Choua was the youngest child of a Hmong clan leader. Their home was continually filled with people coming to her father to settle disputes. Choua was expected to help her mother prepare food for the visitors. "Every single weekend, I was at home cooking for my parents' set of guests who were coming to dispute some issues. After cooking, I sat around and listened to what they had to say. My father was constantly disputing problems. He had cases from domestic abuse all the way to political unrest issues. Some of the stories and some of the problems that I heard were not meant to be heard by young children. But I heard it all."

Choua's older sister was married at fifteen. Within the Hmong culture the gender roles are specific: girls are expected to marry young and have children while boys take on the public role as head of the family. However, because her parents did not have a son, Choua was treated by her father, in many ways, like the son he did not have. This created a peculiar problem for the young girl. "I know that if my parents had had a son I would have become a different person. But I was driven between two different expectations. On the one hand, I'm expected to behave like a girl, to one day become a mother and a nurturer person in my family and to be a daughter-in-law. All these things were being instilled in me: what girls should and shouldn't do. On the other hand, because my parents don't have any sons, they would drive me to the other side that most girls wouldn't have seen. They put more challenges in my way, wanted me to take on more responsibility, to take charge, learn leadership, do things boys would take on."

"A son was always looked upon as better than girls. Girls were not as important in the family. Just a body there. Doesn't mean they don't love them, but just not as important. People would talk in front of me, tell my Dad, 'If only your Choua would be a boy!' I always have a deep feeling of wanting to prove to them that I don't have to be a boy to be successful. I understand the need to have a boy because a boy would be able to remain with the parents during their old age, to take care of them. The boys also maintain the clan rituals. The girls would go off and be with their husband's family."

Choua says that her father was a "figure of importance in my upbringing. Being the only child in the family [after the marriage of her older sister], he encouraged me to strive for more. But in my situation, because my parents didn't have any sons, I took on the role of the boy in the family." Choua's father took her to conferences in their community so that she could meet people who had been successful and would learn from them.

When she looks back on her family, Choua now believes that her mother was the stronger person in her family, the one who held the family together. However, because her parents lived in a male-dominant society "where men were expected to be tough" her father, who had had military training, appeared to be dominant. Neither of Choua's parents attended school. Her father eventually learned to read and write in Laotian but her mother, who speaks five languages, has not become literate.

Hmong society is divided into twenty clans, each with its own surname, and with many subgroups within the clans. As Choua explains it, "There are universal rituals that all Hmong practice, like New Year's, birth of a baby, marriage, death and funeral rites. Then there are specific rituals that only pertain to that clan which serves as an identification. If I go to California, for example, someone would ask, 'What clan are you?' And I would say 'Yang,' because that is the big clan. Then I would say 'Yang Seven,' meaning how we do our rituals versus the Sixth Yang or the Ninth Yang. Once you get to the specific clan then they can trace you to your parents and family lineage."

Hmong are not permitted to marry within their own clan. Choua was born into the Yang clan, but when she married, she became a member of her husband's Lee clan. "You are automatically considered brother and sister within your clan, whether you are stranger or not. If you share the same last name, then you are not allowed to marry that person. So the first thing Hmong girls do is ask a boy what's his last name."

Choua was a good student in school and loved to read, even bringing a flashlight to bed at night so she could read under the covers. Her parents encouraged her to go to college though her father wanted her to study political science and she refused in favor of psychology. She had a negative image of politics, based on watching her father work to resolve personal disputes within the Hmong community and believed that the process ended up being as destructive as helpful. Even after her election to the St. Paul School Board she denied that she was a politician. "I don't want to stigmatize myself as a politician because I hate what politicians do. And yet I also realize we cannot get away from the political aspect of our life because it impacts every waking moment whether we like it or not."

Choua was working with the Hmong Women's Organization when she became involved with the St. Paul Schools over the issue of the English as a Second Language (ESL) program. A group of Hmong women were dissatisfied with the program and asked Choua to be their spokesperson to the superintendent of schools, David Bennett. Choua's visit to Bennett was not satisfactory from her point of view, and, convinced that the program was not meeting the needs of the children, she began to follow the ESL program on her own.

A year later, a friend told her there were three openings on the St. Paul Board of Education and people were looking for an Asian representative. Half joking, she asked him what she should do. The friend said she should run and that he would find her a campaign manager. Choua did not take the conversation seriously until the campaign manager, Patricia Langdon, called on her, gave her a list of delegates, and told her to call them all on the phone. Choua protested, "I don't know these people, I cannot just call them and talk to them." Choua was reluctant to make the calls and waited three days before she dialed the first name on the list. As soon as she started, however, she found the delegates receptive to her ideas and willing to talk with her. "As I called all of those individuals and spoke to them about my concerns with the school district, they started to talk to me about their issues. Throughout the whole process, I grew."

At the age of twenty-three, Choua Lee, a married college student, was elected to the St. Paul School Board in 1992, the youngest individual to be elected to that position and the first Hmong to serve on the Board. As a school board member, she described herself as a person who was persistent but not dominant, a consensus person who liked to work cooperatively behind the scenes. "Through that process I was able to get a lot of things done in the district." In doing her elected job, Choua had more to contend with than her family and her position on the St. Paul Board of Education. She also had clan responsibilities.

When Choua married she took another major role besides that of wife which was that of daughter-in-law. "In a Hmong marriage," she explained, "you don't just marry your husband, you marry his clan and there are responsibilities that come with the job—as being a daughter-in-law for my in-laws." Choua's husband is the oldest child in his family. "So, being the oldest child and the first daughter-in-law, you have more seniority in terms of responsibility. Whenever we have a big gathering, they always look to me to get it done, to organize and get things to go smoothly." Being a daughter-in-law in Hmong society is a difficult task, but for Choua, it was doubly hard because, though her in-laws desired her presence at family and community observances, she at times had to absent herself in order to attend school board meetings.

"You have to deal with the expectations of two cultures," Choua explained. "There are a lot of problems dealing with the in-law issues and the dual roles that you have to play in the Hmong community as well as in the dominant community. I can be as liberated as any women in this country but at the same time be as rooted in tradition as I want to be when the situation calls for it. I think that's one thing that has to do with flexibility. Being flexible is another term that I would use to describe myself. You have to be flexible or it can break you."

Choua is fortunate to have an understanding and supportive husband. When she was elected to the school board, members of her husband's clan came to him and protested. "Why do you let your wife do that, go off to meetings and sit at the men's table and make decisions? You let your wife be the man in the family!" Choua believes that if men are not comfortable with who they are, they will not be comfortable if their wives excel. "It is just a bruise to their manhood having the women more successful than they are."

Choua is understanding of the psychological problems

St. Paul Board of Education Member
Choua Lee

Hmong men, who have come from a society where they are dominant and make all the decisions in the family, face when they come to a more egalitarian society. According to Choua, many Hmong men see her as a threat, fearing that their own wives will imitate her and "want to have the same liberty and equality. It is hard to be a Hmong woman in the public arena. I have men threatening all kinds of things from left to right." Hmong women, however, support Choua's activities. "The women praise me. They say, 'Oh, we're so happy you are doing this. We want role models. You have inspired us so much to want to do more.'"

Choua sees herself as "first and foremost an educator. My role is teacher. I also see myself as a learner because I learn constantly, from students, teachers, parents, from everybody. But at the same time, I also see myself in a leadership role where I organize and take charge of certain projects." Choua served one four-year term on the St. Paul Board of Education, currently serves as a board member for the Institute for Education and Advocacy and is pursuing a graduate degree. She and her husband have one son.

It is not unusual for political women to be first in their positions. The "firsts" racked up by State Auditor Judith Dutcher and Mayor of Eden Prairie Dr. Jean Harris are especially noteworthy. In her initial political race, Judi was elected the first female auditor following nineteen male auditors running back to 1849. Dr. Jean Harris already had a resume of "firsts" when she was elected the first woman (and the first Black woman) to be the mayor of Eden Prairie. She was elected only two years after Minneapolis Mayor Sharon Sayles Belton took office. Both won reelection and, as this is written, currently hold their positions. (The number of Black women holding elective office in the United States has increased from 131 in 1970 to 1,950 in 1990)

From the time she was nine years old until she was in college, much of State Auditor Judi Dutcher's life revolved around swimming. She and her sister, who was a year older, swam competitively and were in the water from two to five hours a day. "When you swim, it is almost like being in an isolation tank," Judi says. "You have a lot of solitude and a lot of time to think. As long as I can remember, I had that time, every day, year round, to think my thoughts. When you're young, that makes an impression on you because you're not having conversation. You're not jumping around. You're directing your body to do a certain thing for two to five hours out of every day." On the other hand, Judi also developed a strong sense of belonging. "I always felt as if I was either part of a family unit or a swimming unit or a group of friends," she remembers. "We always rode our bikes up to the swim clubs in the summer and hung out at the pool all day together. All my best friends swam and I swam and my sister swam."

Judi describes herself as being outgoing, talkative and competitive as well as opinionated and aggressive. "Those are the same things as being strong," she says. "I'm a strong personality." Judi competed with her older sister and with the boys on her swim team for athletic awards and with the other students in school for grades. She was the third child in a family of four and worked to carve out her own place by doing well in school and by winning swimming meets. "Without consciously recognizing it at that point, I knew that by being the best in the class I would get more recognition from the teacher, more privileges and that sort of thing." She also believes that, from an early age, she wanted to make her mark. "I was just much more strident and opinionated about things. I wanted to be noticed."

Judi is closer to her older brother than she is to either her older or younger sister. "I was always Little Dutch and he was Big Dutch. He was diminutive physically and did not go through a growth spurt until his senior year in high school. He was always smaller. He gained recognition for himself by being a big mouth but funny, always very funny. He's the kind of little fellow who makes the wisecracks and then is backed up by guys who are 6'5" and weigh 200 pounds. I wanted to be like him. My older sister was shy and never stood up for herself. I was always the little sister, who, when someone would say something mean to her, would end up jumping into the fray. I just wasn't gonna take any crap from anybody, ever."

Judi and her family moved from Michigan to Bloomington, Minnesota, in 1975, where Judi enrolled in Oak Grove Junior High School. She went from a school where everyone knew her to a school where no one knew her and it was a hard adjustment. By her second year, she had become involved in student government but she participated for only one year because, as she says, "not a lot of the popular kids were in student government. If you wanted to be in those groups [of popular students] you didn't play it up. So I wasn't in student government as soon as I realized that it was probably not the thing to do." The same attitude prevailed about the students who took the advanced placement classes. Judi enrolled in them but she did not want people to know it because accelerated classes were viewed as something the "cool kids wouldn't ever be seen in."

At Jefferson High School, Judi was recruited for the swim team and, like her sister before her, became team captain. The program was an intense one. The swimmers practiced for two hours every day before school and for three hours after school. "Swimming became everything," she remembers. Judi believes that her competition with her sister probably had something to do with her drive for achievement. They were both on the same swim team but fortunately had picked different strokes so they did not have to compete head to head.

When she looks back on herself in high school, Judi feels that she was both competent and confident. "All girls in high school are insecure in some way," she says, "but I really wasn't as much as my friends around me because girls at that age care too much about boys and I couldn't have cared less. You always want to be liked by boys at that age, but I knew that high school wasn't going to be the epitome of my life." Judi did not have to work very hard to make straight A's in school and she found it hard to understand why many of her friends were not devoted to the task of doing well academically.

Judi's father was Jim Dutcher, the University of Minnesota basketball coach. Despite his high-stress job, Judi says that he was a low-key individual who seldom raised his voice. Judi says he never yelled at her in his entire life. "He's just the most easygoing person you'd ever want to meet. My dad's more of a listener. My mom's the talker. People who remember my dad as a coach always said, 'Your dad didn't yell enough, throw enough chairs.' If my dad ever had his pulse rate up high enough to throw a chair, it would be amazing. That's not the way he is wired. My dad was the only one of his family that got to go to college. He went through on an athletic scholarship to the University of Michigan. My grandparents lived a very humble existence. They saved their funds for my cousins to go to college."

Because of her father's notoriety while she was going through school, Judi felt a responsibility to not do anything that would embarrass him publicly or cause him any kind of a problem. She never drank, smoked or experimented with drugs in school. She says that she was not interested in those activities, in part because of concern for her family and in part because she did not want to compromise her athletic ability. She once went to a party where someone put alcohol in the punch and thought it was very funny when Judi took a glass of it. Judi's reaction was to reflect on how incredibly immature and stupid it was, when she chose not to drink, for people to try to trick her into it.

As for her Type A personality, Judi identifies her mother as the source. "Mom always said you can do whatever you want. Mom was very much into holding us accountable for everything. Nothing got by our mom, much to our chagrin." Judi's mother had been valedictorian of her high school class but never went on to college. Academics were very important to her. "That's what she wanted for us and we did it. The psychology behind it is just knowing that you can do it." At one point, the pressure on Judi became too much and she began having dizzy spells and headaches. Her mother took her to the pediatrician who asked Judi, "What are you worried about?" Judi began crying in the doctor's office as she replied, "What do you mean? Everything. I am worried about everything." Judi remembers that she "would always be worried." In retrospect, Judi suspects that, though it was not on a conscious level, she was trying to please her mother. "Daughters always try to please their mothers. 'What's Mom going to say about that?' they wonder. I think what drove me a lot was pleasing her. She's a tough cookie."

Judi's competition with her older sister continued into college at the University of Minnesota. Though her older sister was enrolled at the U, she had lived at home until Judi entered the university. Then her sister signed up for the same dormitory Judi lived in, but on a different floor. Judi was not pleased. "It's my life," she thought. "Go away."

Although Judi was swimming at the University of Minnesota on an athletic scholarship, she soon decided that she wanted to give up swimming. "All my friends were having incredibly too much fun, and I was stuck swimming and being tired and cranky," she remembers. She took the summer off from swimming, her first vacation from the sport in her entire life, and in the fall found herself painfully out of shape. "You take two days off from swimming and you're out of shape." She remembers running up the stadium stairs to try and get her cardiovascular shape back and thinking, "I hate this. I have had enough." Though she was afraid of what her father would say when she told him, she found him in agreement with her decision to drop swimming. The change in her life was dramatic. "That was the first time I hadn't had something to do five hours out of the day in my whole life."

During her senior year in college, Judi clerked for Congressman William Frenzel in Washington, D.C., "It was the first remotely political thing that I had done," she remembers. "I did it because it sounded like a fun thing to go live for a semester in Washington, D.C." While the other interns were mainly graduate students who were eager to help shape policy decisions, Judi was assigned to the receptionist's desk where she greeted constituents and "did the social kind of thing, which was just fine. I certainly didn't walk away from that experience thinking I want to do politics," she says. Judi did not envy her fellow interns who were doing what she called "the grunt work—research issues. I got to do the social job which was fun."

Though she started out in a pre-med program at college, Judi soon switched to law. She was influenced in her decision by participation on the student judiciary board in her dormitory. Students who had broken the student code were referred to the board which would listen to the cases and decide on the punishments. Judi found making the decisions easy. "I just trust my instincts and make a decision. I am not someone who makes a decision and then worries about it afterwards. It's make the call and move on."

Judi says she learned a lot about humility in law school. While she does not like it when someone tells her she is wrong ("I have a healthy ego."), she believes she is willing to listen, is always interested, and wants to hear what people have to say. She finds she enjoys unusual people. "I don't like beige too much. I get a kick out of people who are a little extreme." Judi graduated from the University of Minnesota Law School and became a prosecutor. Realizing that there is an ego element involved in any public job, she suspects that ego involvement, her sense of competitiveness, and the satisfaction that comes from having people know who she is drove her into doing criminal prosecution. Judi says the thing she liked most about working as a prosecutor was the sense that she was doing the right thing. Though she wanted people to like her, she did not care what kind of impression she made on the defendants in her cases.

Judi believes that she was a difficult prosecutor for defense attorneys to deal with. Many issues were "black and white" for her. "An alcohol level is black and white. Domestic violence is black and white. Somebody who just got abused is black and white. If a guy has just beaten up his wife, I don't care if he thinks I am the biggest bitch he's ever met in his life. I hope he does focus his hostility on me. When I prosecuted domestic violence, I would purposely position myself as the person who was causing the problems, not the woman. I wanted to be the target of their anger as opposed to the woman. When you're really clear about that boundary — that domestic violence is not okay — whatever position another person takes is irrelevant."

Not all of Judi's cases were so clear cut. "There were a lot of cases where there was some gray area, and I'd feel a lot less sure, a lot less black and white. But there were certain things that were so repellant to me, domestic violence being one of them, indecent conduct being another. And child abuse cases."

Judi is a student of people's body language and believes she can tell how people are reacting to what is being said. That sensitivity has made her aware of the moves politicians and other well-known people make to both greet and hold off strangers. She first observed this behavior in her father. "My dad was always very nice. You could tell if he knew someone that it would be one thing. But if [the person who greeted him] was a stranger, he'd be very 'Hi! Great!' A quick 'Hello, Nice to see you,' and then he'd move along."

Later Judi would observe Governor Carlson adopting the same behavior ("Great, good to see you") and keep moving. She felt sympathy for the person being brushed off. "You can tell," she says, "that this is just such an important moment in that person's life, talking to the governor. And I'm crestfallen seeing him — thinking that the meeting was so important to the guy — and that the governor should have taken more time." Yet she knows these were survival tactics on the part of her father and the governor. "We used to get phone calls at home in the middle of the night after a game. People would call and just scream." Judi says she learned a lot from her father about how to be normal while in the spotlight of public life.

Judi was recruited to run for State Auditor by Arne Carlson who had held that position before being elected governor. At first, she was concerned about running because she had never held elective office before and she wasn't sure she knew how to run for a state-wide office. Then she told herself that she was qualified for the position of auditor, that she had a good blend of expertise, abilities, and name recognition. She made her final decision to run after a long day of taking depositions in a case of which she had become very tired. She reminded herself that she was someone who would take a chance, that she needed to keep her options open and, above all, not become stuck in one career. "It also didn't hurt to have a sitting governor working for you," and when she saw that Carlson was not going to take 'NO' for an answer, she agreed to run.

Judi regards her decision to run as the best thing she ever did. She did not get into politics because of an unfortunate personal experience but because she sees it as a good career for women. Traditionally men have been the ones to chose a career in politics and women have supported them. Politics, Judi maintains, is also a good option for young women and she urges them to become involved. Judi has found elective office to have been more accommodating to the demands of family life than other job choices.

In the past, women have entered public life after their children were grown, in part to deflect the criticism that they should be home caring for their children. Judi rejects that argument and notes that more and more younger women are entering politics. She points out that much government policy is about issues of working parents and the needs of children and families. Officeholders have the opportunity to exemplify the flexibility, values, and practices reflected in the legislation. Judi had a child while serving as State Auditor and when other women in her office saw how she was able to manage home and career, they too decided to have children. Judi is pleased to have been an example to her co-workers of how they can have both work and children in their lives. "There is a juggling act involved," she admits, "as there is with other working women."

Judi has found the reaction of some women to her professional career surprising, and at times, disappointing. To her dismay, she has observed that many women still measure their self-worth by their appearance. It is her observation that the women she knew through her life who, early on, were struggling to be good looking, failed to develop much beyond that point. She feels it is a value society placed on them which is, in reality, a handicap.

When she was elected the first woman auditor in the state her picture was on the cover of a local magazine. Many of the comments she received were about how she looked in the picture and how she wore her hair, not about how she was doing her job. "Did they read the article?" she wondered. To her bemusement and dismay, Judi finds that many times when she talks to women's groups the comments and questions are more often about her appearance than about the work she does in the auditor's office.

Judi, the highest-ranking Republican woman constitutional officer, made headlines when she announced that she was switching her membership from the IR Party to the DFL. The change, she says, was "for personal and not political reasons." She found that the IR Party no longer reflected the values and goals she had for herself and her family. She said

State Auditor Judith Dutcher

she wanted "to be involved in a party where dialogue would be possible on things that matter." She said that she found a lack of tolerance in the IR Party that disturbed her and little room for a moderate position. Judi said she wanted to be able to go home at the end of the day and look at herself in the mirror and feel good about what was happening.

Judi is proud of the high quality, non-partisan work produced by her office during her two terms as State Auditor and of the quiet manner in which it has been presented to the public. "We have had only about four press conferences in the past five years," she notes. "I only call one when we have something really important to say. The strength of the office speaks for itself and is not tied to anyone's ego." Callers to the State Auditor's office are not greeted with "Judi Dutcher—State Auditor," but simply with "State Auditor's Office." Judi says she will not run for a third term. "I don't want this to be just another job," she says. "I want to leave it while I still have the energy and fire."

Jean Harris, the first black woman mayor of Eden Prairie, grew up in Richmond, Virginia. Richmond is the city that prided itself on being the heart of the Confederacy and the center of massive resistance to school desegregation following the 1954 *Brown v. Board of Education* Supreme Court decision.

"I grew up, the second of three children, in what today we call the 'ghetto,' though in those days we didn't have that word," Jean remembers. "It was a community of people who all looked like me—a very poor community, a community that was so rigidly circumscribed that I did not have interaction on a social or peer level with a white person or a person of another race until I was twenty-one years of age. I grew up riding on the backs of street cars, unable to use the public library, relegated to a small, dirty part of the public beach, unable to swim in the public swimming pools during the summer, understanding generally that I was somehow different and I was somehow second class. I grew up understanding that I had a very narrowly defined role, first as a woman and second as a black. I grew up in a totally segregated school system straight through college."

Jean's parents were both educated. Her mother had her master's degree in social work from Atlanta University, which at that time was a black school. Her father was one of fourteen children of a country preacher who struggled to put himself through high school, then college and eventually through medical school. Though the Harris family lived at a level that was slightly better than many people in their community, they were still poor. Her father was called the "walking doctor" because he could not afford to buy a car. When he finally accumulated enough money to buy an automobile, it was the first car in their black community. Since he practiced in a poverty-stricken area, Jean's father was paid as often in promises and fresh eggs as he was paid in money. Jean remembers a sign in her father's office that said office fees were two dollars, one dollar of which must be in cash. She says that her father never enforced the rule on the sign. Thirty years after he had delivered her baby, one of his patients called on him and finally paid him his fee.

Despite the poverty of the black community and its isolation from the rest of society, it provided a rich life for its members. Since there were no formal government services to help people in need, the neighborhood, mainly through the churches, looked after its own. "The community took care of the disabled, the elderly, the mentally ill," Jean says. Her mother sent meals across the street to an elderly man who lived alone. If children were orphaned or one family had more children than they could care for, the children would be farmed out to friends and relatives. No one was officially adopted, they were just cared for. "There was an understanding that the community had to do these things for its members." Early in her life, Jean learned to take responsibility for other people who were less fortunate. "I learned as a value the need to give back to the community in some way for the privileges I had," she remembers.

Jean's parents supported her aspirations and day after day drilled into her that education was the ticket out of poverty and into the larger world. It became a kind of mantra in the family, one that she believes she heard from the time she was in her crib. The teachers in her all-black school were also dedicated and were determined that the children under their care would learn. When the books provided to the black school turned out to be the handed-down, dirty, discarded texts from the white schools, scribbled in and with pages missing, Jean's mother, all by herself, went to the white school board and protested. Knowing something about politics was a matter of survival. "We knew the systems and could read about the activities of those systems 'outside of' our community because that's the way they appeared to us. They were outside," Jean remembered. "We knew that it was important to be able to deal with them because they imposed their will upon us." From her parents' example, Jean learned that, though it took a great deal of effort, one could change the system. "You weren't going to get any attention unless you did challenge the system in some way."

While still in elementary school, Jean was elected captain of the school patrol, though she was among the younger members. The school patrol had the important task of maintaining order on the playground. Jean had the responsibility for assigning children to specific stations and selecting the periods of time when they would be on duty. She had the authority to evaluate the children's performances and to relieve them if they did not perform well in their selected spots. Although she believes she was much too young to understand how to be a leader, she remembers that she had a sense of fairness that may have been why she was elected captain of the school patrol. "It was very important not to be 'stuck up.' I was always interested in my classmates and what happened to them and what happened to us collectively. I was able to join hands with a lot of very different kinds of persons." Many times Jean had to intervene in disputes among children older than she was. She also brought about a needed change. Because the school patrol was on duty during the noon hour and the members often did not have an opportunity for lunch, Jean went to their teachers and negotiated an extra ten minutes for the patrol members to eat.

By the time Jean was nine years old, she was aware of the tug of two forces pulling on her. One force was the influence of her parents and teachers who insisted that she achieve. She had to be better than white people, they told her, in order to get a decent job. "You have to be better so they can't bypass you," she was told. The other force was the message from the larger society that said, because she was black, that she would never amount to anything or be good enough.

"Girls in those years were taught what I call submissive skills. The messages came both from the female members of my household and from my community. We were taught not to appear too brainy, not to be forthright in our speaking, how to dissemble in order to not affront males of any color—particularly if you wanted to get a husband. We were taught that being beautiful was essential to having a relatively easy life. So even as children being encouraged to excel, we were also warned about appearing too brainy."

In the black community, the beauty standards were those of the Caucasian race—thin nose and lips, fine straight hair. Jean remembers the first time in her adolescence when she really looked at her nose she wanted to cut it off because she thought it was too big. She bought *Seventeen Magazine*, like other teenage girls, but the pictures there only reinforced the negative image she had of herself. "There was no picture anywhere that looked like anyone that I knew." Jean believes that the conflicting messages she received as a young girl created great insecurity in her, and as a result she feels she spent a large part of her life becoming a whole person. She says that it took her a long time to be comfortable with herself.

Jean Harris' role model was Eleanor Roosevelt. Her parents and teachers read stories to her about Roosevelt, Mary McCloud Bethune, and Sojourner Truth. She admired women like Amelia Earhart who had triumphed against difficult odds. Her male role model was her father. "He was kind. He was considerate. He was deliberate. He got ruffled or angry so rarely that we remember every time that he did. He was a true, dedicated servant of the people." Harris remembers her father breaking up fights between adolescent males that the police feared to do. "Nobody would hit Doc. Doc was a real pillar."

After graduating from an all-black college, Harris applied for admission to the Medical College of Virginia. She was the first African American to gain admittance, and she was the first black to graduate. She was also the first black to intern and do a residency in a white institution in the state of Virginia. Later Harris left the state for the District of Columbia where she became one of only two women faculty members at Howard University.

Jean did not become an activist until after she had graduated from medical school. Before that time she was busy learning the social skills of being what she calls "a nice passive female who could attract a good husband because that was how our lives were portrayed for us. Get a good husband." Jean learned to play the piano, becoming a concert pianist, playing for choirs and touring with them. Only as she grew older did other causes, such as issues of women's and children's health, become important to her.

Early in her medical career, it became apparent to Jean that the future of black people was intimately bound up in their ability to become part of the larger system. Moreover African Americans, she believed, had a responsibility to penetrate it. As the Civil Rights Movement opened doors, it was necessary to have people prepared to go through them. During the civil rights years, Harris had a sense of excitement that the world was changing and it was possible to be a part of that change. She felt she had a contribution to make because she was one of those black individuals who was prepared. She was educated and articulate and had a budding sense of her own self. "I had an obligation to myself and to others to take advantage of those opportunities," she says.

Jean Harris' first experience working for a public agency was not as an elected official but as the director of the Bureau of Resources Development for the District of Columbia. The bureau had responsibilities for Medicare and Medicaid. Since these programs were brand new, no one was quite sure how to implement them. Harris says that she did not know either. In her mind the programs represented socialized medicine. Though she had three young children at the time, she decided that by being involved in the implementation of Medicare and Medicaid in the District of Columbia, where she was practicing medicine, she might be able to exercise some control over her professional destiny.

Harris went from that job to the post of executive director of the National Medical Association Foundation — another new agency. "They gave me an agency budget of $40,000 and a secretary and said 'Go forth and do great things.'" Harris did. Within three years, her budget was $7.5 million dollars and she had built a nursing home, established a fellowship program for minority students, begun two research studies, and set up the first black group-medical practice. When she asked the men on her board for a salary increase to bring it up to the level of the man whom she had replaced, they refused, saying "You have a husband who is employed so you don't need a raise."

The response shocked her. "It was one of the most memorable days of my life because I can remember the pain," she says. "I had built that thing up from $40,000 to $7.5 million in three years, and it wasn't acknowledged." It was a Sunday and Harris went back to her office and cried and cried. She realized that if she were going to be recognized as a capable human being, she would have to do it herself. She wrote her letter of resignation, giving the organization three months to find her replacement, and then left to develop a program of community medicine for the state of Virginia.

When Harris took the Virginia job, she discovered that she had sixteen agency heads, fourteen of whom were male Caucasians who had never had a woman as their leader nor experienced a black in top administration. She had a challenging time developing interdisciplinary programs among the schools of medicine, nursing, chemistry, pharmacy, and social work. Nevertheless her program went on to win national recognition for Virginia and earned Harris an award from the National Governor's Association and appointments to two presidential task forces. She was so successful that, six years after she started, Jean — a Democrat in a Republican administration — was appointed to the governor's cabinet. Jean Harris was the first woman in the cabinet and the first black to hold any policy position in Virginia. While in state government, Jean had to steer her Republican governor away from banning abortions to accepting them for women who had been raped or were victims of incest. "I had to literally go to the mat on that one," she remembers.

The governor of Virginia was outgunned on that issue. Jean had seen the ramifications of illegal abortions when she was a faculty member at Howard University. She had seen women come into the hospital on the verge of death from hemorrhage. One of her best four-year medical students had died at home from a self-induced abortion. She had seen women who had become infected from botched back-room procedures and had their reproductive organs either removed or permanently damaged so they could never have children. "I will protect to the nth degree your right to say, 'No, I won't have one [an abortion],'" Jean says, "but I will also fight you to the nth degree if you deny that opportunity to someone who feels, for whatever reason, she must have one. I speak with some fervor about that. I've been there. I've seen that."

Harris was sitting at a meeting of one of the national task forces of which she was a member when she met Bill Norris, CEO of Control Data, who convinced her to come to Minnesota as a vice president of that corporation. She did and worked for Control Data for six years. The first two years in Minnesota she commuted from her home in Virginia. Then she purchased a large home ("so the kids could come home") in Eden Prairie and told her husband, who worked for the Virginia Health Department and had two more years to serve before his retirement, that it was his turn to commute.

Jean lived alone with her fifteen-year-old cat in the Eden Prairie house until her husband arrived. All she did, during that time, was go to work and come home. She says that she and the cat had great conversations. "I would come home and the cat would say 'meow, meow' at the door and we would sit down and the cat would tell me about her day. And I would tell the cat about my day. But when I began to have visions of taking the cat out to dinner at 510 Groveland, I knew it was time to get out of the house. I did not know anyone because I had been working. It was just work, work, work." Jean was reading the paper one evening in her Eden Prairie house when she saw a notice asking for volunteers for Eden Prairie commissions. Realizing that she missed being involved in community concerns, she volunteered and was appointed to the local Economic Development Commission. She had been on the commission only a few months when it was disbanded — wisely, according to Jean, as the community was growing so fast there was little for the Economic Development Commission to do.

A few weeks later, Jean received calls from a city council member and a state representative, both women, asking her to run for the Eden Prairie City Council. Jean replied that, though she had been appointed to office many times, she had never run for elected office before. As she recalls the incident, "They were so persuasive that I decided to go pay my five dollar filing fee and run. But that Friday I was late getting home from work, and when I got to the office it was closed and I couldn't file." The city council member was persistent, calling Harris on Saturday to see if she had filed. The following Monday was the deadline for filing. This time she left work in time to file before the office closed.

Though she had paid her filing fee, Harris still did not think seriously about running. "I paid my five dollars, so what," she thought. "I'm not going to win. I've only been here a little over a year—nobody knows me." But the two women who had persuaded her to run were serious about her candidacy. They called the next day and told her she should organize her campaign committee. Harris knew that one of the women's husbands had run her campaign for her so she asked if he would run hers. "You'll have to ask him," the woman replied. Harris went over to talk to Duane Pidcock and she remembers that he kept looking at her and shaking his head as if he thought she was crazy. Finally he said, "If I run your campaign, you're going to have to work." Harris replied that she would never go into anything that she did not intend to work at.

Duane introduced Harris to his friends. Seven candidates were running for two seats on the Eden Prairie City Council. One of the candidates was an incumbent, so Harris conceded one seat to him, leaving her competing against five white males for the remaining seat. "I knew nothing about Minnesota politics," Harris remembers, "so when the other candidates were talking about streets and sewers and development, I talked about what I know—which is people issues." Harris talked about the people growing older in their homes, the rapidly growing community of upwardly striving young families who couldn't afford to put furniture in their expensive new houses, the teenagers without a structure to meet their needs.

When election night of 1987 came, Harris put a bottle of champagne in her refrigerator in the slight case she might win and made a big pot of cider to serve friends who came to her home to watch the returns. The early returns were discouraging. She lost the absentee vote and appeared to be far behind. But as the precincts reported she began to gain and when she moved from third place to second, she says, "pandemonium broke loose. The hot cider went flying over the kitchen counter and they said, 'Get out the champagne. We're in a real race now.'" Harris remembers the adrenaline surge she felt the first time she realized that it was possible for her to win. "I was a candidate — a serious candidate! It's a real hook." From that point on, Jean carried every precinct. The incumbent won his seat and Jean took the other. When she ran again she ran unopposed and received the highest vote total. Jean went on to win the mayor's seat in 1995 and was reelected mayor in 1998.

Growing up in a black community surrounded by "this sea of others" as Jean put it, gave her a unique perspective on the political process. She learned not to show anger or passion because, as a black person, it could get her in trouble. As a result, she says it is very difficult to make her angry. "I can go through the toughest public hearing, and I never lose my cool because I listen and feed it back in a way that is non-threatening and that allows us to talk." Though she says that "nobody thought about politics" when she was growing up, her parents and friends did learn how to deal with the systems that they saw being imposed on them from outside the black community.

Jean credits her mother and the other women members of her extended family for teaching her how to listen. "Remember, we were not supposed to be aggressive, not even assertive. We were passive. We did not debate. We listened. We derived our argument from hearing what other people said, what the issues were. Then we designed our responses around that. These things just became part of the background static that we picked up."

These experiences gave Jean an appreciation for a sense of humor. "In the worst kind of situation I can find something salvageable," she says. "I can laugh. It can be awful, and I can find the humor in the worst kinds of situations and that helps me to get over it and to move forward — to find the critical pass through whatever it is." Jean uses her morning walks for problem solving. "I think through difficult issues, problems, obstacles, barriers, all those things. And even in the bad ones, most of the time I can see my way through them. But even when I hit one that I know is not going to be resolved, that there is no way to change this person, I can find the humor in the situation. The humor is very important for releasing the tensions and being able to move forward without animosity about the issue or anger with the person."

Jean counts as one of her greatest achievements getting people in Eden Prairie comfortable with the idea of "affordable housing." It was generally believed that lower-cost housing led directly to a degrading of a community. An undefined fear of "those people" underlay the discussion. Jean decided to put a face on the constituency for affordable housing. She pointed out they were teachers and social workers, young couples looking for their first home, seniors wanting to downsize. "Very few of us started life in $250,000 homes," she pointed out. Jean also changed the name of the concept and in doing so redefined it. Instead of "affordable housing," Eden Prairie now has a wide range of housing called "life-cycle housing."

The doctor turned politician fairly bursts with pride in her community. "We honor our past and celebrate our diversity and newness," she says. "Being mayor is great fun." Eden Prairie has been named one of the fifty best places to live in the United States. The rating was based on the quality of local government, physical development of the city, the range of housing available, and the schools.

Jean has strong feelings about community. Her first community was her family, then the black community of shared experiences of discrimination and prejudice. Beyond that is the larger community of women. "When I walk into a room and I see a woman, I'm immediately more comfortable," she says. "I'll go over and talk to the men, but ultimately, I will gravitate over to that woman. Whether I know her or not, makes no difference—she is kinship and there is a bond that is very important to me. I support women candidates across party lines. It makes no difference to me. If you are a women running for office, I know we have had a common experience; we've shared some of the same kinds of pains and the same kinds of joys, though they may have taken a different form. I believe women gravitate toward each other because we are more inclusive, more consensus building. We are more willing to listen. Women are less needy in terms of needing to have the spotlight on us all the time. We are more embracing of differences."

Harris understands that there are times when a politician is not going to win, as in 1990 when she ran for the Republican endorsement for lieutenant governor with gubernatorial candidate Doug Kelley. Once a Democrat, Harris had become a Republican in the early 1980s. In those instances of defeat, she says to "react with good grace, accept the inevitable, determine how best to encompass it within your value system. And remember there is always tomorrow—another day." Her agenda, she says, is people, making sure they have the opportunity to develop their talents to the maximum. She came from a community where very poor people lived rich lives and she is aware that there are people living in impoverished communities who are doing extraordinary things with few resources. She also sees that there are people in wealthy communities who are doing absolutely nothing for the common good.

She has empathy for people who are trapped by the circumstances of their lives, whether it is a lack of education or skills or other problems. But she does not have sympathy for excuses. "Ultimately each one of us is responsible, in part, for our destiny. Circumstances may be inhibitors or obstacles, but ultimately we can either whine or we can set about the task of making a building out of the rubble. We can find a way to climb over whatever it is that is in our path."

Jean has one major regret in her life and from it she has derived a lesson. The regret concerns her mother. Jean's mother delayed doing something she wanted all of her life, which was to visit Hawaii. For most of her life she talked about visiting Hawaii, but instead of taking the trip, she bought shoes for her children, paid their college tuition, or had repairs made on the house. When Jean's mother became ill, Jean was not aware of it. Though her father had written the children that their mother was sick, they had no idea of the seriousness of the illness.

Jean was thinking about her mother one day and spontaneously wrote her a letter. "Mom," she wrote. "You have always wanted to visit Hawaii and never gone. I am going to take you and when I come home for Thanksgiving we will set the date." Thanksgiving that year was November 25, and Jean's mother died on November 19. Though she had written her mother the letter with the invitation, Jean had procrasti-

Eden Prairie Mayor Jean Harris

nated and failed to mail it. Her mother never got the letter. The best a grieving Jean could do was to place the letter in her mother's casket.

From that experience Jean learned that it was "very important to tell people that you love them and say it often." She now says, "Don't delay." She believes in taking joy from life as she is going through it and not delaying giving to others what she has to offer them.

ର Epilogue ଞ

"This is a time in history when women's voices must be heard, or forever be silenced. It's not because we think better than men, but we think differently. It's not women against men, but women and men. It's not that the world would have been better if women had run it, but that the world will be better when we as women, who bring our own perspective, share in running it." – Betty Bumpers

When five women met for tea on a hot July day in upstate New York in 1848, they had no idea that their meeting would have a profound affect on all future generations of American women. One of the invitees was Elizabeth Cady Stanton, who expressed to her friends her frustration at the limitations then placed on women. Finding that they shared similar attitudes, the women decided, rather than merely vent their feelings within their group of five, that they would call a larger meeting. Within two days of the tea party, the group had picked a date for a convention, found a location and placed a small announcement in the *Seneca County Courier*. They called their meeting, later famous as the Seneca Falls Convention, "a convention to discuss the social, civil, and religious condition and rights of women." Though they did not know it, no similar public meeting had ever been called in the history of western civilization.

Women holding elective office today are heirs of those five who dared to challenge the conventional wisdom of their day. Why, they dared to ask, were women's lives being so unfairly constricted? The changes that have taken place over seven generations of women since that afternoon meeting did not happen spontaneously or easily. Nor were women the passive recipients of other's helpful deeds. It was women themselves who made these changes happen through meetings, lobbying, public speaking, and running for elective office.

As the drive for women's suffrage was nearing its completion with women gaining the right to vote, Margaret Sanger, a public health nurse, began the campaign for women to control their own bodies. The movement educated women about birth control methods and spread the conviction that freedom for women meant they must be able to decide for themselves if and when they would become mothers. Sanger and her allies were scorned and opposed for decades. Not until 1936 did a Supreme Court decision rule that birth control information was not obscenity and not until 1965 could married couples in every state legally obtain contraceptives.

The second wave of the Women's Rights Movement began in the tumultuous 1960s when, with Esther Peterson's encouragement, President Kennedy convened the Commission on the Status of Women. The publication of Betty Friedan's book, *The Feminine Mystique*, the passage of Title VII of the 1964 Civil Rights Act prohibiting employment discrimination on the basis of sex and the passage of Title IX guaranteeing equal access to athletics opened previously closed doors to women. One in twenty-seven high school girls played sports twenty-five years ago; one in three do today.

Has the presence of women in elective office made a difference? With the increased number of women members in Congress, the 103rd Congress passed into law thirty bills on women's issues during its first year and thirty-three during its second. The previous record for any year was five.

Since 1920, when women won the right to vote and run for election to the Minnesota legislature, a total of 128 women have served. Thirty-six served in the Minnesota Senate and ninety-nine were elected to the Minnesota House. Seven women, Linda Berglin, Becky Lourey, Sandy Pappas, Donna Peterson, Pat Piper, Linda Runbeck, and Linda Scheid have served in both the House and the Senate. Fifty-seven women are serving in the Minnesota legislature in the year 2000. They constitute twenty-eight percent of the 201 members; twenty-six percent of the 134 House seats and thirty-three percent of the 67 Senate seats.

Women running for political office today no longer have to try to look like men, as Carolyn Rodriguez felt she had to do at the end of the 1970s. "Women can dress any way they want, the same as men, and still be seen as leaders," she noted. Carolyn believes it is not as much of a challenge for women to run for political office now as it was twenty years ago, thanks to the pioneering efforts of the first women to challenge the system. "We had a few strong women in public office who had to fight very hard for recognition and the opportunity to chair com-mittees. Women were not respected and if those strong women had not run for office, nothing would have changed and conditions would still be the same." Carolyn believes women office holders are judged now not so much on their gender but on an individual basis, on how they are doing their job. Women no longer have to challenge the status quo so much, she believes, "and that is exciting progress."

In Minnesota, elected women are still more likely to become chair-persons of caring-oriented committees concerned with aging, children, family service, social welfare, and education rather than other types of committees. That is the focus that women themselves bring to their office, points out Ruby Hunt. Research confirms that women, in the per-formance of their official duties, tend to focus on concrete feelings and people—toward the personal and the particular rather than the theo-retical. Committees such as appropriations, finance, judiciary, and rules—considered preferred or blue ribbon committees—are still chaired largely by men.

A generation ago almost all women holding political office came up through the ranks of the PTA and the League of Women Voters. When Ruby Hunt served on the board of the National League of Cities in the 1970s, she found that almost all of the women elected officials had learned their political skills through the League of Women Voters. The women mayors of San Jose, California, San Antonio, Texas, and Lincoln, Nebraska, had all been members of the League. That has changed. Instead of two avenues, there are now multiple routes to public service for women and, while still significant, the role of the PTA and League of Women Voters as a training school for political leaders has lessened.

When asked if women bring a different style to politics, the women interviewed said that they did. Ruby Hunt says women tend to do their homework more than men. Lona Schreiber believes the differences come from the life experiences of women, that they empathize more easily and are more ready to seek a middle ground in disputes. Joan Growe found women to be more inclusive, better listeners, better at gathering information, and building consensus. "Women are more interested in going into politics for what they may be able to achieve and to get something done."

Women would much rather solve a problem than fight about it, according to Ann Wynia. "Women, on the whole, have less patience with the fighting, the posturing, the proclamations of victory. They just want to get to the business of getting something done." She realizes these are gross generalizations and that there are exceptions both ways. But her observation about groups of both men and women is that the women in the group tend to look for consensus and to seek ways to have more winners than just winning themselves. "They like to figure out solutions to a problem."

Carolyn Rodriguez agrees. "I think men, on the whole, think in terms of win-lose. Men become very involved in an issue and go all out to win. Women, on the other hand, are more apt to look for allies for their positions and to work for a win-win situation. Women look for areas of agreement much earlier than men do."

Sheila Kiscaden has found that women are less prone to use personal power or power politics than are men. Women will try to find the middle ground and will work collaboratively. "It is an extension of the care-giving, looking-out-for-everyone-not-just-yourself trait of women." While there are many men who also work toward consensus ("No one person completely fits any one pattern."), Sheila says that given a group with an equal number of men and women, there will be more women than men working for an agreement that will please everyone.

Roger Moe, Senate Majority Leader, talks about how women have changed the legislature by seeking the middle ground on issues, working toward consensus and focusing attention on what lawmakers had considered to be more traditional women's issues of child-care, family-law and health and human services.

Alice Hausman expresses the frustration that many women have felt over the fact that the state of Minnesota has never sent more women on to Congress or to the governor's office. "Other states have elected women as governors and members of Congress," she observes. "What is different here?" She wonders if women are at times too willing to defer to men. She remembers when Ruby Hunt passed over her opportunity to run for mayor of St. Paul in favor of Ray Faricy. "Do we do that too often?" she asks.

Alice believes there may have been some unsuspected benefits to the discredited "smoke-filled room" of an older style of politics. "The party or community leaders would go into a room and try to figure out who were the emerging leaders and identify them. Then they would go to those individuals and convince them to run, promising to provide resources and help."

"Now we are in an age when individuals self-select for office. They put themselves forward. It requires huge ambition, ego, and a particular, bombastic leadership style. The public says to the candidate, 'Prove to us you can raise money, that you can run a campaign.' That shared responsibility for leadership development has been lost." As to why Minnesotans have not been willing to rally around women leaders to move them to the next level, Alice believes the public does not yet recognize the leadership styles and qualities of women—and because they are not recognized, they are not valued. "Old styles of political discourse still hold Minnesotan's attention and define 'eloquence,'" she said. "We are not open to new voices which may be eloquent in a different way. We see the male bombast and anger and the pounding on the table. . . . and continue to translate that bombast into leadership."

As women bring their own style into the political world, they come with a solid base of development. Many have lived their early lives being connected to and supported by others. They have developed a strong sense of their own personal power, which frequently expresses itself in taking responsiblity to speak out and effect change. The women combine a sense of optimism and hope for the future with curiosity, persistence, and integrity.

Marlene Johnson emphasized the necessity of women mentoring women in the political arena, a process that is not happening often enough. "The informal networks of cohesive support for women in the process of building [a political career] are just not there yet. We don't know what it is that we don't know how to get." As the women who have been pioneers in the political world reflect on their past political experiences, they are challenged to mentor other women to continue their legacies.

Wynia warns that putting emphasis on the fact of being a female candidate for political office instead of a male can be a two-edged sword. "As a woman candidate I could not say, 'Vote for me because I am a woman.' On the other hand, one of the reasons women are running is because they believe they are different. It is a struggle for women to communicate that message—vote for me because I am different, but don't vote for me just because I am a woman." Political campaigns run on short, pithy slogans and thirty-second announcements. The subtleties of the message of why it is important to vote for women candidates can be lost in the sound bites of furious campaigning.

Ultimately, the political process will benefit from a variety of perspectives. The perspective of women is important—first, because women represent over half of the population. Of greater importance is the fact that women have unique insights into how men and women together can accomplish the ultimate goal of politics—the development of a more compassionate and equitable society. That goal will come closer as women continue to narrow the gender gap among those who hold elective office.

Women now hold more political offices in the State of Minnesota than at any previous time in the state's history.

Minnesota Women Legislative Delegation at 1983 Forum for Women State Legislators in San Diego, California. Seated (left to right): Rep. Ann Wynia, Rep. Linda Scheid, Rep. Dee Long. Standing (left to right): Sen. Marilyn Cantry, Rep. Carolyn Rodriquez, Rep. Gloria Segal, Rep. Janet Clark, Bella Abzug, Rep. Lona Minne, Rep. Karen Clark, Rep. Linda Bergland, Sharon L. Coleman, Rep. Pat Piper. (Photo courtesy Lona Schreiber.)

ری References ﮱ

Bondi, Victor, ed. *American Decades, 1970-79*. Detroit: Gale Research, Inc. 1995.

Bondi, Victor, ed. *American Decades, 1980-89*. Detroit: Gale Research, Inc. 1996.

Bourque, S.C., Grossholtz, J. "Politics an unnatural practice: Political science looks at female participation." *Politics and Society*, pp. 225-266. 1974.

Carroll, S.J., Strimling, W.S. *Women's routes to elective office: A comparison with men's*. New Brunswick, New Jersey: Eagleton Institute of Politics. 1983.

Cott, N.F. *The Bonds of Womanhood*. New Haven, CN: Yale University Press, 1977.

Freilino, M.K., Hummel, R. "Achievement and Identity in college-age vs. adult women students." *Journal of Youth and Adolescence*, 14 (1), 1-10. 1985.

Holland, Gini. *America in the 20th Century 1990s*. New York: Marshall Cavendish. 1995.

Johnson, Paul. *A History of the American People*. New York: Harper Collins. 1987.

Jones, W. Nelson A.J. "Correlates of women's representation in lower state legislative chambers." *Social Behavior and Personality*, vol. 9 (1), pp. 9-15. 1981.

Kirkpatrick, J.J. *Political Woman*. New York: Basic Books. 1974.

Kruschke, E.R. "Level of optimism as related to female political behavior." *Social Science*, vol. 41(2). pp. 67-75. 1966.

Layman, Richard, ed. *American Decades 1960-1969*. Detroit: Gale Research, Inc. 1995.

Manza, J., & Brooks, C. "The gender gap in U.S. presidential elections: When? why? implication?" *American Journal of Sociology*, vol. 103(5), pp. 1235-1266. 1998.

Mullaney, M.M. Women and the theory of the "revolutionary personality": Comments, criticisms, and suggestions for further study. *The Social Science Journal*, vol. 21 (2), pp. 49-70. 1984.

Nelson, A.J. "Women's advancement as chairpersons in lower state legislative chambers: 1979 and 1983." *International Journal of Intercultural Relations*, vol. 11. pp. 401-410. 1987.

New York Times, A14, Feb. 4, 1999.

Oglesby, Carole A., ed. *Encyclopedia of Women and Sport in America*. Phoenix: Onyx Press. 1998.

Pfaff, Tim. *Hmong in America: Journey From a Secret War*. Eau Claire, WI: Chippewa Valley Museum Press. 1995.

Plutzer, E., Zipp, J.F. "Identity politics, partisanship, and voting for women candidates." *Public Opinion Quarterly*, vol. 60, pp. 30-57. 1996.

Rimm, Sylvia. *See Jane Win*. New York, NY: Crown. 2000.

Seligman, M. E. P. *Learned optimism*. New York: A.A. Knopf. 1991.

Stanwick, K.A., Kleeson, J.E. *Women Make a Difference*. New Brunswick, New Jersey: Eagleton Institute of Politics. 1983.

Stuhler, B., Kreuter, G. *Women of Minnesota*. St. Paul: Minnesota Historical Society Press, 1998.

Watkins, B., Rothchild, N. *In the Company of Women*. St. Paul: Minnesota Historical Society Press, 1996.

Werner, E.E., Bachtold, L.M. "Personality characteristics of women in American politics." *Women in Politics*. New York: John Wiley & Sons. pp. 75-84. 1974.

ᅇ Index ᅇ

ͼ About the Authors ͽ

Biloine (Billie) Young moved to Minnesota in 1970 when her husband, Dr. George P. Young, became superintendent of the St. Paul Public Schools. Previous homes have been in Guatemala, Colombia, Illinois, New Mexico, and Ohio. She holds graduate degrees in journalism and Latin American history from the University of Illinois and, in her first job in Iowa, was named best woman editor of a weekly newspaper in the United States. She is the author of eight books, including *Grand Avenue, Mexican Odyssey, A Dream for Gilberto,* and *Cahokia: The Great Native American Metropolis.* She has four children and eight grandchildren.

Nancy Deane Wilson Ankeny is a native of Minnesota. She graduated from Mankato High School, went to the University of Minnesota

and graduated with a BA in French literature. Nancy received a Masters Degree in counseling psychology and a Doctorate in psychology from the University of St. Thomas in St. Paul, Minnesota. She is a licensed psychologist with a private practice in St. Paul, which includes contract work at 3M in the Employee Assistance Resource Center as a consultant to employees regarding work and personal concerns. Nancy is married and has two adult children.